Getting Away
with
Murder

57 Unsolved Murders
with Reward Information

Edward Baumann
and
John O'Brien

Bonus Books, Inc., Chicago

95 94 93 92 91   5 4 3 2 1

Library of Congress Catalog Card Number: 91-70965

International Standard Book Number: 0-929387-51-1

Bonus Books, Inc.
160 East Illinois Street
Chicago, Illinois 60611

Printed in the United States of America

To the Charlie Fitzgeralds of the world—those dogged, dedicated, determined street cops who don't win them all, but never give up trying.

CONTENTS

Foreword / ix

Preface / xiii

BOOK I   Suffer Little Children

A Grisly Find in Montrose Harbor / 3
The Sunday Matinee Murders / 13
Chicago's Most Baffling Crime / 20
The Trick-or-Treat Murders / 31
The Corpse in the Hearse / 35
Hitching a Ride with Death / 41
The Sitter Who Never Came Home / 47

BOOK II   Daughters

Murder 101 at the U. of I. / 69
The Senator's Daughter / 75
A No-Show at the Seminar / 85
The Killing a Cop Can't Forget / 89
What Happened to My Daughter? / 91
The Tattooed Waitress / 93
Murder in Movieland / 96

v

CONTENTS

BOOK III   Wives and Mothers

Oh, Those Beautiful Eyes / 107
The Needle-Studded Torso / 112
An Out-and-Out Execution / 119
$1,000 for Elvia's Killer / 122
Death Came Calling / 124

BOOK IV   Job Related, Perhaps

Guns That Go Bang in the Night / 131
The Death of Doctor Smile / 136
Stop at Death's Floor, Please / 139
Who Blew the Foreman's Head Off? / 143

BOOK V   Facing Death Together

I'll Die at Your Wedding / 149
The Missing Wedding Guests / 153
Fifty Grand for Information / 156
Bullets for Broadway Bill / 158

BOOK VI   Not Safe at Home

Sunday Morning Massacre / 181
Who Popped the Pizza Man? / 188
No Sign of Forced Entry / 193
All for One and One for All / 196

BOOK VII   Good Cop-Bad Cop

Stakeout to Murder / 207
Help Wanted—One Killer / 211
The Cop Who Made His Own Rules / 216
The Walkie-Talkie Mob Hit / 221

BOOK VIII   Mob Justice

Murder on a Meat Hook / 229
The Madman of the Mafia / 234
Adios, Godfather / 239
English Wasn't English Any More / 244
The Man Who Knew Too Much / 246

Planted in an Indiana Cornfield / 252
Hit Man with an Empty Gun / 259
No Dinner for Six, at Seven / 263
You're Never Too Old to Die / 266
Torture Wrapped in Mystery / 269

BOOK IX   Murder on the Hoof

"Ya Burnt My *!#!* Shirt!" / 275
Don't Kick a Hood When He's Down / 278

BOOK X   Candidates for Murder

Big Cats Don't Have Nine Lives / 283
It's a Dangerous Game They Play / 296
Is Clem Overparked in the Grant Park Garage? / 299
Anybody Here Seen Sal? / 303
The Mayor Was Marked for Death / 306
The Elks Club Murder / 310

BOOK XI   Murder at Random

Take Two Capsules and Call the Coroner / 321

BOOK XII   Missing and Presumed . . .

Mystery in Candyland / 331
Snatched Right Out of Her Shoes / 337
A Summer Outing to Eternity / 346

Epilogue / 365

Reward Information / 367

Index / 371

FOREWORD

The authors of *Getting Away with Murder*, John O'Brien and
Edward Baumann, are held in high regard and respect by all
police officers who know them. They, like many of the cops
with whom they come into daily contact, have the hard outer
veneer of homicide detectives. But they also have the sensi-
tivity and concern for humanity that most cops have once that
veneer is peeled away. O'Brien and Baumann are talented
reporters who combine detail, such as that found under a
microscope, with the interpretation of that detail into an
insightful and broader presentation.

In addition to the obvious interest people generally have
regarding crime, there is the heightened interest in the
unsolved homicide. In putting together *Getting Away with
Murder*, Baumann and O'Brien have selected crimes which
cross the spectrum of victims from children such as the
Grimes sisters to the prominent socialite Helen Brach; from
mobsters like Sam DeStefano to the dishonored former Chicago Police Commander Mark Thanasauras: and from politicians like Clem Graver to flight attendant Paula Prince, whose
life was taken for no apparent reason.

What degenerate monsters murder the innocent?

What about the other victims of sexual deviates who
murder again and again when released from prison? Who lets

the public know they are back on the street so we can be on guard? Are you against capital punishment? Your husband, wife, or children may be the next victims of one of the animals the authors tell us about in these pages.

For thirty years prior to joining the Chicago Crime Commission I was a Chicago police officer, assigned for the last twenty years to the hoodlum squad of the Intelligence Section. Both the Crime Commission and the hoodlum squad keep a running count of Organized Crime murders committed since 1919. As of the beginning of this year there have been 1,102 such slayings, few of which are ever solved. The usually futile investigation of these homicides lasts about thirty days. But investigations into the murders of innocent women and children go on forever.

I have seen the toughest detectives cry when they had to examine the bodies of children who were tortured and murdered by some indescribable monster. They think of their own wives and daughters when looking at the body of a young woman so badly beaten or mutilated she cannot be recognized.

None of these crimes is ever forgotten. The Organized Crime Task Force consisting of FBI and local investigators works on all unsolved Organized Crime-related murders. There is also the FBI's Violent Criminal Apprehension Program (VICAP), initiated to aid law enforcement units in criminal profiling to solve old murders, or provide significant clues to help identify serial killers. Through the years, investigators have classified many types of homicides. The crime scene itself can suggest what type of person would have committed the murder. Knowing that much, detectives can predict possible future types of behavior. These traits are now recorded and computerized.

With the continued development of new techniques such as VICAP, relatives and friends of crime victims can be assured that law enforcement agencies are effectively continuing their efforts to solve these homicides long after they were committed.

Sometimes even the most insignificant appearing bit of information, added to what investigators already know, is all detectives need to solve a puzzle to mark a long-open case "closed" and bring the perpetrator to justice. If you have any information regarding any of the unsolved murders detailed by O'Brien and Baumann in this book, call the FBI at 312/431–1333, the Chicago Crime Commission, 312/372–0101, or contact the authors through the publisher and they will get in touch with us.

Nobody should get away with murder. Someone out there knows . . .

Jerry Gladden
Chief Investigator
Chicago Crime Commission
March 1991

PREFACE

Not long ago Judith Mae Andersen's brother, James, who still remembers the night his sister walked off into the darkness and met death head-on, put some thoughts down on paper that had been nagging at him for more than three decades. He did it, he said, to relieve his own inner feelings:

> I was only twelve when my sister was murdered at fifteen. Please write something . . . about the many unsolved murders in Chicago. We cannot forget the victims as if their deaths did not happen, and they never lived on this planet. The victims once lived and laughed and enjoyed life. Their families do not want to forget them. The young people who have died because of violent, murderous crimes should not be forgotten because a lot of time has passed. Now it seems that all is forgotten; that these terrible things never happened. I know that my sister was a good person. Has all the world forgotten her, the Schuessler-Peterson boys and the Grimes girls? I haven't.

A lot of people haven't. Police Lieutenant Charles Fitzgerald had Judith Mae on his mind to his dying day. Indiana

State Police Sergeant Edward Burke, though long retired, says a day does not pass that he doesn't think about Ann Miller, Renee Bruhl, and Patricia Blough. And whenever Chicago newspaper reporters of another generation sit around the table and conjure up memories of their days on the crime beat, the names of John and Anton Schuessler, Bobby Peterson, and Barbara and Patricia Grimes always come up.

Somewhere, wherever a homicide case remains unsolved, police officers remember the victim in graphic detail, just as they look back on the agonizing hours they put in trying to bring some faceless murderer to justice.

And somebody else remembers too—the killers, who got away with murder. May the unconscionable acts they committed torment their evil hearts and souls through all eternity.

BOOK I

SUFFER LITTLE CHILDREN

A GRISLY FIND IN MONTROSE HARBOR

Without a doubt, the three most heinous unsolved homicides in the Chicago area during the twentieth century are the slayings of the Grimes sisters, the Schuessler-Peterson boy murders, and the gruesome decapitation of fifteen-year-old Judith Mae Andersen. Of the three, the Andersen case stands out as the most heartwrenching for police in terms of striving to bring the killer to justice.

They pulled out all the stops, resorting even to scenarios right out of Hollywood, but to this day the killer—and they know who he is—smugly walks the streets a free man.

Judy was just two months shy of her sixteenth birthday and preparing for her junior year at Austin High School when she bounced giddily out of her Northwest Side home on Friday night, Aug. 16, 1957, to watch television with her best friend, Elena Abbatacola.

"I was the last one in the family to see or talk to her," recalled her brother, Jimmy. Now a food store employee in a western suburb, he was twelve years old at the time. "On the night she disappeared we had dinner. My mother was washing the dishes. I was drying them and my sister was getting ready to go over to Elena's house. My sister called me into her bedroom and said, 'Pssst. Do you want to know what I got Mom for her birthday?'

"She held a brown paper sack and in it was a little pink ceramic vase. It was like a money bag that you could put coins into. I said, 'Oh, that's real nice. She'll like that.' "

As Judy left for her friend's house, her kid brother followed her out onto the back porch of the home on Lotus Avenue and impishly teased, "Hey, Judy. I'm going to show Mom what you got for her for her birthday." Judy turned, glared at him in mock anger, and playfully warned, "Better not!"

And with that she was off for the Abbatacola home, three quarters of a mile away in the 1000 block of North Central Avenue. She was wearing a loose fitting white blouse, beige pedal pushers, and white leather shoes. A tiny cross dangled from a silver chain around her neck.

At eleven o'clock Judy telephoned home to plead with her mother, Ruth, "Mom, there's a good movie on television. Can I stay 'til the end? Pleeeze?" "No, Judy, it's quite late. You had better come straight home," her mother replied. Judy hung up the phone, turned to Elena and shrugged her shoulders. "I have to go," she said.

"I'll walk part way with you," Elena offered, as she often did.

"No, that's okay. It is late," Judy answered. "It'll only take me twenty minutes or so."

When Judy did not come home her forty-four-year-old father, Ralph, a bookbinder by profession, went out looking for her. Angry at first, but then concerned as the night wore on, Andersen walked the distance between his home and the Abbatacolas' on North Central, covering every conceivable route Judy could have taken—the long way, the short way, and the in-between. At dawn he called the police.

A missing person report was filed, but police were more inclined to treat the matter as a runaway, especially after learning that Judy had been refused permission to stay out late to watch the end of the movie.

Elena Abbatacola did not think so. She came over to the Andersen home to sit vigil with the family Saturday afternoon. Consoling Jimmy and his brothers, Bobby and Ralph, she told the boys, "Judy would never run away just because she couldn't watch an old movie. Your sister would never do that." Elena was painfully prophetic.

Six days later, on Thursday, August 22, boaters in Montrose Harbor, bothered by an old fifty-five-gallon oil drum bobbing in the water, pulled it ashore and found it to contain the dismembered torso of a female. Her head, one arm, and both hands were missing. Without the head or hands there was no way to immediately identify the torso, and members of the Andersen family refused to believe the worst.

Then, on Saturday, August 24, a five-gallon pail floating near the shore was found to contain a severed head, two hands, and an arm.

Through dental records, and a latent fingerprint lifted from a painting of Jesus Christ that hung in the missing girl's bedroom, the body was identified as that of Judith Mae. Prior to being decapitated, she had been shot in the head.

Fishermen on the other side of the harbor told police that several nights earlier they had seen a car back down to the water's edge with its brake light flashing. A well-built man, whom they could not identify in the darkness, got out, opened the trunk, and threw several things into the water with a loud splash. As he drove away they noticed that one of his tail lights was out.

The search for the killer turned into one of the most massive manhunts in the city's history. During the first year alone, 115,000 people were interviewed by police; 2,240 possible suspects were questioned; and 73 lie detector tests were administered. Police checked out 152 reports of shots being heard on the night Judy disappeared, and 81 reports of a female screaming.

Meanwhile police were also busy investigating a series of robberies and unusual sexual attacks on women on the North and Northwest sides. The attacks were uniformly the same. The assailant confronted the women while they were walking alone, frequently just after they had gotten off a bus.

He displayed a knife to menace and cut his victims, often around the genital area. Then they were bound with lengths of rope, each having the same number of twists in the braiding. And, curiously, although the attacks were clearly sexually motivated, none of the victims was raped and no sperm was even found at the scene.

Detective Chief Patrick Deeley formed a special unit consisting of 200 of the city's best officers to investigate the attacks. He put a ruddy-faced bulldog of a sergeant named Charles Fitzgerald in charge.

Essentially a loner, who regularly put in fifteen-hour days "chasing crooks," Fitzgerald was known among his peers as "the Relentless Pursuer of Evildoers." As a Chicago cop he had earned twenty-four creditable mentions, been twice cited for bravery by the city council, and was recognized by the FBI five times. He once solved a murder by piecing together a torn love letter found in a garbage can.

Fitzgerald put his men to work trailing buses from a discreet distance. It was not long before they spotted another car following a bus on Western Avenue near Peterson. Because one of the tail lights was burned out, the detectives ordered the car to pull over, and asked the driver for his license.

The man behind the wheel proved to be Barry Zander Cook, a 200-pound, boyishly handsome twenty-one-year-old construction worker. He clearly matched the description of the suspect who had been attacking women in the area. Not wanting to arouse his suspicion, the officers wrote out a ticket for a tail light violation and sent him on his way.

They now knew his name and address, however, and placed him under immediate surveillance. Fitzgerald was sure he had his man, especially after a check revealed Cook had a previous arrest record.

The next step was for the victims to view the suspect, without him knowing the police were onto him. This was accomplished by taking various assault victims to construction sites where Cook worked, and having the women pick him out from among other laborers on the job.

All went according to plan until Feb. 26, 1958, when Cook recognized one of the victims as she pointed him out at a construction site. He took off running with four detectives in hot pursuit. Several shots were fired, and Cook was slowed down by a flesh wound in the leg. Detective Walter Vallee then brought him down with a flying tackle.

The suspect was taken to Cook County Hospital, where it was discovered that he possessed the genitalia of a six-year-old boy, and was unable to achieve normal sexual gratification.

Fitzgerald attempted to interview him, but he feigned unconsciousness for weeks, refusing to open his eyes or to speak to anyone but his father. This made it necessary to bring victims to the hospital ward to view the prisoner. In order to avoid criticism, police filled Cook's ward with thirty-five patients in their early twenties, and of the same physical description. Police then conducted show-ups in the ward, with victims asked if they could recognize their assailant from among the patients lying on their beds.

As a result of statements taken from victims by Fitzgerald and Patrolman Rudolph Heckscher, the grand jury indicted Cook on seven counts of assault to rob, rape, and murder.

Because of the vicious nature of the attacks, Cook also became a prime suspect in the murders of Judith Mae Andersen and Margaret Gallagher, a fifty-year-old beauty operator, who was slain while sunbathing in Lincoln Park on July 23, 1956, not far from where Judy's remains were found in the lagoon.

The Gallagher homicide became known as the "Spyglass Murder Case," because a resident of a Lake Shore Drive high rise witnessed the slaying while scanning the Foster Avenue beach with a telescope.

Although Cook persisted in refusing to talk to anyone but his father, Fitzgerald was able to persuade the elder Cook that his son could be cleared of any suspicion in the homicides through a routine polygraph examination. Once the father agreed and told his son to cooperate, Fitzgerald obtained a court order to remove the prisoner from the county jail so he could be tested at the downtown offices of John Reid & Associates.

Rather than clear the suspect as his father had hoped, the lie detector indicated that Cook harbored guilty knowledge of the murders of both Judy Andersen and Margaret Gallagher—just as Fitzgerald had expected.

Fitzgerald confronted Cook with the results of the lie test and gently suggested, "You did kill Judy, didn't you?" Cook nodded and told the detective, "I'll tell you everything if my father says it's okay."

Fitzgerald brought in Charles Cook, who had been waiting in an anteroom, and told him that Barry had flunked the lie box, and admitted slaying Judith Mae.

The stunned father pulled up a chair opposite his son and asked him point blank, "Barry, tell me the truth. Did you kill Margaret Gallagher?"

Young Cook looked at his father and nodded, "Yes, I did . . ."

Before he could continue, his father held up his hand and admonished him to be quiet. "Don't say another word to anyone, Barry. Do not talk to anybody."

Stymied at the very moment he felt he was making a breakthrough, Fitzgerald had no choice but to return the prisoner to Cook County Jail where he was consigned to Murderer's Row—a cell block of accused killers either awaiting trial or a date with the electric chair. The youth's father, meanwhile, engaged the services of Frank G. Whalen, one of Chicago's top criminal lawyers, to defend his son. The first thing Whalen did was order Cook not to discuss the murders with anyone, and to discontinue further cooperation with authorities.

Fitzgerald, his Irish dander up, was not about to be outfoxed. He called a meeting with Detective Chief Pat Deeley, Deputy Chief of Detectives Howard Pierson, Chief Tom Smith of the sheriff's police, and Warden Jack Johnson of the county jail. The session was held in a Loop hotel to assure absolute secrecy. When everyone was together Fitzgerald introduced them to Detective Anthony Muranaka and explained, "Here's what I want to do . . ."

Muranaka, a slightly-built Japanese-American, looked like anything but a Chicago police officer. The plan was for Muranaka to be booked into the county jail, on phony charges, where he would try to befriend Cook. It would be a most dangerous assignment. His cell block mates would include James Dukes, George Starcevic, Nicholas LaPapa and Richard Carpenter—all cop-killers—along with mad-dog Gordon De Simone, who had murdered his paramour's husband, and Vincent Ciucci, who would eventually go to the chair for killing his wife and children.

"If you'd rather not go through with this, we will certainly understand, and it will not reflect on your record," Deeley told him. "You know there'll be extreme danger involved."

"I want to help get this guy," Muranaka answered.

After being thoroughly briefed on the Andersen and Gallagher homicides, and on jailhouse behavior, Muranaka was arraigned in court on the trumped-up charges and consigned to the county jail to await trial.

After several days in solitary confinement he was transferred to Murderer's Row. There he struck up an acquaintance with Cook, and as the friendship blossomed over the next two weeks Cook told him how he had murdered Judith Mae Andersen and Margaret Gallagher.

Once he had his information Muranaka was "bailed out," but continued to correspond with Cook in jail.

On June 23, 1958, faced with a platoon of witnesses who had positively identified him as their attacker in the other cases, Cook entered a plea of guilty in criminal court to seven charges of assault and assault to commit rape. He was sentenced to one to fourteen years in the old Joliet Penitentiary.

Authorities, meanwhile, needed more details on the Andersen and Gallagher killings to build their case against the suspect, and Detective Muranaka was called upon to playact once again. On July 8, 1958, with his head completely shaved, he was taken in chains, under heavy guard, to the Joliet Penitentiary where he was confined in the same cell as Cook.

It was like old home week, and Cook, relieved to find a familiar face, took Muranaka into his confidence and, little by little, told him everything he wanted to know. Detective Peter Heidinger, posing as Muranaka's lawyer, visited him daily and relayed the information to Fitzgerald who was waiting outside the walls.

Once authorities felt they had milked Cook dry as far as the unsolved homicides were concerned, Muranaka was "sprung" before any other con might recognize him as the cop who had sent him to jail. Fitzgerald then visited Cook in prison and told him what he knew. Cook was then returned to his cell to mull over the turn of events. The cat was out of the bag, and he realized it.

On Oct. 12, 1958, Cook asked to speak with Warden Joseph Ragen. The warden had the prisoner brought into his office, where he asked him, "What's on your mind, Barry?" Whereupon Cook poured out a full confession to the murder of Margaret Gallagher. The warden called Fitzgerald, and five days later Cook was indicted for the "Spyglass Murder."

In the spring of 1959 the prisoner was returned in handcuffs and leg irons to Chicago to face trial for the Lincoln Park slaying. Lantern-jawed Frank Whalen stood for the defense. It was an incredible trial, which made banner headlines in the four downtown Chicago dailies day after day. And the verdict was a shocker!

Despite the witness who had observed the slaying through a telescope; despite testimony from John Reid that Cook had flunked the lie test; despite Fitzgerald's revelation that he was present when Cook admitted the Gallagher murder to his father; despite Muranaka's testimony that Cook had told him in jail that he killed the woman while she was sunbathing at the beach; and despite Cook's own confession to Warden Ragen—the jury found him innocent after his parents testified that he was home with them at the time of the slaying.

As Clem Lane, the late city editor of the *Chicago Daily News,* frequently observed, "Chicago is a not-guilty town."

Cook was returned to Joliet to finish serving his one to fourteen years for the attacks on other women, Muranaka's cover was blown, and police set about to pick up the pieces. The Gallagher case was history, but there was still the possibility of nailing him for the Andersen slaying.

Of this much Fitzgerald was dead certain, and this is what he reported to his superiors:

Barry Cook's parents were out of town on the night Judy Anderson was snatched off the street on her way home from her friend's house. She may have tried to resist him and he shot her in the temple. She died right there in his car. He then took her body home, undressed her, and cut her into manageable pieces. As for the involved process of dismemberment, Fitzgerald said it took a long time and Cook got "some kind of sexual gratification" from the grisly task. "He enjoyed it."

He took on the arduous task of sealing the torso in the empty oil drum, and the head in the five-gallon bucket, in order to get the evidence out of the house before his parents returned from their long weekend. He then hosed down the basement, making sure that the catch basin was "spotlessly clean."

With Cook's family refusing to cooperate in the follow-up investigation, Fitzgerald and his detectives slipped into their home near Hermitage and Devon avenues while they were at Joliet visiting their son. From basement rafters they recovered several flattened slugs from a .32 revolver, similar to the bullets found in the dead girl's head.

"What we've got to find is the gun, so we can make ballistics tests," Fitzgerald said. The search failed to turn up the weapon, however.

Through the use of eavesdropping devices, Fitzgerald learned that Cook's father had found the gun under some leaves beneath the front porch. He took a post-hole digger, bored the deepest hole he could in the back yard, and dropped the gun in it. He subsequently told Barry, during a prison visit, "I buried it where they will never find it, near the barbecue pit."

Judy Andersen's clothing was never found. Police determined that the cement foundation for the backyard barbecue was poured shortly after the murder. They believe that her pedal pushers, blouse, shoes, and undergarments are imbedded in the concrete.

Until he retired from the force in 1964, Fitzgerald visited Barry Cook in prison regularly, bringing him books to read and other incidentals. And always the talk would turn to Judith Mae Andersen.

"He told me he killed Judy but he would not go into detail or give a formal statement," Fitzgerald told the authors shortly before his death in April 1990. "He said he could tell me a lot of things, but his father wouldn't allow it."

UPDATE

Barry Cook was released from prison in June 1967 after serving nine years for attacks on various young women. He walked out of the penitentiary accompanied by his father, Charles, after which the family moved to Houston.

Fitzgerald, the "Relentless Pursuer of Evildoers," continued to keep an updated file on Cook after his retirement with the rank of lieutenant. In 1973, when a twenty-three-year-old woman was stabbed, sexually assaulted, and left for dead in Houston, Fitzgerald provided Texas authorities with information that led to Cook's arrest. Cook was also questioned in connection with several unsolved homicides there, but was never brought to trial.

The Chicago Tribune offered a $50,000 reward for information leading to the arrest and conviction of the person who murdered Judith Mae Andersen. That reward has never been claimed.

THE SUNDAY MATINEE MURDERS

The slaying of Judith Mae Andersen was actually the third in a series of alarming child murders that horrified the city of Chicago in as many years, snuffing out the lives of six young people. Robert Peterson, fourteen, John Schuessler, thirteen, and his eleven-year-old brother, Anton, were the first, on Oct. 16, 1955.

All three boys attended Farnsworth School, 5414 N. Linder Avenue, where Robert and John were eighth graders and Anton was in the sixth. On this Sunday afternoon in October they decided to go down to the Loop to see a movie, *The African Lion,* at a State Street theater. The Schuessler brothers, who lived at 5711 N. Mango Avenue, picked up Bobby at his house at 5519 Farragut Avenue along the way.

Bobby was wearing a black jacket with a White Sox emblem, a pink flannel striped shirt, blue jeans, an Indian belt, and gym shoes. The Schuessler brothers had blue Chicago Cubs jackets, blue jeans, and gym shoes. John had a brown shirt and tan belt. Anton wore a white flannel shirt with a black pattern.

Bobby had $1.50 in his pocket as the three of them headed for Milwaukee Avenue to catch a bus at 3:30 P.M. The Schuesslers had $2.50 between them.

In the ensuing two and a half hours they made their way downtown, saw the movie, which lasted one hour and forty-five minutes, and hiked two blocks to the Garland Building at 111 North Wabash Avenue. Police from the Special Investigating Unit, headed by Lieutenant Joseph Morris, would later determine that the Peterson boy signed the building register at 6:00 P.M., so he could go in and use the washroom. He was familiar with the place, having gone there previously with his sister to an eye doctor's.

Less than an hour and a half later the trio was back on the Northwest Side, where they popped in at the Monte Cristo bowling alley at 3326 Montrose Avenue. They saw a boy they knew, seventeen-year-old Ernest Niewiandomski, whom they told about the movie. They said they had ridden several subways and buses before they found the right ones to get them back home.

"Do you guys want to bowl?" Niewiandomski asked them. "Not unless you pay for it," they answered, indicating they had spent all their money. After Bobby Peterson and Tony Schuessler used the washroom, they said, "Let's go, John," and the three of them went back out into the rain which had been falling intermittently for the last two or three hours.

At 8:00 P.M. they stopped off at another bowling alley, at 3550 Montrose Avenue. The manager, sixty-one-year-old Waldorf Lundgren, recognized young Peterson, who had been in the habit of accompanying his father, an avid bowler, to the alley at least twice a week. He said the boys stayed only about five minutes before they walked off into the night.

Anton Schuessler, Sr., a tailor, and his wife, Eleanor, became worried when their boys were not home by 8:30 P.M. They telephoned Malcolm and Dorothy Peterson, who hadn't heard from Bobby, either.

Two hours later the concerned fathers, with rain dripping from their coats, walked into the Albany Park Police Station and told Sergeant George Murphy that their sons had not come home from the afternoon movie. Murphy took a description of the youngsters, and notified the sex bureau. He also alerted all squads in the district. The fathers spent the rest of the night walking the streets looking vainly for their sons.

The boys' naked bodies were found two days later in a ditch bordering a parking lot in Robinson's Woods along the Des Plaines River south of Lawrence Avenue. The grotesque discovery was made by Victor Livingston, a fifty-year-old liquor salesman, who had driven to the parking lot to eat his lunch. He drove to the Mello-Rust Stables at 5500 River Road and informed the owner, who telephoned Forest Preserve rangers.

Livingston then drove back to the parking lot, where he was waiting when Ranger John J. Byrne wheeled up in response to the call. "I pulled into the lot here to eat my lunch," he told the ranger. "As I twisted around to get my lunch bag from the back seat, I noticed a body in the ditch. I thought at first it was a store dummy. Then I saw blood on the side of his face."

It was not until he led Byrne to the area, about 300 feet from the lot entrance, that he and the ranger discovered there were three bodies—not one. Byrne relayed news of the grim find to Daniel Conway, chief of the forest rangers, who called the sheriff's office. Milwaukee Avenue sheriff's police and Chicago police, along with Coroner Walter McCarron, converged on the parking lot within minutes.

The boys' bodies were stacked like cord wood. All three had been strangled, and the Peterson boy had been struck repeatedly on the head with a revolver butt or a tire iron.

Dr. Jerry Kearns, the coroner's pathologist, said fingernail marks about the throats of the Schuessler brothers indicated they had been choked to death by hand, while Bobby Peterson had been throttled with a necktie or similar object.

The eyes and mouths of all three boys had been taped, but the tape had been removed before the bodies were dumped into the ditch. A black, oily substance on the boys' feet led police to theorize that they had been slain elsewhere, while barefoot, and their naked bodies were then driven to the parking lot for disposal. Abrasions on one of the boy's backs suggested he had been dragged, and impressions on the Schuessler boys' backs indicated their bodies had lain on a corrugated surface, such as the floor mat of a car.

Sheriff's Lieutenant Walter Fleming cordoned off the parking lot and surrounding area, and detailed 100 men to search the area, walking at four-foot intervals. A plaster cast was made of tire markings found near where the bodies were dumped, and was sent to the police crime laboratory for examination.

Meanwhile Police Lieutenant John Lynch of the Jefferson Park station sent twenty police officers out to search abandoned buildings along Avondale Street for the boys' clothing. The buildings had been recently vacated for construction of what is now the Kennedy Expressway. Their clothing was never recovered.

Although the bodies were found outside the city limits, Police Commissioner Timothy J. O'Connor assigned twenty hand-picked men to work with Sheriff Joseph Lohman's investigators. The Chicago detail was headed by Detective Lieutenant James Lynch, a recent FBI Academy graduate, working with Lieutenant James McMahon, head of the Homicide Division, and Lieutenant John Noone of the old Scotland Yard detail. They had at their disposal two squads of homicide detectives, two crime laboratory squads and five specialists from Scotland Yard.

An examination of the boys' battered bodies showed traces of grain or fertilizer of a type used in stables imbedded in their skin. Perhaps, investigators theorized, the boys had wandered into a stable to get out of the rain, and were killed by someone they encountered there.

Imprints on the backs of the Schuessler brothers indicated their bodies had lain on some type of a mat after they were slain. Crime lab experts determined that the pattern of the imprints matched that of floor mats used in Packard automobiles manufactured between 1942 and 1951.

An autopsy indicated the boys had been dead about thirty-six hours when their bodies were found in the ditch shortly after noon on Tuesday. In all probability, they were killed not long after they left the second bowling alley. The Peterson boy's stomach was empty. However the stomachs of the Schuessler boys, who had eaten lunch a half hour later than Bobby on Sunday, still contained food.

When Malcolm Peterson went to the Cook County morgue to identify his son's body he moaned, "Oh, Robert, what have they done to you?" Both he and Anton Schuessler had to be helped from the room by coroner's aides after viewing their sons' corpses.

Schuessler promptly closed his tailor shop as he and Peterson, a forty-year-old carpenter, both abandoned their jobs in order to work full time with police in the search for their sons' killers. Working with Chicago Transit Authority supervisors, the fathers flagged down Milwaukee Avenue buses and questioned drivers in an effort to further determine the boys' last hours on the night they were murdered.

Schuessler never went back to his little shop at 5200 Sheridan Road. Three weeks later, after sinking into a deep depression over the deaths of his two sons, he suffered a fatal heart attack at the age of forty-two.

As his coffin was being lowered into the ground at St. Joseph's Cemetery, beside the bodies of his slain sons, his thirty-seven-year-old widow, Eleanor, wept, "Your daddy is here, boys. I'll be back before long. I will."

Two men were arrested as suspects while attending the elder Schuessler's funeral. Both were subsequently cleared, but the time and place of their arrests indicated that police were pulling out all the stops in their efforts to find the killers. And they were convinced that there had to have been more than one. As one investigator put it, "Not even the greatest athlete in his prime could subdue three boys—he might seize two, but one would flee."

Police believed that the killers were sexual degenerates, who slew their victims to avoid exposure after molesting them. They were puzzled, however, over why the boys were first blindfolded and gagged with tape, which was then removed before their bodies were dumped. Another mystery: Why had their clothing disappeared completely, while their bodies were left out in plain sight to be found?

With Anton Schuessler, Sr., gone, Malcolm Peterson continued to carry the fatherly burden alone. For years after the triple homicide he continued to visit the Jefferson Park police station about once a week to talk over the case with Sergeant Murphy, who probably spent more time and effort on the probe than any other lawman.

During the course of the investigation, police questioned the owners of 970 Packards built between 1942 and 1951, because of the skin imprints on the Schuessler boys' backs. In each case, the automobile owner was asked to account for the whereabouts of his car on the night the boys were slain.

Sergeant John Hartigan of the special investigating unit advised Chief of Detectives Patrick Deeley that 43,740 people were questioned in connection with the boys' slayings, and 5,866 complaints were investigated. A total of 3,270 actual suspects were interrogated, of whom 244 were given lie tests.

One of them was Barry Z. Cook. Although he flunked a lie detector test in connection with the murder of Judith Mae Andersen, the polygraph indicated he had no guilty knowledge of the Schuessler-Peterson killings or the murders of the Grimes sisters the following year.

Rewards totaling more than $130,000 were offered for information about the boys' slayers, but the money has never been claimed.

UPDATE

Convicted rapist Silas Jayne, who in 1955 operated a riding stable on Peterson Avenue not far from where the boys' bodies were found, was among possible suspects questioned after the murders. Two witnesses had told of hearing screams coming from Jayne's stable on the night of October 16, after which a car with a noisy muffler drove away at a high rate of speed.

The incident took on new meaning in October 1970 after Silas' brother, George, with whom he had been feuding, was shot to death by a sniper in his Inverness home. When agents for the Illinois Bureau of Investigation questioned George's widow, Marion, about possible motives for the slaying, she told them, "Three or four days after the Schuessler-Peterson boys' bodies were found, George came to me and said, 'Well, if Silas gives us any more trouble, I have evidence to put him in the electric chair.' "

A sign painter who formerly did work for Silas Jayne once told police, "A lot of shenanigans went on in that stable on Peterson Avenue." He said he once observed a young blonde woman performing a sex act with a horse under Silas' direction.

Theory: Could the boys have ducked into the stable to get out of the rain, and then been killed to keep them from telling about something they had seen? If, during the struggle, their clothing was stained with manure or something else that would have led police to the stable, it would explain why they had been stripped naked and their clothing was never found.

Silas Jayne was paroled in 1979 after serving part of a six- to twenty-year prison sentence for masterminding his brother's murder. He died in 1987 at the age of eighty, without ever revealing what, if anything, he might have known about the murders of the three Northwest Side boys who went out for a Sunday afternoon movie and never returned.

CHICAGO'S MOST BAFFLING CRIME

The mystery of what happened to Barbara and Patricia Grimes after they left their South Side Chicago home to go to a movie during the Christmas holidays of 1956 ranks among the classics in the annals of American crime.

Barbara, fifteen, a sophomore at Kelly High School, and her twelve-year-old sister, who was in the seventh grade at St. Maurice School, left the house at 3634 South Damen Avenue around 7:30 on the night of December 28, to take in an Elvis Presley movie on Archer Avenue.

Barbara, who was five feet tall and weighed 100 pounds, had brown eyes and long, dark brown hair. Before going out on that frigid December evening she pulled a three-quarter length car coat over her yellow blouse and gray tweed skirt, and tied a gray babushka around her head. Patricia, who was five feet three inches tall and weighed 108 pounds, had brown eyes and dark brown hair like her sister. She had on a warm yellow sweater and blue jeans, a black jacket with white stripes on the sleeves and a white babushka.

Their forty-eight-year-old mother, Loretta, saw them to the door. "I think you both ought to stay home tonight," she suggested. "It's really cold out there." "Mom, we can't miss Elvis," they protested. "I guess I don't understand this current bobby sox craze," their mother sighed, shaking her head. "He can't even sing, as far as I'm concerned."

Barbara and Patricia arrived at the Brighton Theatre at 4223 Archer a short time later. A friend, fifteen-year-old Dorothy Fisher, saw them sitting together. What happened after the movie is where the mystery begins. The only thing certain is that they never returned home.

When the girls were not back by midnight their worried mother sent two of her other children out to look for them. Theresa Grimes, seventeen, and her fourteen-year-old brother, Joseph, stood shivering on a corner two blocks from home as they waited for three late-night buses to go by. Barbara and Petey, as Patricia was called, were not among the bleary-eyed passengers.

When Mrs. Grimes reported her daughters missing early the next morning she had a hard time getting police to take the matter seriously. After all, a couple of teen-aged girls staying out late at night during the holidays was not unheard of. Maybe they had run into a couple of boyfriends.

"My daughters don't date," she insisted. "And they never stay out late without calling me. Besides, New Year's Eve is Petey's thirteenth birthday, but she wanted to celebrate on the twenty-ninth. She's got eight girlfriends coming over tonight for soft drinks and cake."

By the end of the day police, too, were beginning to show their concern, and by the end of the week no less than 150 uniformed patrol officers and detectives were combing the South Side for the missing girls.

On Sunday Mrs. Grimes attended mass at St. Maurice Roman Catholic Church near her home. "I couldn't bear to look at the choir and not see my girls there," she wept afterward. "Barbara and Patricia sang at mass every Sunday."

The worried mother's ordeal grew more agonizing when an anonymous caller telephoned the Grimes home and told Theresa that her sisters' bodies could be found in an alley behind the Archer Avenue theater. Police searched the area, but found nothing. The call had been a cruel hoax.

Pale, with dark circles under her eyes, Loretta Grimes kept a daily vigil, waiting for her daughters to return. She had not been to bed since they disappeared. She napped on a couch in the living room, with a light in the window.

"I am waiting here for news, hoping and praying," she said. "If there was any way for them to get home, I know they would. If someone is holding my daughters, please let the girls call me. I'll forgive them from the bottom of my heart if they let my girls go." Shortly after that Mrs. Grimes received a series of ransom notes demanding $5,000 for the return of her daughters. Police traced the notes to a patient in a mental hospital.

As the days passed neighbors called daily to give the worried mother encouragement. The girls' father, Joseph, a truck driver from whom Mrs. Grimes had been divorced eleven years earlier, was also a daily visitor to the modest, red brick home on South Damen.

The search for Barbara and Patricia grew into one of the greatest missing person hunts in the city's history. Scores of police searched freight cars in the Brighton Park community, and thousands of circulars were distributed with photos of the missing girls.

There were numerous sightings reported by well-meaning citizens. The sisters were reported seen in hotels, at filling stations, in restaurants, theaters from one end of the city to the other, in bus stations in various states, and on cross-country buses. Someone who saw one of the circulars identified Barbara and Patricia as two girls who had been seeking jobs in Nashville, where they could be near Elvis. Someone else was sure he had seen the sisters in a car with two uniformed soldiers. None of the sightings could be confirmed.

A week after the sisters disappeared thirteen-year-old Catherine Borak, a classmate of Patricia's, received an anonymous phone call from a man who said: "We rented a cottage and Patricia took her clothes off but her sister wouldn't. What are you going to do about it, going to call the police?"

"Yes, I am," she replied, and the caller hung up.

Was the call yet another hoax? Or were the girls being

held somewhere against their wills? Police intensified their search. They didn't know what to think.

On January 15, more than two weeks after the disappearance, police received an anonymous tip that the Grimes sisters could be found in Santa Fe Park. Search teams scoured the park, a racetrack for stock cars and motorcycles, frequented mostly by young men with long sideburns and Elvis-type ducktail haircuts, but again they found nothing.

Detectives William O'Malley and Frank Hackel traced the call to a tavern on South Halsted Street. They learned that a fifty-three-year-old steam fitter, Walter Kranz, and another customer had each used the phone at about the time police received the anonymous call. Both men were brought in for questioning. The other patron passed a lie test indicating he had no knowledge of the call, but Kranz flunked miserably.

He then admitted to polygraph operator Walter Gehr that he was inspired to make the call after dreaming that the girls' bodies were in Santa Fe Park. "Psychic powers run in my family," he explained.

If busy investigators didn't have enough to do in their search for the missing girls, now they were chasing dreams.

Early Tuesday afternoon on January 22—twenty-five days after the girls had disappeared—Leonard Prescott was driving east on German Church Road on his way to a neighborhood grocery. Glancing over his left shoulder as he cruised down the two-lane blacktop he spotted what appeared to be two discarded department store mannequins lying along the north shoulder, just east of the Cook-Du Page County line.

After returning to his home in Hinsdale, Prescott casually mentioned the incident to his wife, Marie. Her curiosity was piqued to the point that she wanted to have a look for herself. They drove back down the road, traveled mostly by factory workers from nearby Willow Springs, to a point where the pavement dipped to cross Devil's Creek.

"See, over there, just beyond the guardrail—there they are," Prescott observed. He pulled off to the side of the road so his wife could get a better look. She walked over to the rail, where the snow-covered ground dropped precipitously fifteen feet to the frozen creek, and then hurried back to the car. "Oh, my God, Len. Those aren't dummies," she gasped. "It's two naked girls!"

The Prescotts sped on down the road to Willow Springs, where they alerted police at 1:35 P.M. Within minutes dozens of squad cars from the Cook County Sheriff's office and nearby suburbs lined both sides of German Church Road, red lights flashing, as grizzled lawmen looked down in horror at the grotesque scene.

Chicago police, who had been notified of the grim discovery, arrived with Joseph Grimes. The husky trucker took one look and went to pieces. "Yes, that's Barb and Petey," he choked. "We tried to tell police our daughters didn't run away, but nobody would listen."

The sisters were completely naked. A search of the surrounding area by twenty deputy sheriffs failed to turn up any trace of their clothing or personal belongings. Harry Glos, chief investigator for Coroner Walter McCarron, told Sheriff Joseph Lohman and Undersheriff Thomas Brennan, "The bodies are frozen solid. They've been here for several days, at least. They were covered up by the heavy snow that came down on the night of January 9, and then they were exposed by the weekend thaw."

The bodies were stacked one on top of the other at right angles, in the form of a cross.

Patricia, who lay on top, had three puncture wounds in the chest that appeared to have been made by an ice pick. There were deep creases on her legs and back, apparently from lying in the weeds. Barbara, who was lying on her left side, with her head buried in grass and leaves, bore marks and bruises on her cheek, as if she might have been beaten. Tin cans, bottles, and other debris surrounded the bodies. Both bodies contained numerous rodent bites.

As sheriff's investigators went over the area a heavy snow began to fall. Sheriff Lohman ordered tarpaulins draped over the site to protect any evidence from the elements, and posted a twenty-four-hour guard to remain until the scene had been searched for clues.

The bodies were placed in an ambulance and taken to the Cook County morgue to thaw out. Three of the city's top pathologists, Dr. Jerry Kearns, Dr. Edwin Hirsch, and Dr. A.C. Webb were alerted to stand by to perform autopsies. Crime lab technicians, meanwhile, took scrapings from beneath the fingernails and toenails of the girls.

The unfortunate Kranz, who said he had dreamed of seeing the girls' bodies in Santa Fe Park, was rearrested and taken to the Englewood lockup for further interrogation and follow-up lie tests. He stuck by his story that he had seen the whole thing in a dream.

Santa Fe Park was about a mile and a half from where the bodies were actually discovered. Brennan and Captain Walter Fleming, head of the sheriff's Major Investigations Unit, dispatched several dozen deputies into the Santa Fe Park area to canvass taverns and roadhouses in search of information pertinent to the case.

Chicago Police Commissioner Timothy J. O'Connor huddled with Deputy Commissioner Kyran Phelan, who made fifty Chicago policemen, including twenty-two motorcycle patrolmen, available to assist in the investigation. They joined a task force of more than 200 state, city, county, and suburban police from La Grange, Justice, Bridgeview, Summit, Bedford Park, and Willow Springs, along with forest preserve rangers, who combed the western area of Cook County around where the bodies were found. The searchers came up with two blouses, a belt, and a sweater, but Mrs. Grimes said they had not belonged to her daughters.

On the following day, after the bodies had thawed, the autopsies were performed. But what authorities had hoped would provide answers to what had happened to the girls only deepened the mystery. The five-hour post mortem examination utterly failed to establish the cause of death.

"This is one of the roughest cases I've ever seen in my years with the coroner's office," said Dr. Kearns, chief pathologist for St. Elizabeth's Hospital and a coroner's pathologist for many years before that. "This is the first time in my memory that the cause or evidence of death has been concealed so well on victims known to have met a violent end."

The three pathologists determined that the sisters were both virgins, and had not been sexually molested; that they had not died by strangulation or from carbon monoxide poisoning; and that there were no signs of external violence on the bodies that could have resulted in death. The mortality experts could not even hazard a guess as to how long the girls had been dead, because there was no way of telling how long their bodies had been frozen.

The pathologists determined that the three puncture wounds found on Patricia's chest, believed to have been caused by an ice pick or similar object, were only superficial—none more than three-quarters of an inch deep.

Particles of food found in Barbara's stomach indicated she had eaten three to six hours before she died, whenever that might have been. An analysis of both girls' internal organs confirmed that neither had been poisoned.

A check of weather reports indicated the bodies had to have been dumped alongside German Church Road on the night of January 9, when a storm dumped a foot of snow on the Chicago area. Had they been there earlier, they would have easily been seen by passing motorists.

The pathologists' findings raised the possibility that the girls might have been held prisoner in some lonely, unheated building until they succumbed to the effects of exposure to the bitter cold weather. The condition of the bodies indicated they had not been kept in a warm place for any length of time between the hour of death and the time their naked corpses were left by the side of the road.

The banner headlines in all four Chicago newspapers set the stage for a publicity battle between Cook County's comic opera coroner, McCarron, a trucking magnate who pioneered the manipulation of the media for self promotion, and the college professor sheriff, Lohman, who harbored a chronic case of halitosis that kept even his closest associates at arm's length.

When Republican McCarron called a news conference to announce on television that his office had assumed charge of the investigation, Democrat Lohman hurried down to the County Building press room to declare that the bodies were found in the county, which fell under his jurisdiction.

State's Attorney Benjamin S. Adamowski angrily chastised both of them. "This is the same lack of cooperation between law enforcement agencies that loused up the investigation into the Schuessler-Peterson murders fifteen months ago," he said. "If we let that kind of rivalry get going in this case we're going to wind up the same way—at a dead end."

Stung by the state's attorney's rebuke, Lohman called a harmony meeting in his County Building office to map a unified strategy. Present were McCarron, Adamowski, O'Connor, and Phelan, along with State Police Lieutenant H.W. Moran, Sheriff Stanley Lynch of Du Page County, an FBI representative, the three pathologists who did the autopsies, and Dr. Walter J.R. Camp, state police toxicologist and University of Illinois professor, who had made blood tests on the victims.

The similarities between the Grimes case and the Oct. 16, 1955, slayings of John and Anton Schuessler and Robert Peterson were chilling.

In both cases the naked victims were stacked one on top of the other, a few feet from a road in an isolated area, near a river. In each case, inclement weather might have helped the killers lure the victims into an auto. Both sets of victims had also gone to movies.

The convenient discovery of the bodies pointed to the known habit of a certain type of sex degenerate to make only a halfhearted effort to conceal his victims, usually several miles from where he had picked them up. And the fact that the victims had been stripped naked in both instances deprived police of the opportunity to examine their clothing, which might have yielded valuable clues.

Despite the similarities, Lieutenant Joseph Morris, head of a special police unit still investigating Schuessler-Peterson homicides, discounted any possibility that the two multiple slayings were related. "We are going into this investigation as an entirely new offense," he asserted.

Within hours of Lohman's harmony meeting it was discovered that he had a prime suspect in the slayings under wraps. He was Edward L. "Bennie" Bedwell, a twenty-one-year-old skid row dishwasher. Bedwell was arrested after three witnesses had placed him on skid row with the Grimes sisters on January 6, and four other persons reported having seen him with girls matching their description in Stickney on January 11.

Bedwell denied any knowledge of the slayings, but the professorly Lohman told him, "Bennie, the lie detector tests indicate your story is contradictory and shot through with falsehoods. Why don't you make it easy on yourself and tell us what happened?" Finally, after twenty-four hours of nonstop questioning, Bedwell confessed to the murders, but said he didn't mean to do it. He said he had met the girls on December 29, and thought one of them was named Carol. He was secretly whisked in handcuffs out to the scene on German Church Road, where the spot the bodies were found was pointed out to him.

"Is this the place where you left the girls, Bennie?" he was asked. "Uh huh," he said, hanging his head. "What did you do to them, Bennie?" "I punched them," he answered. "But they were still alive when I left."

Lohman was ecstatic as he breezed pompously into the County Building press room and breathed into reporters' faces that he had solved the Grimes killings. "We've got a full confession," he gloated. "There's no question in my mind. Bennie Bedwell is the killer. He told me personally that he did it."

Bedwell, meanwhile, had already repudiated his confession. Detective Chief Patrick Deeley and Lieutenant James McMahon of the Chicago homicide squad, huddled with the sheriff to discuss the suspect, who had been sprung on other agencies without notice. "If I were convinced that he is innocent, I would release him," Lohman asserted.

The Chicago detectives weren't quite so sure. They put their own men on the case, and discovered that the two girls Bedwell had been seen with were not the Grimes sisters, but Irene Dean, a nineteen-year-old Ottawa Indian, and her eighteen-year-old cousin, Carol King. Both confirmed that they had been with Bennie on the dates in question.

Further questioning of Bedwell indicated the dull-witted dishwasher would confess to just about anything police accused him of. With a little effort, they could have used him to clean up every unsolved homicide on the books. "Bennie is just a lazy, shiftless bum," his mother told detectives who were checking into his background.

Lohman reluctantly had to release his "prime suspect." His clumsy one-upmanship had not only bungled the case, but rang the death knell to his political career, dashing his hopes of one day becoming governor of Illinois.

From that point on Chicago police bore the brunt of the investigation, assuming that whatever happened to the girls took place in the city, near their home, before they were dumped out in the boondocks.

In all, they interrogated 3,341 suspects and ran 73 of them through the polygraph. They checked out hundreds of leads and scores of possible "sightings" of the girls between the night they disappeared and the afternoon their frozen bodies were discovered.

Four detectives, Sheldon Teller, Richard Austin, James Micus, and Albert Marks, determinedly spearheaded the battle to unravel the mystery long after other police moved on to other cases. A solution would be the achievement of a lifetime for any detective. Austin and Teller spent long hours chatting with Loretta Grimes, probing her daughters' pasts for possible clues. But every person they talked to and every trail they followed proved to be the wrong one. The Grimes case stands as one of the most baffling in Chicago police history to this day.

UPDATE

In 1961, Captain Maurice Begner, the city's newly appointed chief of detectives, formed a special ten-man unit to seek solutions to the unsolved series of child murders in Chicago since 1955, including the Grimes sisters, the Schuessler-Peterson boys, and Judith Mae Andersen. Austin and Teller, who had never given up on the case, were named to the team. The investigation dragged on for years, but in the end police were forced to admit that they were not only stumped as to who killed Barbara and Patricia, but also how, when, where, and why.

More than $11,000 was offered in rewards for the person or persons responsible for the girls' deaths, but nobody ever attempted to claim the money.

THE TRICK-OR-TREAT MURDERS

The specter of All Saints' Day still haunts the people of Decatur, a central Illinois community of 94,000 on the banks of the Sangamon River, where every parent's worst nightmare came true that awful night in 1984.

Halloween night was a particularly exciting time for the children of the town, dressed as goblins, spooks, clowns, tramps, cowboys, pirates, ballerinas, and monsters, as they skipped merrily from house to house, holding out their bags of goodies and chanting, "Trick or treat!"

Twelve-year-old Sherry Gordon was out with the rest of the neighborhood kids that night, along with her cousin, Theresa Hall, age nine, and Theresa's seven-year-old sister, Patricia. They weren't wearing costumes, just their regular after-school clothes. They went out to make the rounds, that Halloween night—and never came home.

At 11:00 P.M. their frantic parents, after two hours of walking the streets of their neighborhood calling the children's names, notified Decatur police.

Friends, neighbors, and police officers searched throughout the night, but could find nary a trace of the missing trio.

The next day police conducted a door-to-door search over a twenty-eight-square block area of the city, including a rail yard. They also consulted building department records to get a list of abandoned buildings in the area.

Tension mounted when a pair of red slacks was found on Interstate Hwy. 72 and U.S. 36, west of the city. Blanche Gordon, Sherry's mother, identified the slacks as belonging to her niece, Patricia. Could someone have abducted the youngsters and driven off with them?

"They wouldn't have gotten into anyone's car voluntarily," she told Police Sergeant B.J. Baum. "They would never do that unless someone forced them. They're not riding with anybody." A description of the little girls was broadcast statewide, as police, volunteers, and Illinois National Guardsmen, along with the FBI, stepped up the hunt.

The search ended tragically on Friday morning, November 2, in an abandoned building being rehabilitated for public housing, just a few blocks north of the downtown area near the girls' home. Maintenance men checking furnace pipes discovered Sherry Gordon's little body in one of the upstairs bedrooms. In an adjoining room they found the corpse of her cousin, Theresa.

Macon County Coroner Chris Vallas told Police Chief Patrick Vaughan, "They were both strangled with some kind of cord. As soon as we can post the bodies I'll be able to tell you more."

With the discovery of the bodies, police began a room by room search of the building. The third child, seven-year-old Patty, was found cowering in fear in a closet on the second floor. Assuming that she knew what had happened to the other two youngsters, she was placed under police guard at Decatur Memorial Hospital, where she was taken for observation.

Meanwhile an autopsy on the bodies of the two cousins by Dr. Grant Johnson, a forensic pathologist, disclosed that both of the children had been sexually abused. An examination of the third girl, at the hospital, revealed that she had not been harmed.

In a halting voice the bewildered seven-year-old survivor told police that the three children were lured into the empty apartment building by a man who promised them candy and money for "trick-or-treat" rewards. She said the man first locked her inside a closet, but let her out when she began screaming because she was afraid of the dark. She slipped back into the closet and hid after seeing him strangle her sister with a rope, and her cousin, Sherry, with her own blouse.

Patty, who suffered from a learning disability, was unable to give police a description of the killer. All she could tell them was, "It was a big, bad man."

The youngster was kept in protective custody for nearly a year as police searched for the killer, fearing that he might try to get her, too, to keep her from identifying him. In September of 1985 a judge ruled that Patty could be returned to her family, saying he saw no justification in keeping her in hiding any longer.

In the year following the double murder police compiled 2,000 pages of reports, conducted 2,700 interviews, and collected 2,790 names, including 84 nicknames, of possible suspects. They administered 20 lie detector tests, and the FBI provided authorities with a criminal profile of the assailant. Investigators contacted 28 other police agencies, along with 210 schools, hospitals, and churches in tracking down leads.

"We have a large body of information, including clues collected at the apartment that were processed by the state crime lab," Chief Vaughan said. "We haven't given up. We're just waiting for the right piece to fall into place."

In 1987 it looked like it was going to happen, when an inmate of the Menard State Penitentiary, where he was serving time for abusing a twelve-year-old girl, telephoned Decatur police to say he had information about the murders of Theresa Hall and Sherry Gordon. Chief Vaughan sent detectives to the prison to interview the informant. He told them he had been an eye witness to the killings, and implicated another man as the slayer.

"Let's not jump to conclusions and get the town's hopes up," Chief Vaughan cautioned his men. "I want this guy checked out thoroughly before we do or say anything." It was sound advice.

It didn't take investigators long to determine that the Menard prisoner who said he was present when the girls were strangled had been a patient in a Decatur hospital—under constant monitoring in intensive care—from before Halloween to Nov. 30, 1984. Detective Don Allsop confronted the prisoner with the hospital records, and he admitted that his story had been a fabrication. All he wanted was a little attention.

"We had hopes but it turned out not to be," Allsop said, regretfully. "Our investigation of the case is still going on."

UPDATE

Decatur residents, incensed that small children were no longer safe while out trick-or-treating on Halloween, raised $6,000 in rewards for information leading to the arrest and conviction of the killer. Crime Stoppers, the national crime prevention organization, added another $1,000, bringing the reward money to $7,000—but to this day there have been no takers.

THE CORPSE IN THE HEARSE

On a snowy February afternoon in 1967, the day before Saint Valentine's Day, three adventurous grade school youngsters wriggled through a hole in the wire fence surrounding an auto pound on the West Side of Kenosha, Wisconsin, to play in the abandoned cars. A dozen battered derelicts, forsaken by their owners, were lined up along a four-foot high barbed wire fence adjoining the Chicago & North Western switch yards, where police had ordered them towed because they interfered with snow removal operations.

One of the cast-off vehicles was a once-sleek 1948 Packard hearse. "Hey, lookit over there! That's one a those cars that they haul dead people in," one of the youngsters chirped. "Yeah! Let's look inside. Maybe there's a dead body in it." They giggled with anticipation as they slogged through the powdery snow and clumsily yanked open the rear door with their mittened hands. Abruptly the laughter stopped.

What the three small boys had jokingly expected to find in the back of the old hearse was the last thing in the world they *really* expected to find. They screamed in horror and, leaving the door sagging open in the wind, made tracks for the yard office where they excitedly blurted out their find.

"Mister, there's a dead body in that there hearse. We just saw it!"

"You kids have got no business in the yard. How did you get in here? G'wan home! You could get hurt playin' out there."

"No, honest mister. Honest! We saw it. Go and look!"

The city worker, not happy with his lot in life at the moment, pulled on his jacket and tramped reluctantly out to the abandoned hearse. Best to call the kids' bluff so he could get back to work. He went around to the back where their footprints had trampled down the snow, took one look inside, and ran back on the double to telephone police.

Captain Michael Bruno, chief of detectives, arrived a few minutes later. One look told him what he had feared on the way over. Mary Ellen Kaldenberg had been found.

The seventeen-year-old Tremper High School junior had been missing since Thursday, February 9, from the neat, white bungalow where she lived with her widowed mother, Daniela, and her fourteen-year-old brother, Eddie. Her father, Cecil, had died when she was six.

Mary Ellen had gotten home from school late that day because of band practice. She made herself a snack and turned on the television while waiting for her boyfriend, Jim, who was coming over after supper. At about seven o'clock she told her mother she was going to run over to the Hub Drug Store in the nearby "Uptown" business district, for a bottle of pop. She put on her heavy red ski jacket, went out onto the front porch and down the steps. She turned left, walked past the end of a snow-filled alley running alongside the house, and vanished into the night.

Jim came by at 8:30, as promised, and was somewhat miffed at not finding Mary Ellen home. "She went out more than an hour ago for a bottle of pop. She said she'd be right back," her mother apologized. "Well, I guess I'll go out and meet her," Jim sighed, zipping his heavy jacket back up.

He walked the two blocks to 22nd Avenue and 63rd Street in the bitter cold, expecting to run into Mary Ellen along the way. "Maybe she found someone to talk to at the store," he told himself, blowing into his hands to keep them warm. He got to the Hub just before closing time, pushed the door open, stomped his feet, and looked around. She wasn't there. "Looking for Mary Ellen? Haven't seen her all night," the owner said, noting the confused look on the youth's face.

Puzzled, Jim made a sweep of the neighborhood. He checked the nearby Donut Hole, Bernacchi's pharmacy, the Dutch Maid ice cream store, and other teen-age hangouts, but nobody had seen Mary Ellen. He returned to the Kaldenberg home, hoping she'd be back by then. Her mother hadn't heard anything either. "Well, I'm going home," he said. "Have her call me when she shows up."

He telephoned the Kaldenberg home twice during the evening, but the answer was the same both times. "I can't imagine what happened to that girl. She could at least call so I wouldn't worry." Mary Ellen didn't come home at all that night, and first thing Friday morning her mother alerted the police.

The initial theory that the teen-ager had run away didn't wash. None of her personal belongings were missing. Nothing further was heard until the following Monday after school, when the three boys opened the door of the hearse and found her frozen body, about a mile from home.

Mary Ellen was still wearing the green sweater, black stretch pants, and red ski jacket that she had on when she ran out for a bottle of pop on Thursday night. She was fully clothed except for her shoes, which had been arranged neatly beside the corpse.

A heavy slab of concrete from a broken sidewalk had been placed across her abdomen, as if to hold her down so she wouldn't rise to the surface of some mysterious sea. There was blood everywhere, mixed with the drifted snow that had blown in through openings in the ancient vehicle.

An autopsy, performed at a local funeral home after the body was thawed out, indicated she had been stabbed twelve times in the neck, chest, and forehead. "The nature of the wounds indicates it was a blade-type weapon," Coroner

Edward Wavro advised police. "Two of the wounds in her chest pierced the heart, causing death by internal bleeding. Cuts in her jacket and sweater indicate she was wearing all her clothing at the time she was stabbed."

Captain Bruno ordered the auto pound closed so police could scour the grounds for evidence. The old Packard deathwagon was towed away so crime lab technicians could go over it in the warmth of a downtown garage, and the area where it had been parked was roped off.

Detectives were puzzled as to how Mary Ellen got into the morbid vehicle in the first place. The hearse had been parked there for several months, since the first snows of the season, when it was towed off the street. It hadn't been used to transport dead bodies in more than a decade. Until 1965 a local tavern operator, Frank Renzoni, had used it to haul his baseball team around.

The city lot where the hearse had been towed was locked at the end of each work day, but could be entered by crawling under loose places in the wire fence, the way the kids who made the macabre discovery had gotten in.

If Mary Ellen had been slain elsewhere, the killer would have had to drag or carry her body across the railroad tracks along the south end of the lot in the bitter cold and snow, down a nine-foot embankment, and either over or under the barbed wire fence.

Police could only conclude that she had been slain after getting into the back end of the hearse. The presence of blood in the frozen interior of the vehicle attested to that.

But that left the question: How did she get there in the first place, more than a mile from the corner drugstore where she had gone for a bottle of pop, but never arrived?

Police questioned her friends, acquaintances, school mates, and fellow members of the Tremper band, in an effort to trace her movements, but no one had seen her that fatal night. The only clue police were able to turn up was a witness who said he had seen a blue 1962 Rambler near the auto pound on the night she disappeared. The Ramblers were built in Kenosha. There were hundreds of them in the Southeastern Wisconsin manufacturing town.

An abandoned hearse, a bloody chunk of concrete, a dozen knife wounds, and an elusive blue Rambler. Try as they might, Kenosha police were never able to put the pieces of the puzzle together, and the murder of Mary Ellen Kaldenberg remains a mystery.

UPDATE

Three other young women, all living within a two hour drive from Kenosha, were murdered within the same time frame of the Kaldenberg killing.

Valerie Percy, the twenty-one-year-old daughter of U.S. Senator Charles Percy of Illinois, was stabbed to death by an intruder who attacked her in her bedroom in the Percy mansion in Kenilworth, thirty-five miles south of Kenosha, on the night of Sept. 18, 1966.

Just two months later Dianne Olkwitz, a twenty-year-old receptionist in Menomonee Falls, forty-five miles north of Kenosha, was murdered in the factory where she worked. She had been stabbed more than thirty times. Mary Ellen Kaldenberg was killed three months after that.

And in May of 1968 Christine Rothschild, eighteen, a University of Wisconsin freshman from Chicago, was murdered outside a classroom on the Madison campus. Her gloves had been stuffed into her mouth to keep her from screaming, and she had been stabbed fourteen times.

There were marked similarities in all four homicides. Each of the victims had been stabbed repeatedly, even though one thrust of the knife would have been fatal. None of the victims had been sexually molested. All three of the Wisconsin victims were fully clothed, and Valerie Percy was wearing her nightclothes.

Authorities noted that the four slayings took place in a "Bermuda Triangle" of murder formed by Kenilworth, Madison and Menomonee Falls. They have not ruled out the disturbing fact that all four frenzied attacks could have been the work of the same madman, and if that is true, he could still be out there.

HITCHING A RIDE WITH DEATH

Talk about bizarre twists, the discovery of the bodies of two teenaged girls in Washington Park near the University of Chicago kicked off one of the strangest homicide investigations in the city's history of crime.

There had been a veritable spate of unsolved murders of young women and girls in the Chicago area during the summer of 1972, starting with eighteen-year-old Kathleen Morecraft, who was found beaten to death with a rock in a wooded area near Streamwood on June 22.

Then, on July 9, fifteen-year-old Julie Hanson was found stabbed to death in Naperville. On September 4, Judith Betteley, twenty-four, a tourist from England, was beaten to death while taking a Labor Day stroll through Grant Park. One week later the bodies of twenty-seven-year-old Barbara Flanagan and her eighteen-month-old daughter, Renee, were found in a Mount Prospect church parking lot. The infant had been killed by a sexual attack and the mother died when the attacker beat her head against the pavement. Sally Kandel, fourteen, who disappeared from her home in Carol Stream the next day, was found beaten to death in a cornfield on the edge of town.

And on September 22, fifteen-year-old Amy Alden, who had been missing from her home in Evanston since September 5, was found murdered near a Skokie cemetery.

The next day, Saturday, an early morning jogger in Washington Park came upon the two latest victims a half block west of the National Guard Armory at 5200 South Cottage Grove Avenue.

The fully clothed bodies of the dead girls were lying face down in the shape of a "V" with their feet almost touching. Each had been shot once in the base of the neck, but neither had been sexually molested. Neither possessed any identification cards, purses, or money. One of them was wearing a T-shirt with the wording, "Love is saying it only if you mean it." Coroner Andrew J. Toman said they had been dead four to six hours.

Wentworth Area detectives put out a description of the girls, both white, about sixteen to eighteen years old, five feet seven inches tall and weighing 130 pounds. The bodies were taken to the Cook County Morgue, where every effort would be made to identify the victims, to aid police in their investigation. "If we don't identify them in twenty-four hours—unless something breaks: a telephone call, a piece of clothing—then it's going to get awfully tough," explained Officer William Bodner of the missing persons unit. "So far, we've drawn a blank."

There was one possible clue. One of the girls had what appeared to be a phone number written in ink on her wrist, but it was blurred and could not be made out.

The parents of a number of missing teenagers were brought to the morgue where they apprehensively gazed at the murdered girls. Among them were Richard Pilewicz, a forty-two-year-old Polish immigrant, and his distraught wife, Violet. Their seventeen-year-old daughter, Rosemarie, had been missing since August 10.

Pilewicz could not bear to look, so he stood outside the door, tears welled in his eyes, as his wife went into the chilly room where the two victims were on display. She was in there a long time, fifteen minutes it seemed. This was not how she had planned for her daughter's life to end. Yet there she was, eyes closed in the peculiar way she slept. The pug nose, the short-cropped blonde hair, high cheekbones, strawberry-shaped earrings, and T-shirt. And the phone number written on her wrist—a habit of Rosemarie's. When she came out of the room weeping she told her husband, "You'd better go in and see."

"That's our Rosy," the brokenhearted parents told police. They were so shaken by the ordeal that they had to be helped to their car.

"Now we have something to go on," said homicide Lieutenant Walter Bosko. Once Rosemarie Pilewicz' identity had been established, detectives went to her neighborhood in the 1700 block of West Erie Street to question friends and acquaintances in an effort to find out who the other victim was, and when the girls were last seen alive.

Rosemarie's picture was shown Saturday night on the ten o'clock news, along with a plea from police for anyone having information to contact them. They received their first call Sunday morning—but it was not what they had expected.

At 10:30 A.M. a young man telephoned the Foster Avenue police station and told the dispatcher: "Rosemarie Pilewicz isn't dead." "What do you mean, she's not dead?" "She isn't," the caller insisted. "She saw her picture in the paper this morning, but it isn't her—the one who was killed isn't her. Send someone to the Lawrence Avenue El station and she'll be there." It was most likely a crank call, but the dispatcher told Patrolman John Roberts to drive over to the elevated station to check it out.

As Roberts pulled up at the station a blonde girl with short-cropped hair, wearing blue jeans and a denim jacket, walked over to the squad car.

"Are you Rosemarie?" he asked, incredulously.

"Yes, I am," she replied.

The girl was taken to the Foster Avenue station, where Officer James Allotta put in a call to the Pilewicz home.

Richard and Violet Pilewicz had already made funeral arrangements for their slain daughter. Allotta got the bereaved father on the phone, and tried to explain that he had a girl with him who claimed she was Rosemarie.

The girl grabbed the phone out of the police officer's hand and said, "Papa, you trust me? I didn't do anything wrong. I live with a girl."

It sounded like Rosemarie. Pilewicz asked police if they would bring the girl to their home. When the police car drove up and the girl got out, Pilewicz embraced her and wept, "Rosy, Rosy, we buried you almost. I cried all night."

Rosemarie had run away from home because she felt her parents were too strict. The blonde girl in the morgue could have been her twin. Now, that she had returned from the dead, police were back where they started when the two bodies were discovered Saturday morning.

The only clue they had to the victims' identity was the blurred telephone number on one girl's wrist. It looked like it started with 467. That was the prefix of the telephone exchange serving 10,000 phones in an area bounded by Ohio Street, the Chicago River, Lake Michigan, and the river's north branch.

Meanwhile a new parade of parents of missing teenagers marched through the basement room of the county morgue at 1828 West Polk Street. One woman, in bedroom slippers, her hair in curlers and wearing a raincoat over her housedress, paused longer than the others. She was Sally VanderMolen, who lived in the 5100 block of South Elizabeth Street. Yes, the dark-haired girl was definitely her thirteen-year-old daughter, Carolyn.

"I last saw her Friday morning when she went off to school at St. Augustine's, where she's in the eight grade," she told police. "When she came home from school Friday afternoon she asked my husband if she could sleep over at a girlfriend's house and he said no, but she went out anyway."

Police then had Mrs. VanderMolen look at the other girl—the one who had almost been buried as Rosemarie

Pilewicz. "Yes, I know her, too," the woman said. "That's Debbie Kozlorek. I'm pretty sure. She lives a block over from us on Racine Avenue."

Deborah's father, Edward Kozlarek, a truck driver, was brought to the morgue, where he positively identified the blonde girl as his seventeen-year-old daughter, a high school dropout who worked as a waitress.

The mysterious telephone number written on the girl's wrist turned out to be 767–9040—not 467. It was the number of the restaurant where Debbie worked.

Police now had something to go on. Debbie and Carolyn, good friends despite the four-year age difference, were last seen walking together at 8:00 P.M. Friday in an alley near their homes. How they ended up in Washington Park, nearly two miles away, was explained to detectives by their friends. They liked to hitchhike, and often thumbed rides with strangers to get where they wanted to go.

"They used to stand on that corner and hitchhike rides," said fifteen-year-old Kimberly Fitzgerald, pointing to the intersection of Racine Avenue and 52nd Street. "They would take a ride with anyone who'd pick them up because they didn't want to spend money."

Police theorized that the girls hitched a ride with someone who drove them to Washington Park, forced them to lie facedown in the grass, shot them both in the back of the head, and took their purses.

UPDATE

A twenty-nine-year-old Bible salesman, Lee Clark Jennings, confessed to the murders of Barbara Flanagan and her baby daughter, which occurred after the young mother had answered an ad he had placed for a baby-sitter.

A twenty-year-old Wheaton construction worker, Richard Milone, confessed to the bludgeon slaying of Sally Kandel, and was sentenced to a prison term of 90 to 175 years.

Meanwhile there was yet one more victim in the string of murders that plagued the Chicago area in the summer of 1972. The body of an eighteen-year-old Evanston girl, Robin Feuerriegel, who disappeared August 26, was found three months later in a cornfield near Glenview Naval Air Station. Because of the advanced stage of decomposition, the cause of death could not be established. Ironically, she had been a close friend of the slain Amy Alden.

With the exception of the Flanagan and Kandel murders, all of the homicides remain unsolved.

THE SITTER WHO NEVER CAME HOME

The full moon glowed yellow-bright in the sky over the Mississippi River as its lazy water lapped its way around Goose Island and carried fallen leaves like tiny brown barges downstream toward De Soto and Prairie du Chien. It was the week before Halloween, and a big night in the river town of La Crosse, with the college homecoming and a state high school parley both on the same evening.

But Oct. 24, 1953, will most be remembered around these parts as the night a bright young bobby-soxer named Evelyn Grace Hartley disappeared in a horrible splash of blood, leaving behind her jacket, eyeglasses, and shoes.

The tragic disappearance of the fifteen-year-old baby-sitter remains Wisconsin's number one unsolved mystery. And the ghastly fate she quite possibly met is almost beyond human comprehension.

Evelyn was the daughter of Dr. and Mrs. Richard Hartley. Her father was a biology professor at La Crosse State College. She was a straight-A student in the sophomore class at Central High School, where she was active in both intramural and extracurricular activities. Her family, in addition to her parents, included a married brother, Tom, and a younger sister, Carolyn.

Evelyn had not yet started dating seriously. On the evening of October 24 she was at home with her father, whom she had just helped complete a research project involving fruit flies.

Dressed in a white blouse, red pedal pushers, and oxfords, she was waiting to be picked up for her baby-sitting job. That is how her family will always remember the attractive, dark-haired teen-ager.

Dr. Viggo Rasmusen, a physics professor at the college, stopped by for Evelyn just after 6:30 P.M., and drove her to the Rasmusens' white cottage about a mile and a half away in a new development on the edge of town.

The Rasmusens and Hartleys were close friends, and Mrs. Rasmusen knew she didn't have to give many instructions to the practical young student who was being left in charge of twenty-month-old Janis. "Put the baby to bed at seven o'clock, and cover her up fifteen minutes later," she said. Then the Rasmusens headed for the homecoming festivities, secure in the knowledge they had left their home and infant daughter in the hands of the kind of teen-ager they knew could be "trusted."

As the hum of the Rasmusens' auto faded into the night Evelyn assumed the baby-sitter's lonely vigil. She was, now, a growing child with adult responsibilities in a strange home. She turned on the radio and set the dial at a local station. It was 6:45 P.M. and the gala homecoming parade downtown was about to begin.

The radio helped compensate for the silence that had suddenly taken over the house when the Rasmusens left. Evelyn noted the clock conscientiously, mindful of Mrs. Rasmusen's instructions, and promptly at 7:00 P.M. she put baby Janis to bed, kissed her goodnight, and turned out the light. Before tiptoeing out of the room she set the child's blanket aside to cover her in fifteen minutes.

It would never be done. Evelyn Hartley's time was already running out.

Authorities believe that, even then, someone sinister was

watching the coed's every movement as she tended her chores in the comfortable ranch-style home. Perhaps it was someone hiding in the shadows outside when the Rasmusens pulled away to go to their party, and who felt the unguarded house might be ripe for burglary. Or, as some investigators feel, it was someone specifically on the prowl for a young girl that night of the full moon.

The well-disciplined Hartley girl had a habit of regularly calling her parents from every baby-sitting job. Exactly one hour after her arrival she would telephone home to assure them that everything was under control, there were no problems, and she was all right.

Back home Professor Hartley glanced impatiently at his watch. It was after eight o'clock, and Evelyn had not called. "It's not like her," he told his wife. "I don't want her to think we don't have confidence in her, but I think I'm going to call the Rasmusens' just to make sure everything's okay. He waited until 9:00 P.M. to make the call. There was no answer.

Possibly his daughter was having trouble with the child, and couldn't come to the phone. Or maybe she stepped outside to enjoy the crisp autumn air and gaze at the bright harvest moon. Hartley called the home again. Still no answer.

Concerned now, he telephoned a neighbor of the Rasmusens and asked whether he could see any activity next door. The neighbor peeked out his window. Nothing seemed amiss. Then Hartley called a second neighbor, and a third. All checked outside, but none could see anyone stirring about or anything unusual at the Rasmusen place.

"Maybe I could have dialed the wrong number," Hartley said, trying again. He let the phone ring for more than a minute, but no one picked it up.

Finally he told his wife, "I'm going to take a buzz over there. She wouldn't go away and leave the baby alone, and if there were any problems she would have called us. The worried father got into his car and quickly drove the distance, noticing with some reassurance when he pulled up that the lights were burning in the home. Getting out of the car and going up to the front door, he knocked rapidly and called out his daughter's name. Odd. There was no response.

Nervously he circled the house, banging on doors and rapping on windows on every side. All he got in return was a chilling silence. On one side of the house Hartley noticed a narrow basement window was gaping open. "That's not right," he said to himself. Dropping to his knees he poked his head inside and called out, "Evelyn! Evelyn! It's Dad. Are you in there?"

Hearing no response, Hartley eased himself into the opening, feet first. Feeling around in the darkness, his feet found the top step of a small ladder that had been placed against the wall beneath the window. Resting his feet upon it, he pressed down to make sure it was secure, and then lowered himself to the concrete floor.

Glancing about the unfamiliar basement the college professor spotted something that caused a sinking feeling in the pit of his stomach. It was one of his daughter's shoes.

"Evelyn!" he called out again. "Are you up there?" He could feel the hair on the back of his neck standing out as he methodically mounted the stairs. The radio was playing as he passed through the kitchen and surveyed the cozy living room. "Oh, Lord," he said, as he spied Evelyn's other shoe and her eyeglasses on the carpet. There was also mud on the rug. Fresh mud. Something was terribly wrong.

"Evelyn! Evelyn! Are you in here? It's your father!"

The knot in his stomach tightened as Hartley cautiously went from room to room. The baby was all right. But there was no Evelyn. Baby Janis was home alone. Hartley looked behind the couch, under beds, in corners, and into the darkest shadows of the basement. Evelyn was nowhere around.

For a fleeting moment the idea of a student prank crossed the professor's mind. A prank pulled off in the spirit of the homecoming celebration. Had Evelyn been in on it? Hardly. She would never go off leaving a sleeping infant alone. Hartley knew his daughter better than that.

He located the telephone and reached for it, but pulled back. Something told him not to touch the phone. There might be fingerprints on it. Making a quick check to be sure the baby was all right, he loped across the street to the home of a neighbor and telephoned police.

"Something is wrong. I know there is," he told the La Crosse dispatcher. "My daughter is supposed to be baby-sitting, but she isn't there. She left her shoes behind, and her glasses are lying on the floor. I know this is a busy night, but I really think you'd better send somebody out to take a look."

"Well, professor, it is homecoming," the officer responded calmly. "But I'll send a squad out to take a look. Just sit tight until we get there. Chances are she's close by somewhere."

When two patrolmen arrived Hartley led them around the side of the house to the open window. They flashed their lights around the lawn curiously. One beam picked out a window screen, which had been pried off and discarded on the ground nearby. Adjacent to the open window another beam flashed on a foreboding red stain. Hartley gasped. The police officer's flashlight had picked up a small pool of blood.

"It looks like you're right, professor. This might not be a joke after all."

From that moment on things happened fast.

The patrol officers thoroughly checked the house. They searched the neighborhood, but turned up nothing. Then they radioed for reinforcements. When the Rasmusens returned home at ten o'clock, there seemed to be police everywhere, but their trusted baby-sitter was nowhere to be found.

When Evelyn's mother was told of the blood stains outside the house she sobbed, "I'm afraid my baby is dead."

The search intensified with the rising of the sun, and as stunned neighbors watched from their yards that Saturday morning police discovered an ominous trail of blood leading from the Rasmusen home. The crimson splotches cut a zigzag path for a distance of one block, leading past homes and garages. A hideous red smear defiling the side of a neighboring house bore mute evidence that someone bleeding badly had lurched against the wall.

The ground was muddy throughout the newly developed subdivision, and footprints were everywhere. But there was one distinctive set of prints that captured the attention of detectives. The prints, made by a pair of sneakers, accompanied the trail of blood from the Rasmusen home to where the trail ended by the side of a road.

A joint investigation into the sitter's disappearance was launched by Police Chief George C. Long and Sheriff Ivan Wright. Detective Captain Leo Kihm was placed in charge.

The first thing Kihm did was bring in bloodhounds. But they were able to follow the scent no farther than where the blood drippings stopped in the street east of the home. Backtracking, however, the dogs followed it back to the home, and then north, for more than a block, from the Rasmusens' basement window to a point in a different street.

It appeared that whoever abducted the girl had started from a street north of the home, broken into the house, and carried her off, and then dragged her east, possibly to a waiting car. Investigators questioned residents of a nearby home who said they had been outside around seven o'clock the previous evening, but they could not recall seeing a car, or anyone who did not belong in the area.

Another neighbor, who had been doing her dishes at about 7:15, recalled hearing screams and a "commotion" outside. The view from her kitchen window gave her a good look at the Rasmusen home—but she saw nothing. "I thought maybe it was just kids playing," she said. "I didn't think any more about it until this morning when they found that awful bloody mark on the side of my house."

Still another neighbor, a man, also thought he heard screams while working in his basement the previous evening, but he did not see anything, either.

There was one important clue: When the Rasmusens arrived home at ten o'clock and found the neighborhood crawling with police, the first thing they did was check their infant daughter, and cover her. "The baby's blanket was still neatly folded at the foot of the crib," Mrs. Rasmusen recalled.

Evelyn was a meticulous and dependable girl. She would have put baby Janis to bed at seven o'clock as instructed, and covered her fifteen minutes later, had she been present to do so. This clearly locked the sitter's disappearance into the fifteen-minute time frame between 7:00 P.M. and 7:15.

The citizens of La Crosse were aghast. Nothing of this magnitude had ever happened in the comfortable river town, where folks were not even in the habit of locking their doors when they went out for groceries or to a movie. Now the community was on page one across the country under the classic "Baby Sitter Mystery" headline. Concerned parents kept their daughters in at night, and townsfolk gossiped in hushed tones about the "mad fiend" who had carried off the Hartley girl.

Could it all be just a big put-on to cover up a runaway? Hardly, with all that human blood splashed about.

Evelyn's distressed father became a daily visitor to police headquarters, where he would discuss developments with Chief Long and Detective Kihm. He was the first to volunteer for a lie detector test. After it was over District Attorney John Bosshard declared, "Professor Hartley has been unequivocally cleared of any suspicion in this matter."

Then came the family torment, fostered by sickos, that frequently follows the wake of publicity cases of this kind. The missing girl's mother was heartsick when she received a message from Devil's Lake, North Dakota, asserting, "Evelyn is in my power. You silly people back there, you almost had me once, but I got away. Ransom note will follow."

No ransom note followed. Whoever abducted the girl never communicated with the family. Police saw this as a bad omen right from the start. A ransom note would have given hope that the teen-ager was still alive.

Kihm's investigators, working around the clock, assembled a jumbled assortment of clues that might have been evidence but were, for the most part, insignificant. A great deal of valuable time was necessarily spent just eliminating misinformation.

The hottest lead in the case was turned up by a Chicago newspaper reporter, who found a witness who recalled driving past the Rasmusen home at about 7:20 P.M. on the night Evelyn disappeared.

"I was on the way to pick up my brother-in-law. I didn't think anything of it at the time, because it was homecoming. But I saw this couple—a man and a girl—and he was kind of supporting her. She was staggering, and I just thought they'd done a little too much celebrating," he recalled.

The witness said he drove on to pick up his relative, and as they turned a corner they spotted another automobile. "My headlights picked out a man behind the wheel. And there was another guy in the back seat with a woman, who seemed to be leaning forward."

Reconjuring the fleeting incident in his mind, the witness said he believed the car was a 1941 Buick four-door, two-tone green. Police put out a bulletin for a car of that description, with no positive results. There was no shortage of 1941 Buicks still on the road in 1953.

Not long after Evelyn's disappearance a road grader operator working south of town on U.S. Highway 14 spotted a nondescript garment lying in a ditch by the east side of the road.

Mindful of the search for the missing baby-sitter, he tossed the item, a worn and well-washed denim jacket, into his grader. It lay there a week until he had an opportunity to turn it over to authorities. A short time later a pair of sneakers was found in the same area. The shoes, men's size 11, were lying about 250 feet apart at a spot about 1,000 feet north of where the denim jacket had been discarded.

The sneakers and jacket were turned over to the State Crime Laboratory in Madison, where lab director Charles Wilson took charge of the assignment personally. He determined that spots on the back of the jacket and on the canvas shoes were human blood—of the same type found at the abduction scene.

Other bloodstained garments had been turned up in a widespread search of the area around La Crosse, but the denim jacket took on special significance because of the proximity it was found in relation to the sneakers. They turned out to be the hottest clue yet.

Wilson was able to match the canvas shoes perfectly into the set of footprints found in the mud outside the Rasmusen home. Furthermore, dirt caked in the suction holes matched mud particles found on the living room carpet inside the house.

"There is little doubt that these are the shoes, and probably the jacket, worn by Evelyn Hartley's abductor," Wilson advised local authorities. "They could most certainly lead us to the person who did it." While he used the word "abductor," there was little doubt that he actually meant killer. The frightening trail of blood at the scene convinced the Hartleys and police they would never see Evelyn again.

The tattered jacket and badly worn tennis shoes, along with the witnesses' description of having seen two men holding a girl in an old green Buick, remained the only solid evidence in the case. Autumn metamorphosed into winter and the trail, like the matching Wisconsin weather, grew bitterly cold.

Local investigators, clearly inexperienced in dealing with a crime of this type, were publicly criticized for inaction and mistakes. Townspeople, perhaps expecting a miracle, did not consider what every true detective knows in matters of this nature: No crime is more difficult to solve than one committed by an outsider with no previous links to either the victim or the place where the incident takes place. It is for this reason that so many child slayings are never solved.

Furthermore, a good detective is often no better than his street contacts—his stool pigeons—and if there are none, he can face frustration and defeat. In the Hartley case, nobody knew anything. It was pathetic. There were no tips; no rumbles on the street. Whoever snatched Evelyn must have either been a loner, or from outside the community. The possibilities seemed endless.

Dogged police work continued, however. In February Sheriff Wright dropped dead. Those who knew him maintained his death was largely due to overwork on the Hartley investigation. He was succeeded by Robert Sculin.

After six months, in the face of public clamoring, the La Crosse County Board voted to hire a full-time professional investigator in hopes that he might be able to accomplish what local authorities could not. Alma M. "Joe" Josephson, thirty-three, a crack insurance investigator from St. Paul, was engaged to work exclusively on the Hartley case.

Josephson, who had eleven years of experience as an Army investigator before becoming an insurance sleuth, was given the title of criminal investigator for the La Crosse County Sheriff's Department. He leaped into the case like a lion after raw meat.

He made a beeline for Wausau, over 100 miles away, where a suspect had been nabbed in a rape case. A lie detector test, however, showed that the rapist was telling the truth when he insisted he was in the Montana State Prison at Deer Lodge at the time the Hartley girl vanished.

The experience proved the value of the lie box, however. It could rule out the innocent as well as trap the guilty, and Josephson saw it as a tool in narrowing down the field of suspects. He ordered the biggest mass lie test in history. On May 6, 1954, the Hartley investigator began testing the first of 1,750 male high school and college students in the area.

Josephson decided to run the tests after he and C.B. Hanscom, director of protection and investigation for the University of Minnesota, conducted an exhaustive review of the case and concluded "in theory" that there was a distinct possibility that someone of school age could be involved in the crime.

Polygraph testing began at 9:00 A.M. in Central High School, where Evelyn had been a student. Examinations were also scheduled in Logan High School, Aquinas Catholic High

School, Vocational High School, and La Crosse State College, where Professor Hartley served on the faculty.

"Participation in these examinations will be entirely voluntary, but I feel it is only fair to point out that anyone who refuses to be tested will be thoroughly checked out by the police," District Attorney Bossard stressed. "Anyone could be a suspect at this point, and this is the quickest way a person can clear his name."

Evelyn's classmates came forward in droves. The same milk-fed youths who had helped comb the woods, fields, and gullies and walked the banks of the Mississippi after her disappearance now volunteered to put themselves on the lie box. Twenty students and two teachers were tested the first day. Each signed a statement of consent, and each was asked five pertinent questions concerning the missing girl.

"Everyone is anxious to cooperate, and so far there hasn't been a single protest of any sort from parents," beamed School Superintendent Arthur Jordan.

Unfortunately, all that the lie detector tests produced were headlines. When the school year ended in June, Evelyn's classmates dedicated their 1954 yearbook to her memory. Members of the Westminister Fellowship, a youth organization in which she had been active, donated a stained glass window in the new First Presbyterian Church in her name.

Josephson now became obsessed with the baffling case. He sat and stared at the smiling school photograph of Evelyn Hartley for hours, as though he might miraculously read the answers to his questions in her clear, blue eyes.

Finally he cast every theory aside and began his investigation anew. He visited the scene of the disappearance, and drove out to the ditch south of town where the denim jacket and sneakers were found by the side of the road. Working with federal agents and Wisconsin state crime lab scientists, he painstakingly pieced together what he believed to be the story of Evelyn's last night on earth.

"I think I can tell you everything except the names of the killers," he said. Now it was out in the open. Josephson did not hesitate to use the word "killers" because he felt there was no chance the baby-sitter could still be alive.

"There had to be two men, based on a very obvious deduction," he said. "One man forced his way into the Rasmusen home by tearing off the screen and entering through the basement window. He crept up the stairs and surprised the frightened girl in the living room. We know that, because his shoes left mud on the carpet.

"There was a struggle, and Evelyn's eyeglasses were knocked to the floor. Her shoes, one left behind on the living room rug and the other found in the basement, fell off as the intruder dragged her, kicking and screaming, through the house. When they reached the basement she was grabbed around the waist and shoved up through the window and out into the yard.

"Why didn't she run? Simple. The second man was waiting outside to pounce on her."

Josephson speculated that the screams heard by neighbors were the frightened girl's last faint cries for help as she was being dragged through the window before the outside man silenced her with a blow which caused her to bleed profusely.

"The individual with the size 11 tennis shoes—the one who had gone inside the house to get the girl—picked her up and slunk between houses and garages with the semiconscious girl slung over his shoulder like a sack of potatoes.

"The blood on the jacket shows that. The second individual, meanwhile, doubled back to get the car and bring it around to meet his accomplice.

"As the man in the size 11 sneakers neared the road, where he might be seen, he put his burden down, held her around the waist, and semi-dragged her upright at his side."

Josephson recalled the witness, uncovered by the Chicago reporter, who had told of seeing a man and a staggering female, but thought they had just been partying. "When his buddy came around in the green Buick he shoved her into the back seat, climbed in after her, and they drove off."

Convinced that the girl's abductors were still in the area, the detective sought to smoke them out with a widely publicized reward of $7,000 for the owner of the size 11 sneakers and denim jacket. The items of clothing were publicly displayed in thirty-one surrounding communities, both in Wisconsin and across the wide river in Minnesota, with Josephson standing by like a sentry possessed, eager to talk to anyone who might recognize the articles.

Other police officers remained on the case, of course, even after Josephson took over the investigation. One of them, La Crosse Patrolman Gregory Yehle, became engrossed with the killer suspect's shoes. "This might sound screwy, but I think I notice something special here," he told Josephson. "Look here, the way they're worn across the instep. That could be caused by the pedals of a motorbike. What do you think?"

"It could be," Josephson agreed. "You might be onto something, Greg. Let's check it out further."

The shoes were taken to bike and motorcycle stores, where it was established that the pedals of a Whizzer motorbike fit the shoe wear exactly. The spotlight was now turned on present and former owners or operators of Whizzers. Again, nothing materialized, and summer reluctantly surrendered to fall with its spectacular color changes of the leaves on the trees.

On the first anniversary of Evelyn Hartley's disappearance Police Chief Long begrudgingly admitted that investigators were no closer to solving the mystery than on the night of the full moon when she vanished.

"We had hoped the spring and summer would turn up some trace of her. If her body was thrown into the river, as many believe, you would think someone among all those fishermen and boaters would have found something. If her body was hidden any place else, you'd figure some farmer plowing his field, or a picnicker or hiker or maybe a duck hunter would have stumbled onto it."

More than 3,000 police officers, Boy Scouts, students, and other volunteers had searched an area of 700 square miles and found absolutely nothing. Nearly 2,000 people had submitted to lie detector tests, but were able to provide no clues in the investigation. Suspects were interrogated, some as far away as Texas, whenever a man was arrested on a morals charge, but to no avail. Reports continued to come in almost daily but all led to nowhere.

Evelyn Hartley had seemingly vanished from the face of the earth.

Then Josephson, who had been concentrating all his energy on the size 11 sneakers and the denim jacket, came forth with an amazing deduction: Evelyn Hartley's abductor had been a steeplejack, who worked on metal structures such as water towers, swinging from a boatswain's chair to clean the surface in preparation for painting. Moreover, he was a slightly-built man, five feet seven inches tall, weighing about 140 pounds. And, he had a partner.

The deduction was elementary. Blood on the jacket and shoes was the same type as the girl's, and the shoes had been positively placed at the scene of her disappearance. They gave an indication as to her abductor's physical stature.

The articles of clothing were found in a ditch on the east side of Hwy. 14, which meant they were thrown from a northbound car. It would have been virtually impossible to hit the ditch from the opposite side of the road. That told detectives the abductors were heading back toward town from a drive south, where they might have disposed of the body in an isolated area. It would have been pointless to dispose of the bloodstained shoes and jacket with the victim still present in the car.

The jacket, itself, appeared to have been what was known as a "farm jumper," extending below the hips. It had been cut off with a knife and hemmed with white thread, in the style of a World War II "Eisenhower jacket." The sleeves had been shortened and also hemmed with white thread. The second button from the bottom had been torn off. The resulting tear had been repaired with a zigzag sewing machine stitch in brown thread.

Aside from the bloodstains and a few paint droppings, the jacket was exceptionally clean. The paint flecks were tested and found to have come from base paints for metals. They appeared to have spattered on the jacket while the man who wore it stood beneath a structure being painted.

A crease in the jacket pocket produced a variety of minute, colored fibers. Technicians deduced the jacket had been washed often in a family laundry, where it was customary to save the heavy denims and darker colored items until last. Several other fibers that appeared to have come from a scrub brush were found in an upper pocket.

From a series of folds in the jacket, investigators were able to piece together more of the theory.

"See here," Josephson said, pointing to a series of tiny creases at the top of the shoulders. "These indicate that whoever wore this jacket worked with his hands extended above his head. Furthermore, the right sleeve—but not the left—has been rolled up many times, like a person might do so he could scrub his right arm."

There was still more to learn from the telltale jacket. As Josephson sat pondering it one day in late February 1955, he discerned a faint path stretching across its back. The mark was perfectly delineated, like a belt line, exactly an inch and three quarters wide, as it crossed the back just under the armpits.

Josephson, who was baffled by the almost invisible marking, sent the jacket to the FBI national laboratory in Washington, calling it to their attention. After a thorough examination FBI technicians returned the jacket along with an opinion: "The marking was caused by a strap, harness, or other device worn underneath the jacket."

Now Josephson had something to go on. A belt worn under the armpits could have been for the purpose of attaching the wearer to something—a safety harness to prevent him from falling while working with his arms upraised, for example.

Window washers were ruled out, since their safety belts buckle at the waist. Josephson talked to a number of steeplejacks and learned that they often wore a rope or belt under their armpits to keep from falling or leaning too far back while working in a boatswain's chair suspended by a rope.

The dogged investigator made the rounds of harness manufacturers. He discovered that a La Crosse firm had made two such belts in 1952, one of leather and the other of webbing material. The dimensions of each perfectly matched the mark on the jacket.

Each belt had a metal ring in front that could be attached to a rope. One of the two men who had purchased the made-to-order belts had his right sleeve folded upward and held with a rubber band. Unfortunately, while the manufacturer kept a record of the belt dimensions, he did not record the names of his customers.

"Okay, here's what I would like," Josephson proposed. "Could you make me exact duplicates of those two belts?"

"No problem. We can have them for you in less than a week."

Josephson had the belts made, and tried them on two fellow investigators. They matched the telltale mark on the denim jacket exactly. If the unknown customers of the harness shop were the girl's abductors, this clinched Josephson's theory that they were indeed from the La Crosse area.

"Somewhere we will find somebody who will tell us, 'I know those two men,' and we will have our killers," he said confidently. He circulated hundreds of photographs of models wearing the jacket and harness, but without luck. The suspects might have been traveling steeplejacks, who had the harnesses made while working on a job in or around La Crosse.

Four years and two months after Evelyn Hartley disappeared the world fell in on Joe Josephson. In December 1957 the La Crosse County Board voted, twenty-one to sixteen, to abolish the special crime investigation office because "it cost too much money." Effective Jan. 1, 1958, Josephson was out of a job.

The dedicated detective, who had spent every waking hour for the past three years and eight months working on the abduction mystery, returned to Minneapolis a beaten man.

Josephson established his own lie detection agency, but he was never the same again. He remained obsessed with finding Evelyn Hartley or her killers. Somehow, that summer back in Minneapolis, his tormented mind must have worked out what he thought was a solution.

Alone in the quiet of his home on the night of Aug. 30, 1958, the thirty-seven-year-old detective put his service revolver to his head and pulled the trigger.

Alma M. "Joe" Josephson had joined Evelyn Hartley in death. The coroner's office ruled the shooting a suicide, and he was buried in Fort Snelling National Cemetery.

Tips continued to trickle in, but by the 1980s the number had dwindled to one, maybe two a year. All were checked out. None led anywhere.

In August 1981 a burly, 210-pound, whiskey-reeking factory worker staggered into St. Catherine's Hospital in Kenosha, Wisconsin, and asked for help. "I have something to tell you. I gotta get this off my chest," he told a detective who went to the hospital to talk to him.

"Tell me what? What's bothering you, fella?"

"This thing . . . it's been bothering me for so long. I have to tell you. I killed that girl in La Crosse."

"What girl? Who are you talking about?"

"You know . . . Evelyn Hartley. I'm the guy they've been looking for all these years. I'm the one they're after."

The detective relayed the information to La Crosse police.

"Hold the guy. We'll send someone down to talk to him," responded Police Lieutenant James Dunham. "We'll be there in five, six hours."

"Evelyn Hartley?" Dunham took a deep breath. It was too much to hope for. Could this be the call police had been waiting for for nearly thirty years?

The six-foot four-inch suspect would have been eighteen to nineteen years of age at the time of the abduction. He told La Crosse detectives he lived in Viroqua, about twenty-five miles southeast of there, in 1953. "I strangled her, and buried her at a big construction site outside of town," he confessed.

His admission made new headlines, and stirred La Crosse into hoping against hope that Wisconsin's number one unsolved mystery might finally be over. It was not to be, however. The auto plant machinist turned out to be a man with an unfortunate drinking problem and a vivid imagination. After sobering up he denied everything.

"We checked him out, and he did grow up in the La Crosse area," Dunham said. "The guy was an avid reader, and at some time in his life he apparently read a lot about the Hartley case, and it left a mark on his memory. A lot of people still talk about the Hartley case around La Crosse."

But the burly factory worker could never have squeezed into the small denim jacket, and his feet were considerably bigger than the size 11 tennies worn by the killer suspect who rode a motorbike. He was sent home and told to lay off the bottle before it got him into trouble.

"But somebody, somewhere, does know what happened, and maybe this renewed publicity will prompt that person with legitimate information to come forward," Dunham said. "A case such as this will never be solved without the public coming to the aid of police."

Ironically, Evelyn Hartley had not been scheduled to baby-sit that moonlit October night. She was called upon at the last minute to substitute for another girl. Had she not volunteered, she might be alive today.

UPDATE

The late Judge Robert H. Gollmar, in his book, *Edward Gein, America's Most Bizarre Murderer*, offered a most chilling theory as to the fate that befell fifteen-year-old Evelyn Hartley:

On Nov. 16, 1957, the naked body of a woman who had been beheaded was found, hanging by her feet and dressed out like a deer, on the farm of Ed Gein near Plainfield, a small town about ninety miles northeast of La Crosse. Gein's farmhouse proved to be a veritable museum of grisly, human artifacts. Police found death masks made from human faces; a belt fashioned from female nipples; a wastepaper basket, lampshades, and vests of human skin; soup bowls made of skullcaps; a human heart in a pan on the stove; and a box of assorted female organs. Among the organs were the vulvas of two girls, judged to have been about fifteen years of age. Pathologists determined that the vulvas came from live victims, and not from Gein's nocturnal grave-robbing activities.

Judge Gollmar, who presided over Gein's murder trial, said he is convinced that Evelyn Hartley was one of these unknown victims. Gein, who liked to wear the ghoulish relics as he danced by the light of the moon, was no stranger to La Crosse. He was born and raised in the Mississippi River town, and was visiting an aunt who lived within walking distance of the Rasmusen home at the time Evelyn vanished. Newspaper clippings of the missing baby-sitter mystery were found in his bedroom.

Did the so-called "butcher of Plainfield" carry Evelyn Hartley off by the light of the full moon, as the respected jurist believed? And, did he have help? Only Ed Gein knew the answer, and he died in a state mental hospital in 1984.

BOOK II

DAUGHTERS

MURDER 101 AT THE U. OF I.

Devil's Creek, the rippling stream on whose bank the frozen bodies of Barbara and Patricia Grimes were so wantonly abandoned, meanders through the far western fringes of the county along the Du Page-Cook County line near Hinsdale, through the five-acre wooded estate of socially prominent Dr. Richard Caleel, which he called Devil Creek Farm.

Caleel, a suave, internationally known horseman, enjoyed a lucrative practice as a plastic and reconstructive surgeon in Chicago, after having worked in mission hospitals in remote parts of the world. He was also the author of the book, *Surgeon*, and publisher of *Metro* magazine. As a team captain at the posh Oak Brook Polo Club, he had received an award in 1986 from England's Prince Charles for his horsemanship. His stunning blonde wife, Annette, a former model, was also an accomplished equestrian specializing in a form of horsemanship known as dressage, a highly stylized choreography on the hoof.

The oldest of their four children, Maria Louise, was someone special. Everyone who knew her said she could have been queen of the debutantes, but Maria had a more important mission in life. Her realm would be the animal kingdom. She wanted to make God's creatures well and strong. Birds, cats, dogs, gerbils in general; horses in particular.

While her family dined with princes, collected exotic art from around the world, tracked gorillas in the African jungles, and trekked to the Arctic Circle, Maria mucked out stables. She was described by those who knew her as "hard working" and "down to earth." "You would never know she was rich," a close friend of the family said. "She was as close to a '10' as you could get."

Maria had the wherewithal to buy anything she wanted, but she earned what she got through her natural assets—a fine mind and a driving ambition. A straight-A student at Lyons Township High School, she entered college at sixteen and was an honors graduate from Brown University in Providence, Rhode Island, at the age of twenty. She went on to study veterinary medicine at the University of Illinois in Champaign-Urbana, where she stood at the head of her class with a perfect 5.0 grade point average at the age of twenty-one.

Maria's all-consuming love was horses. She grew up around them, and even took a favorite named Tristan to Urbana to ride during her free time. As Michael Butler, producer of the stage show, *Hair*, and chairman of the Oak Brook Polo Club, noted, "She treated ponies like people treat babies."

"She's one of those people you never hear anybody say anything bad about and there aren't very many people like that," observed one of her instructors, Jonathan Foreman, assistant professor of equine medicine at the U. of I. Maria had been doing volunteer work for Foreman on Saturday, March 5, 1988, her last full day on earth.

There was a day-old foal that had been born seventeen days prematurely. The baby horse had been propped up on bales of hay, covered with blankets and a heating pad at the Veterinary School clinic, and placed under a warming lamp. Maria had gone to the clinic to sit with the bewildered young animal for several hours and to tend to its needs. Around 10:00 P.M. she said she had to meet some friends. She drove back to her apartment on North Lincoln Avenue, two blocks from the campus, to clean up and change clothes.

At 3:28 A.M. a resident of the second floor just below the apartment Maria shared with two other young women heard noises and called police to report a burglary in progress. Two minutes later another resident of the complex telephoned for an ambulance.

Officers Jeff Welborn and Allen Johnson, who arrived moments later, found Maria lying in the third floor hallway, where she had apparently crawled from the apartment. She was wearing a long T-shirt and panties, and was bleeding from a six-inch knife wound in her abdomen. She was still conscious, and was able to give Welborn her name. She seemed utterly bewildered as she looked into the police officer's eyes and whispered, "I don't want to talk. I can't believe . . . I'm going to die."

The ambulance arrived at 3:33 A.M. and rushed her to the Carle Foundation Hospital, where she expired at 5:22 A.M. while undergoing surgery. Her parents were notified of the tragedy as they were preparing to fly to Argentina, where her father was to participate in a polo match.

Six Urbana detectives under the direction of Sergeant Timothy Fitzpatrick were assigned to the homicide investigation. In checking the slain woman's apartment they could find no indication of a forced entry and no sign of a struggle.

Maria had either inadvertently left the apartment door unlocked, or had admitted her killer after being aroused from her sleep. Police said her bed was rumpled, as though it had been slept in.

Coroner Thomas Henderson reported that a medical examination determined Maria had not been sexually assaulted. Furthermore, her body bore no other injuries, such as she might have incurred during a struggle, save the stab wound in her right side. Dr. Stanley Bobowski, the coroner's pathologist, said she died from loss of blood as the result of her aorta being severed.

Alex Crisanto, who lived downstairs of Maria's apartment, told police, "I was asleep, and I thought I heard a scream. I woke up and heard a little rumbling. We heard some unusually hard noises against the floor, like some rummaging around. My roommate and I got up and called Maria's room. It was busy. We figured the phone was off the hook. Fifteen minutes later we heard more rummaging around, and called the police."

In Maria's room police found a letter she had written to a friend in New York, waiting to be posted. In it she told of her work in the wildlife ward at the university's animal hospital.

"You get to feed and handle everything from pigeons to snowy owls to hawks to a bald eagle. Catching them without getting mauled is definitely an acquired skill. One of the hawks got me even through the gloves. They're so gorgeous though," she wrote. "Do you believe it, 1:30 on Friday night and I'm at home in sweats writing letters. Both roomies are away, so I decided to be a vegetable tonight, and boy is it great."

In reconstructing Maria's final hours in an effort to determine whether anything happened that could have led to her being stabbed, police learned that on Saturday afternoon she had driven to the stables south of town where she boarded Tristan and took the horse for a ride.

Afterward she drove the twenty miles back to Urbana and went to the veterinary clinic to sit with the newborn foal.

After she had gone home to clean up, a fellow veterinary student, Matthew Taylor, picked her up at the apartment and they drove to the Campus Town entertainment district to meet friends. The group barhopped between Gully's Riverview Inn and Murphy's Pub on Green Street. Maria did not drink. Taylor told police the evening was just a casual, informal gathering of friends.

Around midnight they joined other students in the old Illini Union, a massive hall where some 800 people had congregated to chat and dance to a reggae band from Chicago. Maria was not among the dancers, but stayed at the table talking. Afterward she and several members of the group went down the street to Garcia's for pizza. One of her girlfriends dropped Maria off at her building at 1:30 A.M., and Maria went up the stairs to her third floor apartment.

Nothing further was heard until 3:28 A.M. when the

second floor tenant was awakened by a disturbance overhead. Police questioned other residences of the complex, but nobody saw anyone else entering or leaving the building.

Maria's two roommates, one from Arlington Heights and the other from Berwyn, returned from their weekend home and went over the three bedroom apartment with police. They could find nothing out of place.

Sergeant Fitzpatrick and Detective Michael Metzler had a long talk with Maria's grief stricken parents, hoping to learn all they could about the victim and her associates. "We learned nothing that we hadn't heard before," Fitzpatrick said afterward. "Maria was an exceptional person." A socialite friend of the Caleels told investigators, "Maria was probably the most outstanding child I have ever known in my life."

As they made preparations to bury their daughter, Dr. Caleel and his wife issued a statement in which they said they would not remember how Maria died, but how she had lived. "This earth was graced by her presence for an all-too-brief twenty-one years," the statement read in part.

"Yet they were years of extraordinary quality, golden years filled with achievement, successes and personal joys few others attain in a much longer lifetime."

Meanwhile the investigation into her death continued. Combining old-fashioned police work and modern technology, police interviewed more than 200 people and gathered a vast assortment of minute physical evidence from inside the murder apartment, which they turned over to the FBI laboratory in Washington for analysis.

"There is speculation in the community that the killer had to be someone Maria knew, like a spurned lover, because there was no forced entry to the apartment," Sergeant Fitzpatrick said. "Did she lock that door, or forget to? If I knew that for a fact it would narrow the type of criminal we are looking for. Maria was security conscious, but she was known to leave the door unlocked on occasion."

Any suggestion as to what really happened that night is pure hunch, he said. It could have been a burglary that escalated to homicide in a confrontation between Maria and the thief, or it could have been a planned crime of violence, such as an intended sexual assault that never came off.

"I won't deny that we are baffled by this case," Sergeant Fitzpatrick said two years after the murder. "We honest to God don't have a theory. We don't know what happened in that place."

Maria's father subsequently sued the hospital for negligence, contending its surgeons had not done enough to save his daughter.

UPDATE

Two new investigators were assigned to the case in late 1990, in hopes of breathing new life into the continuing probe. Sergeant John Lockard and Detective John Koziol picked up where Fitzpatrick and Metzler had left off. Lockard, a twenty-year veteran of the Urbana police department, and his partner confer with Dr. and Mrs. Caleel on a weekly basis to keep them informed of their progress, and to trade information.

"This has always been a two-pronged investigation, focusing on friends and acquaintances on one hand, and a would-be burglar or rapist on the other," Lockard said. "My theory is that Maria did not know her assailant, or at least could not identify the person. From what she said to the officer at the scene, she did not know why she had been stabbed. It was too dark for her to see much. Her apartment was completely dark."

A local Crime Stoppers organization offered a $1,000 reward for information leading to Maria Caleel's killer. The Champaign News-Gazette added $2,000 to the amount, and Maria's parents offered another $5,000. When that brought no response her family added another $20,000. A year later they increased it to $30,000. They subsequently raised the family's offer to $45,000 which, coupled with $5,000 offered by other agencies, brought to $50,000 the rewards offered for information in the case. There have been no takers.

THE SENATOR'S DAUGHTER

Maria Caleel was by no means the first vibrant young socialite, bright eyed and brimming with expectation, whose promising future was cut short by a mindless intruder in the night. Being of the manor born is no insulation from some furtive madman lurking in the shadows with murder in his heart.

Charles H. Percy, the millionaire Chicago industrialist who in the fall of 1966 was the Republican candidate for United States Senate, also had a beautiful twenty-one-year-old daughter. Valerie Jean Percy had just graduated from Cornell University in Ithaca, New York, with grades well above average, and had come home for the summer to work on her father's election campaign.

The Percys lived in a lakeshore Tudor mansion on an estate called "Windward" in the northern suburb of Kenilworth, a silk-stocking community of 3,000 nestled cozily between Winnetka and Wilmette. In the seventy-five years since its founding by Chicago businessman Joseph Sears in the early 1890s, Kenilworth had never had a homicide.

In the early morning hours of Sunday, September 18, Percy and his thirty-seven-year-old wife, Loraine, were asleep in the master bedroom at Windward. Valerie and her twin sister, Sharon, occupied adjoining rooms down the hall. The Percys' youngest daughter, Gail, thirteen, was asleep in her room as well. Eleven-year-old Mark was staying overnight with friends and the oldest son, Roger, nineteen, was away at college. Loraine, who had married Percy after the death of his first wife, was the mother of the two younger children and stepmother to Roger and the twin girls.

At 5:05 A.M., the wail of a siren on the roof of the Percy home cut through the night, awakening Dr. and Mrs. Robert Hohf who lived just south of the Percy estate at 303 Sheridan Road. Nydia Hohf tumbled out of bed, pulled on a robe, and ran out into the backyard. From that vantage point she got a clear view of the south side of the Percy home and private beach. She saw no one.

At almost the same moment the telephone jangled in the Hohf home. The doctor picked it up and heard the anxious voice of his neighbor. "Bob, it's Chuck. Valerie's been hurt. Please come right away."

Percy was waiting at the door when Dr. Hohf, a surgeon at Evanston Hospital, breezed in, his trousers pulled on over his pajamas. He went straight to Valerie's room on the second floor, where he found her lying across the bloodstained covers on one of the twin beds. Her skull had been crushed by repeated blows from a heavy object, and she had been stabbed ten times in the throat, chest, and abdomen.

There was nothing Dr. Hohf could do. Slowly he went back downstairs and told the Percys that their daughter was dead.

"I thought I detected a pulse beat in her wrist just before you came over," Mrs. Percy said hopefully. "I'm sorry, Loraine," the doctor replied.

While the doctor was upstairs, Percy had telephoned Kenilworth police. Police Chief Robert H. Daley put in a quick call to Chicago Police Superintendent Orlando W. Wilson asking for assistance, before heading for the Percy estate. Daley arrived at the home a short time later, along with several crime lab technicians from the city. They were soon joined by Chicago homicide Sergeant James Moore and Detective Hartwell McGuinn. Since none of his officers had ever investigated a murder before, Daley welcomed all the professional assistance he could get. Cook County Coroner Andrew J. Toman and his assistant, Sidney Berman, also sped to the scene from their homes.

As her husband comforted her, Loraine Percy told the detectives a frightening story. "I was awakened by the sound of someone moaning, and I got up to see what was the matter," she related. "I paused outside Sharon's room, but it was quiet. Then I realized the sound was coming from Valerie's room farther down the hall."

As she opened the door, she said she observed the figure of a man bending over the blood soaked bed, shining his flashlight on Valerie's body. As she gasped in surprise, the intruder swung around and beamed the flashlight into Mrs. Percy's eyes, blinding her momentarily. "I took a step backward, turned, and ran back to our bedroom. I awakened my husband and pressed the central burglar alarm button that activated the siren on the roof," she said.

In the precious seconds that elapsed before Percy could reach his daughter's room, the killer fled down the stairs and out through the French doors leading from the music room to a patio. A pane of glass had been broken in the French doors, indicating the intruder had entered the same way.

The next day, after recovering somewhat from the numbing event, Mrs. Percy was able to give Chief Daley a vague description of the man she had seen bending over Valerie's body.

He was a dark-haired man, about five feet eight inches tall, and weighing around 160 pounds. She also noticed, during the brief encounter, that he was wearing a checkered shirt.

In examining the entryway between the music room and the patio, police observed that a four-inch square section had been cut from a screen door. Markings on the glass in the French door indicated that a glass cutter had been used to outline one of the panes, which had fallen into the room. The intruder apparently reached through the opening, unlocked the door, and let himself in.

Crime lab technicians lifted a clear fingerprint from the section of glass which had fallen from the French door.

Mrs. Percy recalled being semi-awakened earlier by the tinkle of breaking glass, followed by a clicking sound, as though someone with hard heels were walking across the tile floor. "I thought maybe someone had knocked a water glass off their nightstand, and went back to sleep," she said. In a home where a major political campaign was being mustered, it was not unusual to hear people up walking around at all hours.

On Saturday night, as a matter of fact, Valerie and her stepmother had entertained two young Percy campaign workers for dinner, discussing how to appeal to young voters and to activate neighborhood campaign centers. The campaign workers left around ten o'clock, and Valerie went up to her room.

Sharon, who had been out on a date, told police she got home at 11:30 P.M. and went up to Valerie's room to return a borrowed raincoat. "Val was in her nightclothes, sitting up in bed watching television," she said. She was the last person known to have seen her twin sister alive.

Percy, who had resigned as president of the Bell & Howell camera firm to enter politics, had been making a campaign appearance in Chicago. He arrived home at 12:30 A.M. He said he and his wife watched television for an hour or so and retired for the night.

Percy was not only the GOP candidate for senator, he was Kenilworth's most illustrious citizen. Often described as a "boy wonder" in business, he had fought his way up the ladder in Horatio Alger fashion, earning his millions the hard way, not through inheritance.

Chief Daley met with the mob of reporters outside the Percy home the morning after the murder and assured them that the killer would be caught. State's attorney's police, under the direction of Lieutenant Nicholas Juric, along with six Illinois State Police detectives commanded by Lieutenant Richard Robb joined Daley and the Chicago detectives in the investigation.

From that point on police literally moved into the seventeen-room mansion, where they worked on the slaying around the clock. The best clue they came up with was five bloody palmprints left on the banister as the killer fled down the stairs and out of the house.

Suspecting that the killer would have wanted to rid himself of the incriminating weapons as soon as possible, scuba divers combed the sandy bottom of Lake Michigan off the Percys' private beach where he might have thrown them. They dragged the bottom with an iron bar equipped with powerful magnets and dredged up an old army bayonet, which may or may not have been used to stab the victim.

They had hoped to find the glass cutter and the object the killer had used to smash Valerie's skull. The bludgeon weapon had left a series of cone shaped depressions in the victim's head. Police theorized it could have been a ball peen hammer with one end sharpened to a point, resembling a tool used by jewelers or silversmiths.

One thing that bothered police early on was the fact that the family dog, a Labrador retriever named Li Foo, had not barked when the murderer broke into the home. Yet the animal, who was roaming the grounds, vigorously protested the arrival of the first Kenilworth police officers on the scene. Could the killer have been someone so well known to the family that the dog paid him no mind?

Various family members were asked about this, and they explained that Li Foo seemed to have a thing about people in uniform. He always barked at police officers, deliverymen, and letter carriers, but rarely barked at anyone not in uniform. As a matter of fact, the Percy home was regularly so full of campaign workers coming and going that the dog learned to ignore strangers. Li Foo's name, ironically, meant "guardian" in Chinese.

Police were puzzled over a motive in the slaying. The intruder took no money or other valuables from Valerie's room. And the position of the body did not indicate she had awakened and caught someone in the act of ransacking the room. For all appearances she had been beaten about the head as she lay asleep, and then stabbed as she lapsed into unconsciousness.

It seemed almost a certainty that someone had broken into Windward and gone to Valerie's room for the express purpose of killing her. This meant, of course, that it had to have been someone familiar with the layout of the home. Possibly the slayer was someone who had once been a guest, and who still had a key. The cut screen and broken glass in the patio door could have been a smoke screen to throw police off the scent.

Detectives delved into Valerie's many political friend- ships, as well as a number of young men she had dated. They questioned and requestioned members of the family, along with the maid and the live-in butler, but no one could think of anyone who would have wanted Valerie dead.

In a bizarre sidebar, Coroner Toman and his assistants all had to be fingerprinted so they could be ruled out as suspects. This came about after a Kenilworth police officer disclosed that the coroner's men had carelessly handled objects and leaned against an ornamental iron railing, leaving their palmprints all over the place the morning of the murder.

Percy and his family went into seclusion after the incident. Two weeks later he called a press conference to announce that he would resume his campaign for the Senate. "This is what I must do and it is what my family wants me to do," he said. He went on to win the election in November, unseating long-time Democratic Senator Paul Douglas. When Percy went to Washington he sold the estate in Kenilworth. His wife was too terrified to stay there any more.

As the investigation continued, a flurry of excitement developed when an eighteen-year-old Arizona man admitted to police in Tucson that he had been paid seventy-five dollars by a stranger "to kill anyone in the Percy home." FBI agents determined that the youth, an AWOL sailor, was nowhere near Kenilworth at the time of the slaying. In all, nineteen men would confess to the murder over the ensuing years, and police would waste valuable time checking out each man's story before discounting it as a publicity stunt or the ramblings of a kook. Other men would be falsely accused.

Among them, for example, was a tree trimmer who had worked around the Percy estate. A Stateville Prison inmate tipped off police that the trimmer had told him he killed Valerie.

The suspect was from southern Illinois and spoke with a pronounced drawl. A state policeman from southern Illinois was taken out of uniform and put to work as a tree trimmer for the same company as the suspect. He befriended the suspect, moved in with him, and joined him in drinking bouts. Weeks passed, and the suspect showed no more than a passing interest in the slaying, and then only when the undercover cop brought the subject up.

Investigators finally requestioned the Stateville convict and put him on the lie box. He flunked the test. He then admitted that he had falsely accused the tree trimmer to get him out of the way because they were both interested in the same girl.

In the first two years following Valerie's murder, police interviewed some 10,000 people and investigated 1,226 suspects, including burglars, drug addicts, sex perverts, Peeping Toms, boyfriends, former boyfriends, domestic employees, and campaign staff workers.

One possible suspect, whose name was turned up by Chicago detectives, was a cross-country burglar named Frederick J. "Freddie" Malchow. Known to police mostly along the East Coast, Florida, and the Gulf states, Malchow was a career thief who traveled by commercial airliner from city to city to pull off scores, often hopping the next plane home the same day.

FBI agents interviewed the forty-year-old Malchow in a Pennsylvania jail where he was awaiting trial for rape and robbery in connection with a home invasion in Norristown. He steadfastly denied any involvement to the Percy murder. After the agents left, however, Malchow confided to a fellow inmate that he feared he might be linked to the slaying through an old pair of trousers.

A jailhouse informant passed the tip on to authorities. Armed with that information, agents recovered a pair of Malchow's pants that had red stains on them. Lab testing determined that the stains were blood, but the stains were too old and faded to determine whether the blood was human or animal.

Before Malchow could be questioned again, he broke out of the Norristown jail in the spring of 1967. He plunged to his death from a railroad trestle over the Schuylkill River as police moved in to recapture him.

As the trail grew colder, and each new lead fizzled out, police gradually want back to other pressing business. By 1969 the twenty-five investigators from various agencies assigned to the Percy homicide had dwindled to two, State Police Agent Robert Lamb and his partner, John Nevergall. They set up an investigative office in the state police station on West Irving Park Road, where they would continue for years on what would be their permanent assignment.

Curiously, the name of Freddie Malchow kept coming back like a bad dream. In 1970 another inmate of the Norristown jail, Harold James "Jimmy" Evans, twenty-four, said that Malchow had once confessed the Percy killing to him. Evans, a former Chicago truck driver who had just been arrested in connection with another home invasion, said he and Malchow were cellmates in the Montgomery County, Pennsylvania, jail when Malchow told him of his involvement.

According to Evans, Malchow said he had flown up from Texas to burglarize the Percy home, and Valerie awakened while he was in her room. "Freddie didn't mean to stab her, but she kept rising up, and Freddie kept pushing her down on the bed. With one hand, he pushed her down, and with the other hand, in which he held a knife, he stabbed her," he said.

Lie tests administered to Evans indicated he was telling the truth.

However Montgomery County District Attorney Milton O. Moss, who directed the polygraph examination, pointed out that there was no way of knowing whether Malchow was also telling the truth when he "confessed" to Evans.

In 1973 a German born woman who had been spurned by her boyfriend fingered him as a suspect in the Percy slaying. The man, Francis Leroy Hohimer, forty-six, a convicted burglar, had reportedly told his brother, Harold, on the day after the murder, "I've been on a score. There was some trouble, and I had to do somebody in. I had to 'off' somebody." When his brother asked him what he meant, he reportedly answered, "It's in all the papers."

Police questioned Francis Hohimer, who gave authorities details about the Percy case which had not been given out to the public. Hohimer blamed a member of his gang, Norman Jackson, for the killing. But before authorities could talk to Jackson, he died in a mysterious plunge from a Chicago building. Hohimer, who was subsequently sentenced to a thirty-year prison term in Iowa for burglary and interstate transport of stolen goods, later told investigators who questioned him in prison that it was another member of his gang, Freddie Malchow, and not Jackson, who had killed Valerie Percy.

The two most likely suspects were both dead, however, and could not defend themselves from the accusations. After moving to Washington, Senator Percy offered a $50,000 reward for information leading to the arrest of his daughter's slayer, but no one was ever able to claim the money.

UPDATE

Lamb, the last full-time investigator in the Percy homicide, retired from the Illinois State Police with the rank of captain, and is now chief of police of the northwest Chicago suburb of Barrington Hills.

"To this day I am convinced that Freddie Malchow was the killer, and that he acted alone," Lamb said. "We considered Malchow our prime suspect for several reasons: (1) He was a professional burglar who specialized in nighttime home invasions; (2) we were able to place him in Chicago at the time of the murder through the purchase of an airplane baggage ticket; and (3) at least two of Malchow's underworld associates have said that Freddie admitted the murder to them."

If Lamb is correct, that blows the "revenge" theory of earlier investigators clear out of the water. The Valerie Percy murder case remains one of the most perplexing mysteries in Illinois history—and all of the money and political influence in the world have been unable to solve it.

A NO-SHOW AT THE SEMINAR

Nobody ever tried harder to find out what happened to a loved one than Berit Beck's devoted family and friends in Sturtevant, Wisconsin.

Berit, an attractive eighteen-year-old blonde with blue eyes, held a summer job as secretary for the Boldt Construction Company, of Appleton, which was working on a project at the J.I. Case tractor works on the Racine lakefront. She intended to go to college in the fall, and had signed up for a three-day computer seminar in Appleton.

At nine o'clock Tuesday morning, July 17, 1990, she climbed into her 1987 gray, two-tone GMC van at the Racine construction site to begin the 135-mile drive to Appleton, where she had reservations at the Holiday Inn. A co-worker had highlighted the route for her on a map, following Interstate Hwy. 94 and U.S. Hwy. 41. Berit carefully recorded the van's odometer reading before leaving, because the computer school had agreed to reimburse her for her mileage. That was the last anyone ever heard from her.

When she failed to call home to report her safe arrival, her father, Dave Beck, forty-two, called the Holiday Inn and discovered that she had never checked in.

He then organized a search party among friends, relatives, and fellow members of the Racine Bible Church. They retraced the route between Racine and Appleton they figured Berit had taken, along with several alternate routes, but could find no trace of her or her van.

They then reported her missing, and the Sturtevant Police Department put out an alert for the van and its driver, described as five feet ten inches tall, weighing 140 pounds, and wearing blue jeans and a red shirt.

Police Chief Ronald Kittel expressed fears Berit might have been abducted, after a check of hospitals along the way revealed no young woman matching her description had been admitted. "She could be missing voluntarily. I hope that's what it is," he said. "But she had a very bright future ahead of her, and it's not in her character to do something like this."

"All kinds of things are running through our minds, but we're trying to think positive thoughts about this," her forty-one-year-old mother, Diane, told friends who called to join in the search. "We just hope that whoever has her will return her safely to us."

On the Thursday after Berit disappeared, friends again followed the route from Racine to Appleton, stopping at every place she might have visited along the way, and distributing photos of the missing teenager. Her father, mother, and fifteen-year-old brother, Ben, meanwhile, set up a schedule for monitoring the telephone around the clock.

Shortly before noon on Thursday her van was found abandoned in a K-mart parking lot in Fond du Lac, thirty-eight miles south of Appleton. Her clothing, purse, and items of food she had purchased at the store were still in the vehicle. A receipt found in her purse indicated she had purchased sundries at a nearby Walgreen Drug Store at 11:03 A.M. on July 17. Curiously, the van's odometer showed 462 miles more than it should have registered for the trip up from Racine.

The discovery of the van brought the Fond du Lac police, under the direction of Captain John Hoffman, into the search. It appeared obvious that Berit would not have left her purse in the vehicle if she had gone somewhere voluntarily.

By week's end the search party consisted of more than 200 friends and fellow church members, who drove to Fond du Lac where they fanned out in all directions looking for the missing woman. Special songs and prayers were offered for her and her family at the Racine Bible Church on Sunday.

Hundreds of photographs of Berit were distributed in fast-food restaurants, convenience stores, truck stops, gas stations, and motels throughout the area, and huge banners bearing her likeness, eight feet high and forty feet long, were affixed to the sides of semi-trailers parked on the outskirts of Sturtevant and Fond du Lac. The banners, containing Berit's description and phone numbers to call with information, were donated by a graphics firm from Union Grove.

During the Experimental Aircraft Association's annual Fly-In Convention at Oshkosh two weeks later, a plane flew over the crowd pulling a long banner that urged "Please Help Find Bery." A similar plea appeared in lighted letters, four feet high, flashing outside the Milwaukee County Stadium during major league baseball games. Giant photographs of Berit were posted at 100 locations throughout the State Fair Park in West Allis, while other pictures were tacked up on bulletin boards in food stores, banks, and other places of business. Her face appeared on television newscasts, and on network broadcasts of Milwaukee Brewers' ballgames.

By early August it was impossible to go anywhere in Southern Wisconsin without seeing a picture of Berit Beck. Pink ribbons filled the trees and bushes around her home, and virtually every car in town carried a "missing" poster in its window.

The Beck home in Sturtevant, just west of Racine, had become a vast operations center directing all aspects of the search. Dave Beck, who shut down his independent construction business so he could devote full time to the search, said, "It's our little girl that's missing. To us nothing can be more important than that."

Sturtevant and Fond du Lac police, working with the FBI, checked out hundreds of "sightings" of Berit throughout the country, but all proved false.

The tireless search ended tragically five weeks later, on Wednesday, August 22. Farmer Michael L. Pluim was pulling a steel-wheeled hay rake behind his tractor about fifteen miles southwest of Fond du Lac in the Town of Waupun, when he came upon her decomposed body near a grove of trees at 3:07 P.M. "I was going real slow and that's how I happened to see her," he told Sheriff Jim Gilmore. "The only thing I could see was the head. I pulled the grass away and there lay the whole body. I couldn't believe it."

Berit's body was fully clothed. A red bandanna had been tied tightly over her mouth as a gag.

The remains were removed to the Wisconsin State Crime Laboratory in Madison, where Fond du Lac County Coroner Susan Casper confirmed identification through dental records. Due to the condition of the body, pathologists were unable to determine the cause of death. They said, however, that Berit did not appear to have been sexually molested.

So, if she was not robbed, and was not sexually assaulted, why was she killed?

UPDATE

The absence of a motive has been a real stumbling block in attempting to determine who killed Berit Beck, according to Fond du Lac County Sheriff's Lieutenant Ed Sheppard. "It forces us into several theories and down several avenues," he said.

The one clue investigators have is her van, which poses yet another question: Who put the extra 462 miles on the odometer, and why?

THE KILLING A COP CAN'T FORGET

When twenty-one-year-old Beth Buege modeled a swimsuit while standing on a dock near Milwaukee, her mother said, "She stopped traffic on the lake." She was that kind of girl—a vivacious, exciting, beautiful young woman with that freshly-scrubbed look of the girl next door.

On Sunday morning, June 3, 1990, Beth's body was found in her car parked in the 4900 block of North 49th Street in Wisconsin's largest city. She had been strangled.

For Detective James Gauger the murder was a shocker. While going over the victim's car for clues after her body had been removed, he came upon an old report card showing that Beth had enjoyed perfect attendance in Sunday school at Abiding Savior Lutheran Church during 1977. "It was signed by me as Sunday school superintendent," he said. "I was her Sunday school teacher."

The thirteen-year-old Sunday school card had been in the car because Beth was in the midst of moving some of her things.

Police and her family think her killer had to have been someone she knew. There had been no sign of a struggle in the car. It was almost as if Beth had been strangled while in her sleep.

"Beth was a fighter," her mother, Bonnie, told Detective Gauger, a family friend for fifteen years. "Two years ago she'd been assaulted on the East Side. Someone jumped her from behind and knocked her down. She jumped up and kicked him where it hurts, knocked him to his knees. She had karate training."

Beth's last words to her family were, "I love you, Mom." She and her mother had talked by phone the afternoon before her body was found. Her father, Robert Buege, had just returned home from a church convention, and Beth was invited over for dinner. Unfortunately, she told her mother, she had already made other plans for dinner Saturday night. But she didn't say with whom.

Gauger believes the unidentified dinner date was Beth's killer.

She was extremely popular and had many male friends. All of her known male acquaintances except one attended her funeral, where five of them served as pall bearers. Her family thought it strange. The one man who didn't come to the service knew the family well, had been a guest in the Buege home, and had dined out with them. Yet he never even phoned Robert or Bonnie Buege when their daughter was killed. Instead, he hired a lawyer.

UPDATE

Bonnie and Robert Buege have offered a reward of $5,000 for any information given to police that leads to the arrest and conviction of their daughter's killer.

"We're almost sure we know who did it," said Detective Gauger, who wants to solve this case more than any other he has ever worked on. "But right now we're stymied."

WHAT HAPPENED TO MY DAUGHTER?

Patricia Wisz Field's family would give almost anything to find out what happened to her. Field, a thirty-four-year-old Chicago lawyer, was last seen alive on Sept. 3, 1989, when she left her home in the Rogers Park neighborhood on the city's far North Side. She was reported missing when she failed to return that evening.

Five days later, on September 8, workers came upon a badly decomposed body near the Chicago & North Western Railway commuter viaduct over Devon Avenue at Ravenswood. Due to the condition of the corpse, police were unable to immediately determine the sex, and it was listed in the Cook County Morgue as a "John Doe."

It was more than ten days before pathologists got around to determining that they had a "Jane Doe" on their hands, not a "John." Thus no effort had been made to associate the report of a missing woman with the body of the unidentified "male" in the county cooler. Furthermore, due to the advanced stage of decomposition, doctors were unable to determine the cause of death.

It was six weeks before Patricia Wisz, a suburban nurse, learned that the unclaimed body in the morgue was that of her thirty-four-year-old daughter.

Police were partly led to the erroneous conclusion that the dead person was a male by a pill container with a man's name on the label, found near the body. The pills had actually belonged to Patricia's boyfriend. When he went to his hospital pharmacy to have the prescription refilled on October 18, he was told, "The police advised us the person this prescription was issued to is in the morgue." He contacted Patricia's mother, who gave police her daughter's dental records.

The mystery of where she had been was solved, but that only led to a new one: What had happened to her?

"After we found out that she was in the morgue and we got a positive identification, the detectives who were assigned to the case went out to look, but the area had been hosed down," Mrs. Wisz said afterwards. "It seemed like everything went against any kind of solution. We don't know what happened to her."

UPDATE

In an effort to solve the mystery, the dead woman's mother has posted a $10,000 reward for information as to what happened to her daughter. On Sept. 3, 1990, members of the family hung a large banner from the railroad overpass at Devon Avenue, where it couldn't be missed by passing motorists. It said: $10,000 REWARD for information leading to conviction in the death of Patricia Wisz found here 1 yr. ago. 708–337–3468.

"Maybe people will remember where they were on that date. Maybe somebody there knows something. Maybe they will come forward. Maybe $10,000 will be the stimulating factor for them," the concerned mother said. "If this [sign] gives me an answer, it gives me an answer. If it doesn't, it just cost me a sign."

THE TATTOOED WAITRESS

Her body was found lying in a ditch alongside County Highway Z near Twin Lakes, Wisconsin, by two highway department workers picking up debris on the morning of Dec. 19, 1983. It was a heck of a way to begin the week.

The young woman had been savagely beaten. Her face was badly swollen and discolored by bruises, and she had bled profusely. She looked to have been in her late teens or early twenties. She was five feet six inches tall, weighed around 110 pounds, and had dark brown, shoulder-length hair.

Her body had been partly hidden by snow and spray from passing vehicles, and the two highway workers first thought it was a bundle of clothing dumped by the side of the road.

She wore a beige corduroy jacket, a white sweater with a maroon pattern across the front, white slacks, and brown suede shoes with laces. Sheriff's Captain Roger Zeihen could find no identification in any of the clothing, nor could his deputies find a purse or billfold anywhere near the scene.

Kenosha County Coroner Thomas Dorff held the body overnight in a Twin Lakes funeral home, hoping the sheriff's men could come up with some identification. She remained a

Jane Doe, however, and the body was then removed to the State Crime Lab in Madison for an autopsy.

The only clue authorities had to her identity were three tattoos. The victim had a half-moon with a small star in one corner on her right ankle; a small heart with the initials "DM" drawn over the letters "JB" on her upper abdomen; and a peace sign near the index finger of her left hand.

It was not the tattoos, but fingerprints, that finally led to the victim's identity a week and a half later, on December 30. She was twenty-one-year-old Jody Lynn Davis of Chicago, a waitress at the Sportsman Lounge on Roosevelt Road in Berwyn.

Her mother, father, step-father, grandmother, two sisters, and her steady boyfriend all drove up to Kenosha County, where they made positive identification. Jody's mother, Joanne Bedner, told Sheriff Daniel Piencikowski that she had last seen her daughter on December 17, two days before the body turned up in the ditch on the outskirts of Twin Lakes.

In all probability, the young woman had been beaten to death somewhere in the Chicago area, and then driven over the state line and dumped. Kenosha County investigators went to Chicago, where they worked in tandem with Windy City police on the case, but they were never able to determine who killed Jody Davis, or why.

UPDATE

There is a haunting follow-up to the unsolved murder of Jody Lynn Davis. In 1980 she and a friend named Marcy Jo Andrews lived as roommates in an apartment at 3322 North Lakewood Avenue, on Chicago's North Side. On Feb. 14, 1984, less than two months after Jody's body was found discarded in the Wisconsin ditch, twenty-four-year-old Marcy Jo also disappeared.

Police found a witness who placed her in the Iowa Street apartment of a thirty-four-year-old ex-convict, Casey Nowicki, on Valentine's Day, where she appeared to be high on marijuana. Police questioned Nowicki, who admitted Marcy Jo had been in his apartment, but contended she left and never came back. He declined to take a lie test, however.

In May 1984, police searched an eighty-acre farm owned by Nowicki's mother in Pulaski County, Indiana, after informants told them the missing woman's body could be found there. They found nothing.

In another bizarre twist, on April 6, 1985, a farmer walking along Highway Z near Twin Lakes, at almost the exact spot where Jody Davis' body had been dumped two years earlier, came upon a rolled-up carpet. He unrolled the rug and discovered yet another dead body.

The occupant of the carpet was identified as thirty-one-year-old Michael J. Moriarty, III, a painter who lived on Chicago's North Side. He had been tied up, beaten, and shot in the head and chest.

The disappearance of Marcy Jo Andrews, and the murders of Jody Lynn Davis and Michael Moriarty remain unsolved, and authorities have been unable to determine whether they are in any way connected. One thing appears evident, however. Somebody has discovered a handy dumping ground for corpses in Kenosha County.

MURDER IN MOVIELAND

At Girl Scout camp one summer, when she was a little girl, she made her parents a ceramic plate on which she inscribed, "To Mommy and Daddy from Cookie." Her real name was Karyn. Daddy was the nationally famous gossip columnist for the *Chicago Sun-Times*, Irv Kupcinet, and Mommy was Kup's wife, Essee, the former Esther Solomon.

Although she was a plump little girl, who thought of herself "Miss Five-by-Five," Cookie had visions of becoming an actress. When she grew older she went on a stringent diet and, at five feet three and one-half inches in height, got her weight down to 105 pounds. She indeed developed into a beautiful young woman who saw her dreams come true.

After Wellesley College Karyn went on to New York to study at Actor's Studio before heading west to make her name in Hollywood. There were some who said her father's many West Coast contacts opened magic doors for her, but Karyn's friends would be the first to tell you that she was making it on her own.

In 1963, at the age of twenty-two, she appeared in the Jerry Lewis film, *The Ladies Man*. She also had roles in Lewis' television show, the Gertrude Berg series, and "Perry Mason."

The world was still reeling over the assassination of President John F. Kennedy when, shortly after Thanksgiving, Karyn wrote to tell her parents she was excited over a forthcoming trip to Palm Springs. On Friday night, November 29, they put in a phone call to her in Hollywood, but got no answer. "She's probably gone out with some friends," Kup told his wife. "We can try again tomorrow."

For Karyn Kupcinet, however, there would be no tomorrow.

On Wednesday night she had been a dinner guest in the home of actor Mark Goddard, twenty-seven, and his twenty-five-year-old wife, Marcia, the daughter of Hollywood publicist Henry Rogers. Two of Karyn's closest Hollywood friends, the Goddards, too, had called her home Friday and got no answer. When they tried to reach her again Saturday night, without success, they became concerned and decided to go over to her apartment near Sunset Strip.

After getting no answer to his knocks, Goddard tried the door and found it unlatched. He called out Karyn's name several times, but got no response. He and his wife cautiously entered the eerily quiet second floor apartment and looked around. There was an empty coffee cup on the floor, and an empty brandy snifter. There was an overturned coffee pot in the kitchen, and unwashed dishes in the sink. Karyn was lying naked on the couch, face down, surrounded by the sickening aroma of death.

Goddard called the Los Angeles County sheriff's office, and several deputies were dispatched to the apartment, along with Lieutenant George Walsh. Walsh noted that, except for the upset coffee pot, there was no sign of a struggle. And there were no visible marks on the body, which had already begun to decompose.

In going over the apartment Walsh found several bottles of pills in the bathroom, which he would take to the lab for analysis. There were no notes in the apartment, nor anything to indicate the death was a suicide. The sheriff's investigator just wanted to make sure he was covering all bases.

Back in Chicago, Kup and his wife were attending the opening of a new Sara Lee plant in the northern suburbs when they learned of their daughter's death. Kup's midnight television show on WBKB-TV was instantly cancelled as he prepared to fly out to Los Angeles to see what he could do.

He was driven to the airport by his close friend, Sid Luckman, the Chicago Bears football coach. Kup, a former pro football player himself, was also accompanied by sports broadcaster Jack Brickhouse and his wife, and Kup's brother, Joseph.

While waiting to board his plane the grief stricken father sat in an airport lounge with his face in his hands, weeping. He had been placed under sedation, and by the time his plane was airborne at 2:20 A.M. he was asleep in his seat. Kup, his brother, and attorney Arthur Morse were met by Hollywood lawyer Sid Korshak when their plane touched down in Los Angeles.

An autopsy on Karyn's body Sunday morning revealed that her death was no suicide. She had been strangled. "Death was caused by asphyxiation due to manual strangulation, which fractured the hyoid bone in the throat," Dr. Harold Kade, assistant chief county surgeon who performed the postmortem examination, told Walsh. "That's the little U-shaped horizontal bone at the base of the tongue. Whoever did that to her might have used one or both hands."

The condition of the body indicated she had been murdered not long after returning home from the Goddards' party on Wednesday night, the pathologist added.

"She knew her killer, no question about it," Walsh asserted, after talking to acquaintances of the slain starlet. "She would never have opened her apartment door to a stranger. Whoever did this has got a three-day head start on us."

The Goddards told Walsh that Karyn arrived at their place around 7:30 P.M. Wednesday, an hour later than she had been expected. She explained that she had been delayed by a phone call from her boyfriend, actor Andrew Prine, with whom she'd been having problems.

The Goddards added that Karyn had dated a number of young men in the television and writing fields, but Prine was the one with whom she had been keeping steady company. "Karyn didn't stay long at our house Wednesday night," Goddard added. "She had only a few bites of food, and nothing to drink. She went home around 8:30."

In attempting to determine who might have wanted Karyn Kupcinet dead, police came up against a blank wall. "This girl had more friends than anybody I ever heard of—and not a knocker in the bunch. They all loved her," Lieutenant Walsh told the press.

The sheriff's investigation soon focused on the twenty-six-year-old Prine, and three other male acquaintances of the slain starlet—free-lance writer Edward Stephen Rubin, who also went by the name of John Edward Manson; and actors Robert T. Hathaway and William Mamches.

Rubin and Hathaway, who said they knew Karyn through Prine, admitted having been in the apartment on the night of the murder.

"I went over to Karyn's around nine o'clock," Rubin stated. "I knocked on the door and she let me in. She seemed to be troubled about something, and a little while later she went out for a walk."

Hathaway told Walsh that he happened to be in the neighborhood around 9:30 P.M. when he saw Karyn walking around the block. "She said she just wanted to get some air," he related. "She told me that Rubin was in her apartment, and invited me to come up also."

The two men said they spent several hours with the young starlet, having cake and coffee and watching television. "After awhile she said she was getting tired," Hathaway said. "She went into her bedroom, undressed, and went to bed. Rubin and I both left. We pulled the door shut behind us, and made certain it was locked."

Walsh's earlier examination of the murder scene indicated that Karyn apparently had indeed gone to bed. Her bedclothes and pillow were rumpled. She evidently got up to admit someone who knocked or rang the bell—undoubtedly her killer—who had to have been someone she knew.

Mamches, who like Hathaway and Rubin said he knew the young actress through Prine, told investigators he had not seen her in three weeks. "The last time I talked to her I would say she was very nervous, very upset, and frantic about problems in her romance with Andy," he added.

Prine, who was divorced from actress Sharon Farrell, and who had been appearing in the NBC television series "Wide Country," was picked up for questioning.

"I called Kary at her apartment around 6:30 Wednesday night," he told Walsh. "We had a slight misunderstanding, a lovers' quarrel, and I hung up. I went to a movie, and I called her again a little after midnight to try to straighten things out. We had agreed recently not to see so much of each other and not to get too serious. Actually, we hadn't seen each other since last Sunday."

"Did anyone see you at the show, anyone who could verify that you were there?" the detective asked Prine.

"I didn't go by myself," he said. He explained that he had taken a young actress, Anna Capri, to see *A Streetcar Named Desire* at a Hollywood little theater. Afterward they had dinner at the Via Veneto restaurant on Sunset Strip. "I took Anna home about midnight, went back to my place, and called Kary."

Prine and his three friends all agreed to undergo lie detector tests. Unfortunately, the tests proved inconclusive, possibly because the men were all mentally tired after having been questioned at length by detectives.

Prine voluntarily returned the following day for additional interrogation, during which time he introduced a new element of mystery into the murder case.

"Kary and I both got death-threat notes pasted to our doors," he told police. "I just figured they were the work of some crackpot, but now—after what happened to Kary—I'm a little concerned."

"What kind of 'threats' were they," asked Floyd W.

Rosenberg, chief of the sheriff's detectives. "Exactly what did they look like, and what did they say?"

"They were not coherent threats," Prine responded. "They were a series of frightening words like 'you are going to die' and things like that. They had no name signed."

"Where these threatening letters written or printed, or what?"

"They weren't handwritten. They consisted of words clipped from newspapers or magazines and then pasted on a sheet of paper," Prine explained. "They weren't really letters. They didn't go through the mail. They were pasted onto the outside of our doors by someone who knew where each of us lived."

After he and the victim moved to different apartments, the notes ceased coming, he added. Prine had kept seven of the notes the couple had received, and turned them over to Rosenberg. One of them read:

"YOU MAY DIE WITHOUT NOBODY. WINNER OF LONELINESS WANTS DEATH UNTIL SOMEONE SPECIAL CARES."

"Like I said, they don't make much sense," he told the detective. "I'm going to stay with friends for the next few days, in case you're looking for me. I don't feel like seeing anybody, but I don't want to be alone. I'm a little nervous. I don't know who did this to Kary. Maybe they might also try me."

Kupcinet, meanwhile, sadly accompanied his daughter's body back to Chicago. More than 1,500 people, including Governor Otto Kerner and Mayor Richard J. Daley attended services for the slain actress in Temple Sholom on Lake Shore Drive.

Back in Hollywood, detectives located Anna Capri, an eighteen-year-old Bavarian beauty who had come to Hollywood only recently. She corroborated Prine's story of the movie and restaurant dates. "Andrew dropped me off at my apartment about a half hour after midnight," she estimated.

The investigation into Karyn's murder, meanwhile, took a truly bizarre twist when crime lab technicians put their microscopes to the threatening notes that had been affixed to Karyn's and Prine's apartment doors.

"This is the damndest turn of events I've ever seen," Sheriff's Captain A.W. Etzel told Walsh and Rosenberg. "Our identification section personnel have positive identification of a fingerprint on the bottom side of the scotch tape used on one of the words and the note. It's the right middle finger of Karyn Kupcinet!"

Faced with the possibility that the murder victim had originated the threatening notes herself, detectives gathered up magazines found in her apartment and began going through them, page by page. Sure enough, they found a number of pages that had words clipped from them.

The discovery sent the homicide investigators back to square one. If Karyn had sent Prine and herself the threats, then the notes—which police had considered their hottest clues—apparently had no bearing on her murder. "Perhaps they were meant for some reason only known to her," Etzel surmised.

Then Kup's New York counterpart, Walter Winchell, who happened to be writing his column from Los Angeles at the time, decided to solve the case on his own. "I promise you I'll find out who did it—and this will win a Pulitzer Prize for me," he told Kupcinet.

Eventually Lieutenant Walsh phoned Kup and begged him, "Please get this guy off our back. He's interfering with the investigation." So Kup called Winchell and politely asked him to quit playing detective and stick to his typewriter.

So, who killed Karyn Kupcinet?

UPDATE

"After more than a quarter of a century of agony, that question still haunts us," says Kupcinet, who is still writing his *Sun-Times* column at the age of seventy-eight. In his autobiography, *Kup—A Man, An Era, A City* (Bonus Books) he offers his own thoughts on who might be responsible for his daughter's death:

"What disturbs us most was the failure of the Los Angeles Sheriff's police to pursue the evidence that Essee and I thought pointed directly at David Lange, who had been a friend of Cookie's."

Lange, described by Kupcinet as a heavy drinker, a hanger-on, and a gofer, occupied the apartment directly below Karyn's on the night of the murder. He was in his bedroom with a girl friend when they heard a commotion, followed by the sound of a lot of people running up and down stairs. Lange ignored the excitement and did not leave the bedroom to see what was going on, even after someone knocked at his door and told him what had happened.

"Police suspect . . . he chose not to appear on the scene because he already knew what had happened. That enabled him to stay clear of the authorities," Kupcinet surmised.

"If that behavior was suspect, there also was a 'confession.' The police report includes a statement from a friend of Lange who reported that he told her that he was the person who killed Karyn.

"Essee and I pressed the sheriff's police to pursue such a revealing statement, but their response was that they had tried with no success because Lange by this time had moved into the home of his sister, Hope, and she had retained attorneys who refused to let him answer any questions."

BOOK III

WIVES AND
MOTHERS

OH, THOSE BEAUTIFUL EYES

In 1988 Lisa Kopanakis, a twenty-two-year-old business student at Indiana University Northwest in Gary, tied for second place in a contest for the "Most Beautiful Eyes in Indiana." A year later, just seventeen days short of her first wedding anniversary, the light in those eyes went out forever in one of the state's most grotesque homicides.

A violent electrical storm packed with rain had whipped through the Portage area in Northwest Indiana on Aug. 4, 1989, the last day the attractive young bride was seen alive. Her husband, George, a mechanical engineer, was in Knoxville, Tennessee, on business. He tried to call home the following day, but got only a recorded message from the phone company saying telephone service had been temporarily interrupted.

He then put in a call to his sister, Niki, who lived a few miles away in Lake Station, and asked her to drop by the apartment to make sure Lisa was all right. He had been apprehensive about his wife's well-being ever since a macabre incident that had darkened their lives shortly after their marriage.

On March 19 the newlyweds had come home from a late supper to find their two pet dogs on the blood-smeared kitchen floor with their throats cut. Lisa became hysterical over the deaths of the year-old cairn terrier and year-old fox terrier, which she referred to as "my babies."

While she and her husband were out dining an intruder, who disturbed nothing else in the apartment, had taken a butcher knife out of a kitchen drawer and slashed the animals' throats. The killer then wrapped the knife neatly in a blood-soaked towel and placed in on the counter top.

Lisa's mother-in-law, Sophia Kopanakis, a seamstress, told authorities at the time that her son and daughter-in-law had been having trouble with neighbors who were involved in devil worship. Portage police checked on her report but found no substance to it. They did learn, however, that Sophia Kopanakis had been bitterly opposed to her son's marriage to Lisa, and there had been ongoing friction between the two women.

Shortly after the pet dogs were killed George and Lisa moved to their present townhouse in the Cherrywood Trace apartment complex. George bought Lisa a Pomeranian puppy to try to take the place of the slain animals.

Lisa and her mother-in-law continued to squabble, and had one particularly bitter dispute over the removal of two photos of the young couple's Hawaiian honeymoon from their apartment. When Lisa discovered that the photos had been taken, she complained to her father-in-law about Sophia.

When George called from Tennessee asking his sister, Niki, to check on Lisa after the storm, Sophia insisted on going along. They found the apartment at 5237 Rachel Street locked, and got no answer to their ringing of the bell at 4:30 P.M. The two women let themselves in with a spare key the in-laws kept, and found Lisa dead in a sticky pool of congealed blood on the kitchen floor.

It was a repeat of the dog incident, except that this time the victim was their young mistress. Her throat had been so violently slashed that she had been all but decapitated.

Portage Police Sergeant Warren Lewis and Detective Roger Kiser were mystified as to a motive. The murder weapon, a knife taken from a kitchen drawer, had been rinsed of blood, wiped clean of fingerprints, and placed upon the body. A kitchen throw rug had also been laid across the body, as if to indicate the dead woman was nothing more than a door mat.

There had been no forced entry. The killer either had a key, or the victim had admitted the killer as someone she knew.

The body was fully clothed, and a sanitary napkin was still in place, ruling out a sexual attack. Furthermore, the dead woman still wore all her jewelry, including a necklace. Robbery certainly could not have been the motive. A check of the apartment revealed that nothing appeared to be out of place.

It was clearly a crime of passion. Porter County Coroner John Evans, who performed an autopsy, told investigators the victim had died of "a combination of sharp and blunt trauma." He said Lisa had been stabbed eleven times in the back before her throat was cut. She also had a crescent shaped wound on her forehead.

Kiser determined that the forehead injury had been caused by a heavy drinking glass, found in the kitchen. Like the murder knife, it had also been wiped clean of fingerprints.

In reconstructing the crime, Kiser, working with Detectives David Reynolds and Keith Burden, figured the young woman had been entertaining someone she knew. Perhaps she was handing the visitor a glass of iced tea, when the intruder took the heavy tumbler and slammed her in the forehead with it, knocking her unconscious. The visitor then took a knife from the kitchen drawer and plunged it into Lisa's back, again and again, in a murderous frenzy of hate.

Then, rolling the dead or dying woman over, the killer twisted her head grotesquely to one side and all but sliced it off.

Afterward the killer more or less washed dishes, cleansing the knife of blood, and wiping both the knife and tumbler free of fingerprints. The kitchen counter top and drawer pulls were also wiped clean, as was the floor around the body, to remove any bloody footprints.

It was a violent murder scene devoid of clues. The only witness appeared to have been Lisa's new puppy, the Pomeranian, which was wandering around in a state of bewilderment with blood on its fur.

The slaying of Lisa Kopanakis caused police to take a fresh look at the unsolved murder nine years earlier of her uncle by marriage, Gus Raftopoulos. Gus, known as "Nick the Barber" because he had shops in Lake Station and nearby Gary, was found bludgeoned to death on a country road on May 13, 1980.

Gus' wife, Demetra, and Lisa's mother-in-law, Sophia, were sisters who lived near one another in Lake Station.

According to Detective Kiser, Gus had been killed by blows to the back of his head with a baseball bat or other blunt instrument which crushed his skull, possibly in his home in Lake Station. The killer then dressed the corpse, put the body in the family car, and drove about five miles to Portage, where the body was dumped alongside Willowcreek Road just north of U.S. Hwy. 6 at around 5:00 A.M.

"After he was dumped out of the vehicle, someone ran over his hand with the car," Kiser recalled. "There were tire marks on the ground near his body."

The most puzzling aspect of the barber's murder, however, was a piece of string. After he had been killed a length of string, similar to the kind used in gardening, was tied around his head, partly covering his eyes. It was still in place when Gus' body was found by a passing motorist.

Kiser and other detectives felt the string had significance, but were unable to find out what. Despite extensive talks to members of the closely-knit Greek community, and interviews with University of Chicago experts on Old World customs and Greek mythology, they could find nothing to explain the presence of the mysterious string.

Demetra Raftopoulos was questioned in connection with her husband's slaying. She told police she last saw him the previous evening, when he left the house with $800 in cash to buy a car. A Lake County grand jury investigating the murder in 1985 called Gus' widow as a witness, but no charges were ever brought against her.

Kiser and his fellow investigators determined that there was no relation between the two homicides—although the victims were relations.

They now had two unsolved murders linked by two sisters—one the wife of the first victim, and the other the mother-in-law of the second.

UPDATE

The Porter County Crime Stoppers program posted a $1,000 reward for information leading to the arrest of the Lisa Kopanakis' killer. Since her step-father, Steven Handlon, was the former Portage city attorney, a group of fellow lawyers initiated a reward of their own. The initial fund of $2,200, from eleven local attorneys, grew rapidly to more than $7,500. Added to the Crime Stopper bounty, rewards for Lisa's killer totaled nearly $9,000, but the money was never claimed.

"We have a pretty good idea as to the identity of the killer, but there is no proof," Detective Kiser said. "We continue to hope that someone will remember something that happened on the night of the storm when Lisa died—perhaps they saw someone enter the building and thought nothing of it, because the visitor was someone who had been there before. We keep hoping that someone with information will contact us."

THE NEEDLE-STUDDED TORSO

At the age of thirty-one, Dorothy Tapper of Oak Park, Illinois, was every black child's role model. A sixth grade teacher at Corkery Elementary School on Chicago's Southwest Side, she was one of five teachers who had organized a drug-and-alcohol abuse program at the school. She was married to Dr. Edward Tapper, a seemingly well-to-do white obstetrician.

In 1977, Tapper, like many other young resident doctors at Rush Presbyterian St. Luke's Medical Center, was trying to learn his craft and make ends meet on $15,500 a year while carrying a grueling workload. By 1982, he had clearly won the struggle, and had turned a West Side Chicago clinic into a booming business that enriched him to the tune of nearly $150,000 a year.

That was the year Dorothy and Edward met. Dorothy Goods was a patient at Presbyterian St. Luke's, where she had undergone minor surgery, and Dr. Tapper was the attending physician. He had just shed his second wife, and after Dorothy's release from the hospital they began dating. They were married two years later, in June 1984.

Later that same year Dorothy Tapper took a maternity leave to await the arrival of the couple's son, Alan. She had been due to return to the classroom after the Labor Day weekend in 1985, but she never made the first day of school.

She was reported missing on Sunday night, September 1, by her mother and stepfather, Ora and Walter Thomas. They told Oak Park Police Chief Keith Bergstrom that they had not seen nor heard from their daughter since August 29. Her thirty-six-year-old husband filed a belated missing person report himself on Monday, September 2. Detectives Patrick Kelly and Frank Kennedy interviewed the obstetrician-gynecologist twice during the ensuing week, but he could shed no light on his wife's disappearance.

By week's end the schoolteacher's frantic parents, clutching at straws, telephoned WLS-Channel 7 in Chicago in hopes of getting something about their missing daughter on the TV evening news.

Meanwhile Channel 7 reporter Russ Ewing was putting together a gruesome story on the discovery of a headless torso in Porter County, Indiana. The naked torso, stuffed into a plastic bag, was found at 1:30 P.M. Saturday, August 31, alongside the Baltimore & Ohio Railroad tracks running beneath the Interstate Hwy. 94 overpass in Portage, a community of 28,000 people about forty-five miles from Chicago.

From every indication, the sack had been tossed from a passing car on the overpass.

Porter County Coroner John Evans had the torso taken to the South Bend Medical Foundation, where Dr. Rick Hoover, a forensic pathologist, identified the remains as those of a black female between twenty and thirty years of age. He estimated she had been slain eighteen to twenty-four hours before a track walker came upon the body. The hiker first poked curiously at the green plastic bag with his walking stick. Then he took a peek inside—and called the police.

The victim had been brutally tortured before being killed. In addition to being beaten so badly that all of the ribs on one side of her body were broken, a number of long surgical needles of the type used to perform spinal taps had been imbedded into her chest, back, and heart. Several of the needles were still protruding grotesquely from her chest when the torso was found.

Pathological findings indicated the victim had been tortured for two to four hours, and was still alive when the dismemberment process began. Her head, arms, and legs had been neatly severed. "This woman was cut up by an expert," Dr. Hoover told the coroner. "Possibly by somebody with some medical background, or someone who knows how to gut a large animal."

Ewing's assignment editor, Gera-Lind Kolarik, suspected a possible link between the Oak Park teacher's disappearance and the Indiana torso, and told Ewing about the missing woman. Ewing passed the information on to Coroner Evans, who obtained copies of Dorothy Tapper's medical records from Oak Park police. Although the head, arms, and legs were missing, Dr. Hoover was able to positively identify the torso as Tapper's through surgical scars and X-rays of her spinal column taken during her stay at Presbyterian St. Luke's.

Once identification was accomplished, police in Indiana and Illinois huddled over who would take jurisdiction of the case. At the moment nobody knew who killed Dorothy Tapper, where the deed took place, or why. Bergstrom agreed with Portage police that since the torso had been found in their community, they would assume primary responsibility for the homicide investigation, while Oak Park police would continue their inquiry into the victim's disappearance.

Portage Detective Lee Allen, who headed the murder investigation along with Detective Sergeant Roger Kiser, met with Oak Park investigators Kelly and Kennedy to compare notes. The only clue police had was the green plastic bag in which the torso had been wrapped, which was of the type used by medical laboratories, and the ominous needles.

Oak Park police learned that the last time Ora Goods Thomas saw her daughter alive was Thursday afternoon, August 29, when the victim and her ten-month-old son waved good-bye to grandma as they went into Dr. Tapper's Near West Side clinic. Dorothy, who taught school under her maiden name and was known to her pupils as "Miss Goods," had just returned from the Chicago Board of Education headquarters where she had signed up to resume teaching sixth grade following her year-long maternity leave. After not being able to reach her daughter for three days, the older woman called police.

Detectives learned that the Tappers' marriage had been floundering. Dr. Tapper had become immersed in drug use, and was having severe financial problems. His wife had told relatives, "I'm ready to leave him. I want a divorce." If he did not agree to the divorce, she threatened to expose his drug abuse, relatives told police. As a matter of fact, a close friend and associate of the doctor had just been arrested by Chicago police for drug trafficking after an unidentified informant blew the whistle on him.

Dr. Tapper was questioned extensively by Oak Park police and investigators for the Porter County coroner's office. They learned that the couple had engaged in a "heated argument" that Thursday afternoon in the doctor's office, after which Mrs. Tapper called a taxi and left with her infant son. Dr. Tapper quit the couple's Oak Park home later that same evening and moved in with a relative. Little Alan, meanwhile, was being cared for by Dr. Tapper's sister.

Officials from the Portage, Chicago, and Oak Park police departments met with prosecutors in the Cook County state's attorney's office to exchange information in the case. They were of the unanimous opinion that Dorothy Tapper had been tortured with the surgical needles in an effort to force her to admit that she had been the confidential police informant who brought about the drug arrest of her husband's close friend. The long surgical needles stuck into her chest, back, and even her heart were strategically placed so that they would not kill quickly.

Search warrants were issued for the couple's home and Dr. Tapper's clinic, but nothing was uncovered that would implicate him in his wife's murder.

Whenever violence befalls a married person, police immediately zero in on the surviving spouse. In delving into the background of Dr. Tapper, the homicide investigators learned that he was a young man who once appeared to have everything going for him. He had been an Eagle Scout, an A-student at Brother Rice High School, a trumpet player in the school band, and was the only one of five brothers and sisters in his family to go on to college.

Somewhere along the line his life went sour. His father, seventy-two-year-old Albert Tapper, a retired railroad worker, told authorities he had barely spoken with his son in three years—ever since he accused his son of burglarizing his home of sixty dollars in cash and credit cards.

More recently, investigators determined, Dr. Tapper had been under investigation by a Cook County grand jury in connection with nearly $287,000 worth of bad checks written to drug companies with which he did business. Ten major pharmaceutical companies were involved in the grand jury probe. Investigators learned that nearly 150 checks were being scrutinized, and that about 80 percent of them were for drugs, such as amphetamines, depressants, and codeine-based cough syrup. More than $70,000 worth of the bogus checks had been penned within a six-day period in February.

Investigators had attempted to question Dorothy Tapper in the couple's Oak Park home about her husband's financial dealings in May, however the doctor returned home unexpectedly and ordered an end to the interrogation.

But that wasn't all. The Illinois attorney general's office was also looking into charges of duplicate billings for Medicaid patients at Dr. Tapper's clinic, which had received more than $208,000 in Medicaid reimbursements since 1983. And in addition to the claims by the major pharmaceutical firms, four other companies had sued Dr. Tapper, claiming he owed them $291,000 for loans, drugs, and electronic equipment.

According to court records, Dr. Tapper had filed for bankruptcy in 1979, near the end of his four-year residency at Rush Presbyterian St. Luke's. Three years later he filed for protection from creditors in bankruptcy court, and a judge absolved him of $90,000 in debts, including thousands of dollars in student loans. Yet he continued to rake in money. Where had it all gone?

On September 13, two weeks after his wife was found murdered, the Cook County grand jury indicted Dr. Tapper on charges of bilking pharmaceutical houses out of $289,000 in drugs and medical supplies. He was charged in eleven separate indictments with a series of deceptive acts over a seven-month period, ending in June.

The doctor was taken into custody by detectives of the Chicago Police Financial Crimes Unit at his West Side clinic. He was ordered held in the Cook County Jail in lieu of $250,000 bond. His elderly father expressed amazement at his son's financial problems. "I never could figure it out," he said. "These doctors are pretty well fixed for money."

The case against Dr. Tapper dragged on for more than a year, until November 1986, when he pleaded guilty to writing $145,000 worth of bad checks to obtain drugs from pharmaceutical companies, which he later resold illegally.

He was sentenced to thirty months probation, and ordered to perform 500 hours of community service.

The doctor was still on probation on April 6, 1988, when he was arrested on a charge of illegal possession of cocaine, after tactical unit police found a quantity of cocaine on the kitchen counter of his low rent apartment on Chicago's South Side. A woman who shared the apartment with him was also charged with drug violations.

Police had originally responded to a call of a burglary in progress shortly after midnight, when they apprehended Dr. Tapper running from the scene carrying a large brown plastic garbage bag containing a videocassette recorder. When they escorted him back to his nearby apartment for questioning they found the narcotics paraphernalia and cocaine on the kitchen counter.

It appeared that drugs were the root of all of his troubles, and had reduced the once successful obstetrician-gynecologist to little more than a pathetic junkie, stealing from his neighbors to get money for his next fix.

UPDATE

Dorothy Tapper's skull turned up several years after her body was found. A fisherman retrieved the grim relic from a retention pond, not far from where the torso had been dropped from the highway overpass. Her arms and legs were never recovered. No one was ever arrested for her murder.

Dr. Tapper's troubles reached a climax on Nov. 17, 1989, when U.S. District Court Judge George M. Marovich in Chicago sentenced him to forty-one months in prison for mail fraud involving phony or inflated medical insurance claims, conspiracy and distribution of controlled substances. Dr. Tapper had pleaded guilty to the charges, telling the judge that he was a drug abuser. Assistant U.S. Attorney Stephen Sinnott, who prosecuted the woebegone physician, said, "He wrote prescriptions to anyone for anything, just for the money."

AN OUT-AND-OUT EXECUTION

The young married couple in the Wyndham Court Apartments in an unincorporated area of northwest suburban Palatine kept pretty much to themselves. When their next door neighbor, Gary Faegenburg, said "Hi" to them, they kept right on walking and didn't answer. One day when they were getting out of their car with their arms loaded they dropped a package on the ground. Faegenburg offered to help, but they said "No thanks," and went inside.

Little wonder that neighbors were inclined to let well enough alone on that cold February night in 1988 when they saw twenty-eight-year-old Dana Rinaldi slouched in the front seat of her late model Ford Mustang with her legs sticking out the door on the driver's side. Finally at midnight, as February 17 came to an end, someone called the sheriff's office and let them worry about it.

A squad car rolled up at 12:30 A.M., Thursday, to see if everything was all right. It wasn't. Dana Rinaldi was dead of unnatural causes. She had been shot five times in the head with a small caliber weapon at close range.

Dana was fully clothed. Her purse was in her lap and the car keys were lying beside her on the seat. She had apparently been shot through the open door of the car as she was getting out, after coming home from her job as clerical supervisor on the three to eleven shift at GTE Directories Corp., in nearby Mount Prospect.

An autopsy showed she also had gunshot wounds to her hands, as though she had held up her hands to fend off the bullets.

Detectives, under the direction of Cook County Sheriff's Captain George Nicosia, went into the apartment complex and began knocking on doors to awaken neighbors. Nobody had heard any gunfire. Nicosia broke the news to the victim's twenty-nine-year-old husband, Joseph, when he arrived home at 4:30 A.M. to see police and neighbors crowded around his wife's blue Mustang. He burst into tears.

Rinaldi, the vice president of a Franklin Park construction company, had an airtight alibi. He said he had been out nightclubbing with a friend in Chicago, and had two time-stamped receipts to prove it. Both he and his associate volunteered to take lie detector tests, which they subsequently passed.

"This is a baffling mystery. We have no motive or suspects," Nicosia asserted. "We have absolutely no idea why anybody would want to do this."

Nicosia assigned ten detectives to the case, working under Lieutenant Leonard Marak and Sergeant Charles Schenk. In questioning residents of the apartment complex, they learned that several neighbors had seen two men sitting in a red sports car about a half a block from the murder scene not long before the body was discovered. The 1988 Nissan Pulsar was idling in the roadway with its headlights on.

One witness said he saw the red Nissan pull into the only available parking space in the area. "I was miffed, because I'd been driving around looking for a place to park," the witness said. "A few seconds after I had passed they pulled out of the parking space and drove past me."

Were the men in the red Nissan the killers?

"It appears that Dana Rinaldi may have recognized or known her assailant, based on examination of the crime scene," said Lieutenant Marak, who remains in charge of the investigation. "She was holding her purse on her lap. There was no sex attack. She was plain out executed. This was a blitz attack designed to kill her."

UPDATE

Three years after the Rinaldi assassination police believe they know the identity of the shooter, but do not have enough evidence to make an arrest that will hold up in court. "Getting the evidence is the task we face," Lieutenant Marak explained. "The one thing on our side is time. Somewhere down the line someone is going to make a mistake. Someone is going to say something."

$1,000 FOR ELVIA'S KILLER

The only thing Elvia Johnson ever did that a newspaper deemed noteworthy enough to put her name in print was get killed.

She was one of the little people of the world, people who go about their own business, trying to eke out a living, pay their bills, raise their kids, do the right thing, and hope for the best.

Elvia, who was twenty-five years old, lived in an apartment on Broadway Avenue in North Chicago with her five-year-old son, Jason. She worked as a tax representative for Sears Mortgage Corp., in northwest suburban Lincolnshire, driving to and from work in her blue 1986 four-door Alliance.

When she failed to come home on the night of Feb. 10, 1988, her family reported her missing at 6:00 P.M. Concerned friends went out looking for her, and around midnight they found her car parked in an alley off Broadway near her home, just east of Sheridan Road. Her naked body was found in the back seat. A red cloth cord had been wrapped tightly around her neck. Her clothing was found rumpled on the floor, and her body had frozen in the bitter February cold.

Lake County Coroner Barbara Richardson determined that the young mother had been raped and strangled.

North Chicago Police Chief Ernest Fisher put out a plea for anyone who had seen her the previous evening, or knew who she might have been with. When last seen around 10:00 P.M., Elvia, who stood five feet six inches tall and weighed 130 pounds, was wearing a red sweat shirt with a North Chicago girls track team logo and blue jeans.

Chief Fisher said the victim might have been raped and killed elsewhere, and her body driven to the spot where her car was abandoned. North Chicago police tracked down a number of leads, and even went all the way to Seattle to question a suspect, but have been unable to come up with a clue to the identity of the slayer.

Co-workers at Sears Mortgage, stunned at the slaying, established a trust fund to help pay for young Jason's education. Who killed Elvia Johnson, however, remains a mystery.

UPDATE

The North Chicago Crime Stoppers organization posted a reward of $1,000 for information leading to the arrest of the killer. The case remains open, and anyone knowing anything about the brutal slaying of Elvia Johnson is asked to call 708–662–2222, anonymously or otherwise. "We are still following up on leads," Chief Fisher said. "Our department has a good homicide clear-up rate."

DEATH CAME CALLING

Shortly after nine o'clock on Friday morning, Aug. 17, 1984, Indiana housewife Darlene Hulse, twenty-eight, answered a knock at the front door of her home just outside of Argos, a town of 1,500 in the north-central part of the state. A deliveryman stood on the stoop with a package in his hands. Her husband, Ronald, a supervisor at a local aluminum siding and door manufacturing company, had already left for work. She was alone in the house with the couple's three daughters.

Mrs. Hulse stared suspiciously at the blond haired man, in his late twenties or early thirties, who stood before her with his offering. "I'm not expecting a package or anything," she told him, moving to close the door. Before she could complete her move the deliveryman pushed his way inside, and a violent struggle ensued in the living room.

The intruder displayed no weapon. Tossing aside the package he grabbed a poker from in front of the fireplace, and brought it down forcefully and repeatedly on the woman's head and upper body as her children looked on in horror.

The two older girls, ages six and eight, were in the bathroom, and overheard the exchange of words between their mother and the blond haired stranger as he barged into the home. As their mother struggled with the assailant the eight-year-old, ignoring the danger, ran to the telephone to summon help. Before she could make a connection, however, the poker-wielding man grabbed the instrument from her hand and ripped the phone off the wall.

The girl and her sister then bolted out the back door and ran a quarter of a mile to the home of their grandmother, screaming, "Grandma! Grandma!" as they got within earshot of her house. The older woman calmed them down, listened to their story, and called police.

Within minutes, officers from Argos pulled up at the scene, a secluded area near old Indiana Hwy. 31. Several Marshall County Sheriff's deputies and Indiana State troopers were right behind them.

There was an eerie quiet about the Hulse home as the lawmen approached with weapons drawn. Fresh bloodstains on the front stoop told them that the frightening story blurted out by the two little girls had not been the figment of childish imaginations.

Sheriff Richard E. Tyson, no stranger to the criminal mind, warned his fellow lawmen to proceed with caution. A World War II marine, Tyson had been in law enforcement for twenty-two years, serving as police chief of the nearby town of Bremen before taking over as sheriff in January of 1983.

Once inside the house, the lawmen found the Hulses' one-year-old daughter unharmed, but covered with her mother's blood.

Except for the child, the house was empty. A thorough inspection indicated that nothing was missing except Darlene Hulse and the fireplace poker.

"Good lord, when you stop and think about what happened here, we could just as easily have had four homicide victims," the sheriff said, surveying the bloody home.

The two older girls gave the sheriff a description of the deliveryman, and police immediately fanned out in search of the woman and her blond haired abductor. Roadblocks were thrown up in all directions and police units were alerted to be on the lookout for a two-tone green automobile, possibly a

General Motors make, that had earlier been seen parked near the Hulse residence.

Neighbors told deputies, "It was an older four-door model with rust on the doors."

Ronald Hulse, who had been at work when his wife was abducted, joined the sheriff's men and state investigators in searching for her, but no trace was found until the next afternoon, Saturday, August 18. A timber buyer, tramping through the woods some seven miles west of the Hulse home came across her battered body at 2:30 P.M.

Darlene Hulse was lying face up on the ground. She was fully clothed in a skirt and blouse. The blood-stained poker lay at her side. Sheriff Tyson observed that her body bore signs of drag marks. "It looks like whoever did this dragged her body into the woods from the road," he said. Fresh tire tracks were noted in the gravel road, a distance of sixty-two feet from where the body was found.

An autopsy confirmed that Mrs. Hulse had been bludgeoned to death, but had not been sexually molested.

An investigation into the Hulse family background failed to turn up any motive for the slaying. "The Hulses are pretty much a church-going, all-American family," Sheriff Tyson observed. "This community is a pretty quiet one. What happened here is a real shocker."

Based on a description of the deliveryman by the two children, police prepared a composite drawing of the suspect. It would fit almost any blond haired man around the age of thirty.

Authorities were never able to determine a motive for the slaying. It wasn't rape and it wasn't robbery. Whoever took the life of Darlene Hulse just seemed hell-bent on violence.

UPDATE

Several suspects were questioned in connection with the Hulse homicide, including one man who was extradited from

Colorado. All were released, however, after the girls who witnessed their mother's brutal slaying failed to identify any of them.

In the end, Marshall County Prosecutor Fred R. Jones was forced to admit, "I can say that we have no one individual who is the suspect."

The Marshall County Sheriff's department continues to run down all possible leads, numbering "in the hundreds," according to Detective Sergeant David Yoquelet. "It is not uncommon for burglars to pose as deliverymen to determine if anyone is home," he said. "This might have been what took place, although there is no clear motive for what happened."

Ronald Hulse erected a protective chain-link around his rural home after the slaying, but the memory of the nightmare that had taken place inside was more than he could live with. Ultimately he packed up his three little girls and moved away.

BOOK IV

JOB RELATED, PERHAPS

GUNS THAT GO BANG IN THE NIGHT

When ruggedly handsome Charles E. Merriam failed to show up for work at his Amoco Oil Company office, his colleagues called and asked a neighbor to check his home on the grounds of the Rob Roy Country Club in Prospect Heights to see if everything was okay. It wasn't. Through a window of the house at 457 Sutherland Court the neighbor could see the fifty-two-year-old senior marketing executive's pajama-clad body lying on the floor in a pool of blood.

The neighbor called paramedics and Cook County Sheriff's police, who entered the home where Merriam's body was sprawled in a foyer near the front door. He had been shot three times. There was also a bullet hole in the door.

The medical examiner's office was notified, and Merriam was pronounced dead shortly after 11:00 A.M. on Thursday, Nov. 5, 1987.

Captain George Nicosia, commander of the sheriff's investigations section, figured that Merriam, awakened during the night, had opened the door in response to the ringing of the doorbell and then tried to slam it when he saw who was out there.

Whoever it was fired one shot through the door, striking Merriam in the chest. The visitor then forced his way in and shot Merriam two more times, once in the head and once in the chest. Two shell casings from an automatic pistol were found inside the foyer, and another outside the front door.

The last person known to have seen Merriam alive was his secretary, who told sheriff's investigators she left the house about ten o'clock Wednesday night. Earlier in the evening Merriam had kept a dinner engagement with a family friend. En route to the restaurant he had used his car telephone to talk to his wife of twenty-eight years, whom he had met in college and married in Hawaii—but from whom he was now living apart.

A neighbor, Bonnie Loudan, told Nicosia that she heard what might have been the fatal shots being fired around 1:00 A.M. "I heard a boom—a loud noise," she related. "Noises like that during the night attract attention because they're so rare around here. I was raised in Montana and am familiar with the sound of gunfire."

Aside from the empty shells, no weapon was found at the scene. Nor was there any sign of a struggle or forced entry, and nothing appeared to be missing from the house. From all appearances it was an out-and-out assassination.

But why? What was there in Merriam's background that would cause someone to come to his door in the dark of night and shoot him dead? Nicosia's detectives probed into the slain executive's background for an answer.

Merriam was the scion of one of Chicago' most respected families. His late father, Charles J. Merriam, had been a patent attorney, and his uncle, Robert E. Merriam, was a former reform alderman from Chicago's Fifth Ward, and one-time member of President Dwight D. Eisenhower's White House staff. His grandfather for whom he'd been named, Charles E. Merriam, had been a University of Chicago political science professor, reform alderman, and unsuccessful candidate for mayor in 1911.

The slain man had joined Amoco when it was known as Standard Oil Company of Indiana in 1956 after graduation from DePauw University in Greencastle, Indiana. He spent the next thirty-one years working his way up the corporate ladder until being named manager of the Chicago district, the company's largest, in January 1986.

As the head of more than 1,000 Amoco service stations in Illinois, northwest Indiana, and southern Wisconsin, Merriam was responsible for deciding how the company outlets should be operated, and whether any should be closed. He was always the first one at his desk in Amoco's district office in Des Plaines, which was why co-workers became concerned when he failed to show up for work Thursday morning.

In talking to the slain man's family, police learned that Merriam, the father of three grown children, had been acting "disturbed" over something in recent months. About six weeks before his death he moved out on his wife, Carol, and into the home in Prospect Heights, where he lived alone.

A neighbor of the family in west suburban Elmhurst told police, "He surprised his wife about Labor Day. He gave her two or three days' notice he was divorcing her. She had no indication it was coming." Since leaving his wife, Merriam had been seeing a young divorced woman.

Police also learned that Merriam had told colleagues of having received three death threats. His co-workers said they believed the threats had come from disgruntled service station operators who were unhappy about their stations being transformed into mini-marts. The change-over would cause full-service operators to lose lucrative auto repair work.

Merriam, an ex-marine, was a tough taskmaster. Investigators immediately saw two possible motives behind the slaying.

Could a gas station operator, distraught at seeing his life's work as a mechanic going down the tubes, have wiped out the management person who caused it to happen? Or could Merriam have incurred the wrath of an ex-husband or boyfriend of a woman he'd been dating?

The president of the Illinois Gasoline Dealers Association, Bob Jacobs, bristled at hints in the press that Merriam might have been slain by a disgruntled service station operator.

"Certainly many dealers are angry over the current policies of Amoco Oil, which are eliminating many of them from business. But many of Amoco's own staff had grievances against Chuck for demotions, lateral moves, and firings," he asserted. "If I were to point an accusing finger, it would be against the company itself that set these policies for him to initiate and enforce. To his employers, Amoco Oil Company, I say shame on you. Look what you have wrought."

Jacobs said Amoco policies, which Merriam was charged with enforcing, in addition to conversion to mini-marts, included outrageous rent increases; 3 percent charges for credit card users, driving some customers to Shell; and mandatory twenty-four-hour operation, even in high crime areas.

Amoco spokesman Charles Miller said it was not unusual for executives of large corporations to receive threats from a variety of sources in the course of business activities. In acknowledging that Amoco was going through a period of transition, he said many customers, as well as station operators, were unhappy over the change from full-service with repair bays to mini-marts.

Sheriff's investigators pored over company records in an effort to determine whether Merriam's murder could have been job related. They also interrogated a number of station operators in Merriam's territory who were having business difficulties as a result of Amoco policies. Their names were fed into FBI computers to determine whether any of them had criminal backgrounds.

Meanwhile Dr. Robert J. Stein, the Cook County medical examiner, had some startling news for detectives working on the case. Stein, who performed an autopsy on the slain man's body, told investigators, "He was killed with two different guns. I removed a .25-caliber steel-jacketed bullet from the victim's head, and took a copper-jacketed, .380-caliber slug out of his body. The third bullet went right through him, but it was the shot in the head that killed him."

This meant one of two things: Either there were two killers standing on the stoop when Merriam opened the door, or Merriam was shot to death by one person blazing away with one gun in each hand.

About twenty-five divers, under the direction of Sheriff's Lieutenant Ray Olson, searched the murky water of two ponds on the golf course near the victim's home for the murder guns, but came up with nothing but a lot of lost golf balls. Detectives also probed 100 sewer openings and tunnels in the area around his home, with the same discouraging results.

Police checked out more than 275 leads, interviewed hundreds of Amoco employees from management offices to grease pits, and examined reams of company records, but could never come up with a definite motive, much less a suspect, in the Merriam homicide. The local Crime Stoppers posted a $50,000 reward for the killer, and Amoco matched the amount, but the death of Charles Merriam still defied solution.

UPDATE

Despite rewards totaling $100,000, the investigation into the murder of Chuck Merriam remains at a virtual standstill. "There are no leads, no new information at all," said Major Thomas Newman, commander of the Cook County Police investigation section. "Detectives review the case file from time to time, but to date no clearcut suspect or motive has emerged."

"I think it is solvable," said Detective Warren Schwartz, a twenty-five-year veteran of the sheriff's department who is assigned to the case. "Chuck Merriam was known as a tough wagon master, whose job made him enemies. That's no secret."

THE DEATH OF DOCTOR SMILE

Dr. Burton Isaacs, a forty-four-year-old Chicago dentist whose friends called him "Mr. Smile," was finally starting to get his act back together. The road along the way, however, seemed to have been paved with speed-bumps.

First there was the unexplained death of his ex-wife Ilene, on April 25, 1977. A maid found her body in her car, parked in the family garage in Northbrook with the motor running. The coroner listed the cause of death as carbon monoxide poisoning. Northbrook police could find no "conclusive proof" that the death was a suicide, nor could they be sure that it wasn't.

Then there was a mysterious home invasion in 1981, while Isaacs was away. A lone intruder posing as a telephone repair man shot the dentist's second wife, Marlene, with an electric stun gun, tied up her and two of the couple's children, and stole an undetermined amount of jewelry.

That was followed by the 1983 separation from his second wife, which threatened to get ugly. He listed his base salary from his dental practice at $126,000 a year in divorce papers, but Marlene countered that he was earning closer to $600,000.

After Isaacs moved out on his wife she complained that an unidentified assailant attacked and beat her unconscious in the family garage—the same garage where the first Mrs. Isaacs had died.

By 1984, however, all Dr. Isaac's problems seemed to have been put behind him. "He was beginning to enjoy himself for the first time in many years," his friend and associate, Dr. Robert Hessberger, would relate afterward. "He was taking vacations because he had me to handle his practice. He was ready to cut a couple of deals to enhance things."

At 6:00 P.M. Monday, January 30, after they had closed up shop for the day, Isaacs and Hessberger sat down and went over details for working out deals with insurance companies to beef up their already flourishing practice at 3847 North Harlem Avenue. From there Isaacs drove through the cold and wintry night to Northfield for a session with his psychologist.

At 8:15 P.M., as he was leaving the psychologist's office at 464 Central Avenue, someone walked up from behind and shot him three times, in the back, the back of his head, and right shoulder. He fell to the ground, dead, alongside his yellow 1979 Cadillac.

His body was still warm when a janitor found him a short time later, lying in the snow. Thinking he had suffered a heart attack, the janitor phoned paramedics. It was not until they had moved him into their ambulance that the paramedics discovered Isaacs had been shot. By then the crime scene had been trampled and disturbed and the killer's footprints obliterated.

"From all appearances the killer either followed him to the psychologist's office, or knew he had a regular Monday night appointment and was waiting for him when he came out," Northfield Police Chief Richard Klatzco speculated.

Robbery was quickly ruled out as a motive for the killing. The victim's expensive Rolex wristwatch and a gold chain were still on his body, and his wallet and credit cards seemed undisturbed.

A task force of ten investigators from surrounding suburbs was assembled to work with the twenty-six member Northfield police department in investigating the slaying. Detectives searched Isaacs' high-rise condominium overlooking Lincoln Park, they interviewed his accountant, they went over his books, and they questioned scores of friends of the slain man but could find no clue as to why anyone would shoot him dead. No matter who police talked to, the answer seemed always the same: Mr. Smile was a guy with a dazzling personality and a talent for raking in big bucks.

The psychologist, M. David Liberman, told investigators that Isaacs had not appeared upset or unusually worried during their session.

Ballistics tests showed that the dentist had been shot with a .38-caliber revolver. Police also learned that Isaacs had $1.4 million in life insurance coverage, not counting double-indemnity provisions.

In digging into the victim's background, police learned Isaacs had once received Mob-style threats, and that a smoke bomb had been thrown into a building near his office. The incident occurred after he turned down an offer of a high-interest "juice" loan from the mob to alleviate early financial problems. After the threats were made on his life in 1976 he began carrying a pistol, and had his nurse walk out the door ahead of him when he left the office.

"Someone wanted him killed very, very badly," a relative of the slain man told police. "But why? I was his friend for twenty years. If he gambled, we didn't know it. If he was mixed up with the mob, we didn't know it. He may have had a hidden life. He may have had a side none of us knew."

UPDATE

"We've had so many leads, but they all went to a dead end," Police Chief Richard Klatzco says today. "The victim was into a lot of investments—all losers. He invested in film deals, a garbage disposal business . . . None made money. You wouldn't think he'd be killed for losing his money, would you?

"I always figured it looked like a professional take-out. If that's the case, the killer's identity might only come to light in a federal mob trial, from the lips of a government witness."

STOP AT DEATH'S FLOOR, PLEASE

Whoever killed four Park Ridge, Illinois, men on the night of July 21, 1977, gave new meaning to the term, "taken for a ride." The one-way ride, as a matter of fact, originated in Chicago, and its victims usually ended up in the trunks of their own cars or in a ditch by the side of the road. In the Park Ridge case, they ended up in an elevator.

Joseph LaRose, thirty-five, his brother-in-law, John F. Vische, thirty-two, Donald Marchbanks, fifty-three, and Malcolm Russell, thirty-five, were partners in U.S. Universal, Inc., a burglar alarm outfit with upstairs offices in a pleasant two-story building at 516 West Higgins Road.

Their second floor suite was located just off a balcony overlooking an airy atrium dotted with potted palms and ferns. It was a lovely setting for a murder.

All four partners in Universal were known as "high rollers." They drove expensive cars and liked to flash big wads of bills. There was also some suspicion that, as businessmen, they might have been straddling the line of legitimacy.

A federal grand jury had been poking around into the operation of Universal, as well as into the previous dealings of at least two of the partners. The feds were looking into complaints that Universal, which was incorporated to sell home fire alarms and burglar alarm systems, was actually a "pyramid" sale operation set up to bilk investors. Salesmen or purchasers of prospective franchises claimed they had been talked into paying $1,750 for a sales kit of alarms worth only $400.

On the evening of July 21, the fast-talking partners held a "seminar" for prospective salesmen in their Park Ridge headquarters. During the Thursday night presentation they flashed $500 and $1,000 bills at their audience as part of the sales pitch.

The seminar broke up some time after ten o'clock, and the would-be alarm salesmen filed out of the office. At 10:55 P.M. Vische telephoned his wife in suburban Country Club Hills and told her, "We're finished. I'm leaving and coming home."

He never made it. Nor did LaRose come home to Inverness that night, or Marchbanks to Palos Heights, or Russell to his home in Chicago.

On Friday morning a middle-aged secretary for a vacuum cleaner sales firm located in the brick structure drove down the ramp and parked her car in the basement garage. She got out of her vehicle, walked across the concrete floor to the sliding doors, and used her security key to activate the elevator. To her utter horror, the metal doors slid open to display a ghastly tableau.

Stacked inside, and covered with blood, were the bullet-riddled bodies of Joseph LaRose, John Vische, Donald Marchbanks, and Malcolm Russell. It was a condensed version of Chicago's St. Valentine's Day massacre of 1929, in which seven members or associates of the Bugs Moran gang were cut down by Al Capone men disguised as cops.

All had been shot at close range. There were powder burns surrounding the bullet holes in the victims' three-piece suits. The front pockets had been ripped out of the suits of LaRose, Marchbanks, and Russell, as though someone had angrily demoted them in rank before pumping them full of lead. The $500 and $1,000 bills the promoters had waved at their audience the night before were gone, yet they still wore their expensive wrist watches and diamond rings, and had other cash in their pockets.

Judging from the patterns of the numerous bullet holes, all four had stood facing their executioners as the fatal shots were fired. Before fleeing, the killers had meticulously retrieved dozens of spent shell casings from the elevator floor. In removing the bodies police found four .22-caliber shells that the killers had overlooked.

Park Ridge police and sheriff's investigators, working under the direction of Lieutenant Frank Braun of the Cook County Sheriff's Department, searched the Universal offices, but could find nothing that might have pointed to the killers. They interviewed hundreds of friends and associates of the victims and pursued dozens of leads, all of which led nowhere.

In going through the pockets of the bloody suits after they were removed from the victims at the morgue, detectives found three safe deposit keys. Two of the bank boxes contained nothing of use in the investigation, and the third was empty. Police also analyzed business records and telephone bills of the firm, along with records of the victims' personal phone calls, but came up with nothing. Among possible suspects questioned were twenty West Side Chicago women, whose names investigators found in the records of phone calls made by the men during the previous two weeks.

One of the things that plagued investigators from the start was that there was anything but a shortage of suspects. The four big time operators apparently had not gone out of their way to win friends, and people they influenced ended up with negative impressions. They knew nothing of value.

From all indications, the slayings took place around 11:00 P.M., right after Vische phoned his wife to report that he was on his way home. The killers no doubt knew when the victims would be leaving, and were waiting with guns drawn when they rode the elevator down to the parking level to get their cars.

An early theory, that went nowhere, was that any of the scores of Universal salesmen who had been duped into purchasing the $1,750 sales kits might have decided to make an out-of-court settlement in the elevator. Investigators compiled a lengthy "grudge list" and questioned plenty of people who would not have been unhappy to see the quartet dead, but made no arrests.

For a brief while a former partner, who had engaged in a bitter dispute with his associates, loomed as a prime suspect. Fortunately, for him, he had an airtight alibi for the night of the murders.

The neatness with which the killers cleaned up the spent shell casings pointed to a professional job—possibly a crime syndicate hit—but again police were unable to give credence to the theory.

Who mowed down the men in the elevator, and why, remains a mystery to this very day.

UPDATE

The best guess, according to Sheriff's Lieutenant Braun, is that the motive was robbery, pure and simple. Earlier in the evening the four men had arrogantly waved $500 and $1,000 bills in the faces of those attending the seminar—many of whom were out-of-work salesman looking for a way to earn a fast buck.

To lie in wait for the high rollers and relieve them of their wads of cash might have been a temptation too big to pass up, even if they had to cut some hired gunsels in on the deal.

WHO BLEW THE FOREMAN'S HEAD OFF?

The old parking lot is overgrown with weeds now, and International Harvester Company's Wisconsin Steel Works on the far southeast corner of Chicago has long been shuttered. But whenever old-timers get together they still talk about that spring day back in 1954 when someone killed their foreman.

Dennis Delph was fifty-four years old, a boss on the midnight shift in the open hearth laboratory of the plant at 2701 East 106th Street. He'd been a minor league ball player once, and had studied to be a physician like his brother, before switching to chemistry. Delph was well liked; a man who led by example.

It was the habit of Ed Smerciak, foreman on the 4:00 P.M. to midnight shift, to meet Delph in the parking lot every night to brief him on what had transpired during the evening shift before Delph went into the plant. He was heading out to the lot shortly before midnight on April 3 when a company chemist, Donald Pomeroy, Jr., stopped to talk to him.

As Smerciak and Pomeroy chatted they saw Delph's car pull into the lot at the 110th Street gate, followed by a second auto. Delph parked in the row just south and about twenty-five feet west of the entrance, facing north.

The second car pulled alongside, facing south. Smerciak and Pomeroy saw the lights of Delph's car flick off and heard the car door slam shut as he got out.

Then they heard what they would afterward describe as a "thud." A second later the second car spun out of the lot and zoomed north on Torrence Avenue, disappearing into the night.

The two men waited a bit for Delph to join them, but when he didn't come by they hiked over toward his car to meet him halfway. They walked all the way to his car before they found him, lying on the ground with blood flowing from the space between his shoulders where his head was no longer attached.

Police Lieutenant Edward Barry, who arrived minutes later with Patrolman Joseph Jakucyn of the East Side District, observed that someone appeared to have slashed Delph's head almost clean off as he got out of his auto. His car keys lay on the ground where he had dropped them, along with a book and a newspaper, when he fell. His lunch bucket was still clutched under his arm.

The dead man's pockets had not been rifled. If he had been attacked by robbers, they ran off before they had a chance to take anything.

Delph's body was removed to the Cook County morgue, and police drove to his home on Komensky Avenue in nearby Worth to break the news to his wife, Catherine. She knew of no reason why anyone would have killed her husband. "He was in good spirits when I packed his lunch bucket and he went out the door," she wept.

Dr. Jerry Kearns, the coroner's pathologist who performed an autopsy the following day, had news for police. "The guy wasn't slashed, he was shot," Kearns told Lieutenant Barry. "I found fifteen lead pellets and two pieces of cotton wadding in his neck. It looks like someone came up from behind, put a shotgun on his shoulder, and pulled the trigger. The arteries on both sides of his neck, leading to the brain, were severed."

The shotgun pellets were sent to the crime lab for examination, but proved of little evidentiary value.

Police were never able to establish a motive for the slaying, much less the identity of the killer or killers. They thought, perhaps, that the murder might have been the aftermath of a traffic altercation.

A coroner's inquest jury, meeting in the morgue on June 5, ruled that Delph met his death at the hands of "person or persons unknown."

UPDATE

The subject of Delph's murder came up Oct. 17, 1990, at a luncheon of Wisconsin Steel Works retirees on the Southeast Side. Among those present was Chester Lulinski, who had worked as a research chemist under Delph. He offered a theory that had been kicked around by Delph's fellow workers thirty-six years earlier.

Dennis Delph was well liked, and there was no reason why anyone would want to kill him. There was a worker in another department, however, who was vehemently disliked among his associates in the plant—and he drove a blue automobile almost identical to Delph's. It is entirely possible that the murder was a well-planned ambush, and the killers hit the wrong guy.

BOOK V

FACING DEATH
TOGETHER

I'LL DIE AT YOUR WEDDING

On Saturday, March 19, 1988, Richard Esparza, a twenty-seven-year-old ironworker from Chicago's Northwest Side, got all decked out in his best suit to attend his mother's wedding. His twenty-six-year-old wife, Rebecca, a secretary for a Loop brokerage house, wore her finest gown. They left their three-year-old daughter, Stephanie, with a baby-sitter, figuring it was going to be a long night.

After the marriage of his fifty-year-old mother, Patricia, to Chicago Police Sergeant Russell LaBarber, they joined about sixty other relatives and friends for a reception and dinner at Sy and Mary's Lounge and Banquet Hall, 5301 West Newport Avenue.

"It was a small sitdown dinner; they were all real nice folks," owner Sy Soszynski would tell police afterward. "It ended at midnight, but I heard some of the people say they were all going to go someplace else to have another drink."

Richard and Rebecca, along with some of the others, adjourned to the City Lounge at 4735 West North Avenue. About an hour and a half later Rebecca felt a bit woozy and Richard took her outside for some air. Another member of the party, Harold Koppel, gave the couple the keys to his van so she could lie down. When the rest of the group came out later, the van was gone. They figured Richard had taken it to drive Rebecca home.

Early Sunday morning two fishermen on their way to Flatfoot Lake noticed a white 1985 Ford van parked on a muddy path in a remote area of Beaubien Woods, nearly thirty miles away on the city's far South Side. One of them told his wife about it when he got home, and she notified police. Officers from the Pullman Area violent crimes unit drove over to the forest preserve at 8:30 A.M. and checked it out. The Esparzas were still in the back end. Both had been shot in the head and left for dead.

Richard Esparza, still dressed in his go-to-wedding suit, with a flower in his lapel, was pronounced dead at the scene. Rebecca, her clothing in disarray, and bleeding profusely from a head wound, was semiconscious and mumbling. She was rushed to South Chicago Community Hospital, where her condition was listed as critical.

Police searched the area, and found the woman's purse in the water nearby. Although it appeared to have been rifled, it still contained more than twenty dollars. Her dead husband's wallet was still in his back pocket. The keys to the van were missing. Police and scuba divers searched the area on the west side of the lake for the keys and the murder weapon, but found nothing.

"We don't know if they were shot in the forest preserve or on the Northwest Side and driven here," observed Sergeant Rutherford Wilson of the violent crimes unit. "This is a real mystery."

How the couple ended up so very far from home was another part of the mystery. Lieutenant Philip Cline, commander of the unit, pointed out that the van was parked in an obscure area, about a mile south of Lake Calumet, reachable only by someone familiar with the forest preserve.

Police questioned Rebecca Esparza as soon as she was able to talk, but she could tell them nothing. Dr. Lawrence Ferguson, director of neurosurgery at Michael Reese Hospital, where she had been transferred, said that the bullet wound in her head had bruised her brain and caused "retrograde amnesia," in which she was unable to remember events leading up to the shooting.

It was not until the following November that police were able to get their first lead in the case. The break came when Dr. Kenneth LeFebvre of Northwestern Memorial Hospital placed the wounded woman in a hypnotic trance, in which she saw the faces of her attackers.

She told Pullman Area Detective Thomas Shine that she and her husband were sitting in the back of the van, with the motor running to keep warm, when two men entered the vehicle and abducted them. After shooting Esparza in the head, the killers drove the van across town to a remote corner of Beaubien Woods near 134th Street and the Calumet Expressway, where they beat the woman with a club, assaulted her, and then shot her as she begged for her life, pleading, "I have a three-year-old daughter at home."

The last thing she remembered was hearing one of the assailants say, "I'm going to kill you and throw you and your husband into the lake where you'll never be found."

She described her attackers as dark-skinned. One was twenty-seven to thirty-five years of age, five feet seven to five feet nine inches tall, weighing 165 pounds, with bad teeth. The other was thirty to thirty-five, more than six feet tall, and weighing 230 pounds.

"We were in limbo for months. We didn't know who they were—black, white, pink, or whatever," Shine said. "Now we have something to go on."

Since that day police have interviewed more than 1,000 people, including everyone who attended the wedding reception and tavern celebration. Undercover agents also visited bars near the Flatfoot Lake area, in hopes of overhearing someone boasting of the murder, but none of the legwork turned up any solid leads.

The most likely scenario, according to Lieutenant Cline, is that two South Siders, prowling the Northwest Side in the early morning hours, came upon the van with the motor running and decided to steal it. When they discovered the Esparzas in the back end, the caper escalated to murder. They abandoned the vehicle afterward in the forest preserve near the Altgeld Gardens housing project, so they could walk home.

UPDATE

With the police investigation up against a blank wall, friends of the Esparzas have offered a $10,000 reward for information leading to the arrest of the killers. Paul Knyuch, a former classmate of Esparza who helped organize the fund, said, "We're hoping to stimulate someone's interest or conscience."

THE MISSING WEDDING GUESTS

Eight years before the Esparza murder a young couple from just outside of Fort Atkinson, Wisconsin, also attended a wedding from which they never returned.

If anyone could have been described as the typical All-American couple it would have been Timothy Hack and his girlfriend, Kelly Drew, a pair of fresh faced nineteen-year-olds who had been sweethearts since their sophomore year in high school. Tim worked on his father's farm, where he was getting ready for a big tractor pull, and Kelly was enrolled in a beautician school.

On the night of Aug. 9, 1980, they attended a wedding reception in a Concord dance hall halfway between Milwaukee and Madison, about thirty-five miles north of the Illinois border. They were last seen leaving the hall, after telling other guests that they were on their way to meet friends in Fort Atkinson, fifteen miles away.

They never made it to their car. Tim's locked auto, with his coat, checkbook, wallet containing sixty-seven dollars, and keys still inside, was found in the dance hall parking lot the next morning.

What happened to the young couple became Wisconsin's biggest mystery. There were rumors that they had eloped, but it didn't make sense that they would leave Tim's car behind with his money in it. Chief Deputy Harry Buerger of the Jefferson County Sheriff's Department knew they hadn't eloped when all of Drew's clothing except her shoes was found strewn along a stretch of highway leading out of town four days later. Several items of her apparel showed evidence of having been slashed with a razor.

The discovery touched off the most extensive missing person search in Wisconsin's history. In addition to scores of lawmen from surrounding counties, the FBI, and the state Division of Criminal Investigation, along with members of the Wisconsin National Guard and volunteers who tramped through the surrounding fields for miles around, the search included aerial infrared photos and consultations with psychics.

The search for the couple ended two and a half months later, on Sunday, October 19, when hunters came upon their skeletal remains. They were lying about 150 feet apart in a corn field and woods near Ixonia, about eight miles from the Concord dance hall. Tim was still dressed in the suit he had worn to the wedding. Kelly was naked. She had been bound with rope, tied in peculiar knots.

Chief Buerger said the bodies appeared to have been dragged from a vehicle to where they were found, but no attempt had been made to hide them. "They've probably lain here since the night they were abducted," he said.

Jefferson County Coroner Ewald Reichert used dental records to positively identify Kelly. He identified Tim by the clothes he wore. Because of the advanced stage of decomposition, pathologists were unable to pinpoint the cause of death.

"I guess we all realized they probably wouldn't be found alive," Tim's mother, Pat Hack, said on learning that her ten weeks of praying were over. "But Kelly's mother and I didn't want to find one without the other. We knew how they felt about each other. We knew they would want to be together and we wanted them together."

After a joint funeral in St. Joseph's Catholic Church in

Fort Atkinson, they were buried side by side in the Hebron Cemetery, next to the Hack home.

Buerger speculated that whoever abducted the couple had to be from the area, because the backroads used to get to the location where the bodies were found would have been unknown to strangers. He and his eight detectives would spend more than 4,500 hours on the case, interviewing some 700 people, including everyone who attended the wedding.

But all they ended up with was a filing cabinet full of reports. Nobody even saw the couple leave the parking lot.

In 1983 a Milwaukee private detective, Norbert Kurczewski, claimed he had uncovered evidence linking the couple's murder to three other mysterious deaths and disappearances in Jefferson County. He said the deaths involved a Satanic cult run by a Watertown man with a criminal record for child molestation.

Kurczewski said he uncovered maps belonging to the suspect that had drawings of devils in the margins. The tails of each devil pointed to the location where each of the bodies was found.

Sheriff Keith Mueller, who checked out the report, and even questioned the suspect's divorced wife, called the private eye's reports "highly irresponsible."

UPDATE

The parents of Kelly Drew and Timothy Hack raised $10,000 in reward money for information as to the fate of their children, but the money went unclaimed.

The case file remains open. "There isn't a month that goes by when we don't get something to check out concerning their deaths," said Rick Wellner, who succeeded Buerger as chief investigator for the Jefferson County Sheriff's Department. "We are adding to their file constantly. We keep checking out everything we get. Most is related to murders and disappearances in other states. Any time another agency comes up with anything at all similar, we check it out."

FIFTY GRAND FOR
INFORMATION

The thing that made the deaths of a west suburban River Grove couple so fascinating was the lengths their friends went to afterward to find out who could have done them in.

It was early Friday morning, Sept. 4, 1987, when the body of thirty-nine-year-old Frank A. Matous was found in the trunk of his burning car on a rural road near Algonquin, just inside the McHenry County line. Before being stuffed into the trunk he had been shot in the head.

Sergeant Charles Terrell, chief investigator for the McHenry County Sheriff's Department, ran a check on the license plate on the burned out auto and learned that it was registered to an address in River Grove. He notified River Grove authorities, who went to the home at 9013 West Grand Avenue to notify the next of kin.

Unable to get anyone to answer the front door, officers went around to the back, where they found the apartment door open, went inside, and discovered another corpse. The body of the dead man's twenty-three-year-old girlfriend, Donna Hartwell, was lying facedown, fully clothed, on the living room floor.

A search of the apartment turned up drug paraphernalia, but no illicit drugs.

An autopsy performed by the Cook County medical examiner's office determined that the young woman had died of a cocaine overdose. A postmortem examination of Matous in McHenry concluded that he had been shot once in the head with a handgun.

River Grove Police Sergeant Dennis Raucci, working with Sergeant Terrell, concluded that both Frank Matous and Donna Hartwell died within the same general time span.

There were suspicious marks on the woman's body, indicating the overdose might have been induced by her boyfriend's killer to eliminate witnesses. Her death was not listed as a homicide, however, since it was impossible to determine whether she was force-fed the lethal dosage of cocaine or took the drug voluntarily, Raucci pointed out.

Police in neither county were able to get a line on the killer, but friends of the victims were determined to find out who was responsible for their deaths.

Leon Falcon, an Elvis Presley impersonator and close friend of the couple, spearheaded a fund drive to establish a reward for the killer. The victims' friends put together $10,000, but didn't stop there. On July 23, 1988, they held a luau in a Northwest Side restaurant in Chicago, which doubled the fund to $20,000.

Despite the efforts of police, and the posting of the reward that continued to grow in size from month to month, the identity of the killer, and the motive behind the deaths, remains a mystery.

UPDATE

The reward for information leading to the arrest of the person or persons responsible for the deaths of Frank Matous and Donna Hartwell eventually reached $50,000. Their friend, Leon Falcon, subsequently opened a tavern in Chicago, which he named for the victims in their memory.

BULLETS FOR BROADWAY BILL

The eighteenth of March, 1981, was the day the Chiwaukee Prairie ran crimson with blood. It was a brisk Wednesday morning, still winter jacket time in southeastern Wisconsin, hard by the Illinois border, when naturalist Phil Sander set out to look for signs of spring. But what he found was murder.

The tall, lanky Sander, a director of the Kenosha County Historical Society, lived on the edge of the prairie just south of town, and had an abiding interest in the area's colorful history as well as its future.

So named because it lies almost halfway between Chicago and Milwaukee, hugging Lake Michigan's shore on the Wisconsin side of the line, this was once a hunting ground for Indians. Youngsters hiking through the rolling sandy area, covered with a brush all its own, still come upon an occasional arrowhead or spot a deer peeking skittishly from a clump of trees.

Great plans were envisioned for the 1,500-acre windswept tract in the 1920s when Edith Rockefeller McCormick, one of the world's richest women, fancied the site for a city of the future.

The daughter of John D. Rockefeller, along with promoters Edwin Krenn and Edward Dato, purchased the virgin land several miles south of Kenosha for $1,000 an acre. The Chicago socialite named it Edithton Beach, in her own honor, and poured $4 million of her own cash into the venture, personally supervising and planning the landscaping.

There would be a yacht basin, an airport, a municipal golf course, and a school in a twenty-five-acre park. Sites for elaborate Spanish castles and Atlantic City type hotels were marked off. The Chicago & North Western Railroad, which ran along the western edge of the property, planned a luxurious station where its puffing trains would deliver the wealthy to their newfound playground by the lake.

The only building ever constructed was a clubhouse on the edge of the lakeshore golf course. Then the stockmarket crash of 1929 brought Edith Rockefeller McCormick's dreams to a bitter and frustrating end. Three years later she was dead. And for the next half a century the unique plant life on the prairie thrived undisturbed.

As the 1980s approached, and the industrial city of Kenosha began extending its tentacles outward, a group of environmentalists called the Nature Conservancy began acquiring the land, now renamed Chiwaukee Prairie, in order to preserve it from future developers. A women's club in Kenosha had purchased several parcels of the land and donated them to the nature group, of which Sander was a member. And on this Wednesday morning he decided to hike out and inspect the acquisition.

As Sander approached the area, just west of a narrow blacktop road running along the shoreline, he noticed that a patch of the winter-brown prairie grass glistened red in the rays of the morning sun. There was no mistaking it. It was fresh blood—lots of it. Sander's first thought was that an archer might have wounded one of the deer still roaming the area.

The naturalist gingerly followed the bloody trail through waist-high weeds for about twenty-five feet, and then stopped. Directly ahead he spied a well-dressed man and an auburn haired woman, lying motionless on the matted ground. He knew instinctively that they were dead. Retracing his steps so as not to disturb the surroundings, Sander raced to the nearest phone to call the sheriff's office.

Sheriff Gerald Sonquist sped to the scene, a straight shot down Sheridan Road from his headquarters in the center of town and a left turn toward the lake on the last road before the state line. With him were Lieutenant Lee Ormson, detectives Robert Hubbard and Dale Crichton, and evidence technician Dennis Chartier. Sander was patiently waiting for them by the blood-soaked weeds.

"Good god, what next?" muttered the sheriff, tromping through the brush. The normally-quiet university town had endured eight homicides in the past six weeks, compared to only three in all of the previous year. Six of them had been solved by arrests. These two latest ones did not look so easy.

Bringing the hand-held walkie-talkie to his mouth, Sonquist pressed the send button and advised his dispatcher, "Get hold of Tommy Dorff, the coroner, and tell him we've got two more for him."

The victims were both white and fully clad in expensive clothing. The male was well built, possibly a former athlete. He appeared to be in his late forties or early fifties. He had receding brown hair with streaks of gray. He was wearing light brown corduroy slacks, a gray crew-neck pullover sweater, and brown patent leather loafers.

His partner in death, a striking redhead in her late twenties or early thirties, was attired in a kelly green corduroy jump suit with a French label, and knee-high black leather Gucci boots.

Both had suffered massive head wounds. The condition of their bodies indicated they had not been dead more than a few hours.

"It sure as hell doesn't look like robbery, does it?" Sonquist mused, pointing to an expensive gold Omega watch on the dead man's wrist. He also wore a gold wedding band, a gold neck chain, and a religious medallion. The woman wore a platinum wedding ring, a gold neck chain with a medallion, had gold earrings and a gold watch.

Kenosha County's feisty coroner, Thomas J. Dorff, a one-time boxing promoter, arrived and inspected the bodies. "Looks like they've both been shot," he commented. "Look here. The girl's got a hole through her right hand, as if she's been trying to ward off the bullet."

Dorff also noted that both victims were heavily suntanned, in contrast to the pale skins of the sheriff and his men who had just weathered another long Wisconsin winter. "I'd say they both spent a heck of a lot of time lying on a beach somewhere, and not around here," he concluded.

While the sheriff's deputies combed the area for possible evidence, Dorff authorized removal of the bodies to a Kenosha mortuary where the coroner's pathologist, Dr. John Sanson, would perform postmortem examinations.

The male victim measured five feet nine inches in height and weighted 180 pounds. He had light blue-gray eyes, but no scars, tattoos, or other identifying features. The woman was five feet six inches tall and weighed 110 pounds. She had blue eyes, beyond shoulder-length hair, and a four-inch abdominal scar.

In addition to the hole in the woman's hand, Sanson determined that each had been shot three times in the right side of the head. The slugs were from a .22-caliber automatic pistol, a newfound favorite among professional assassins. The same type of weapon had been used to execute Chicago Mafia boss Sam "Momo" Giancana a few years earlier.

The pathologist estimated the couple had been driven out to the prairie and executed on the spot around 5:00 A.M., just before sunrise.

Before proceeding any farther with the investigation Sonquist and his detectives would first have to establish the identities of the victims, determine where they had come from, and with whom they associated. This proved easier said than done. In going through the victims' clothing deputies found that all personal identification had been painstakingly removed. Yet whoever killed the couple did not bother to take $1,573 in Canadian currency stuffed in the dead man's pants pocket.

"This is an out-and-out execution. No doubt about it," the sheriff surmised. "Somebody wanted these people dead, and left unknown. He, or they, weren't at all interested in the victims' valuables."

In addition to the more than $1,500 in his pockets, the man was wearing a $5,000 timepiece, an Omega with a genuine reptile band. This was determined by a local jeweler who examined the victims' watches at the request of investigators. "This Omega is a model manufactured in Switzerland in 1956, and not available in the United States," he told them. "The woman's watch is a Swiss-made Rotary worth about $100. It's a model sold only in Switzerland and South Africa. By the way, the man's watch was set on eastern standard time and the woman's on central standard."

"From those suntans and the wad of dough the guy was carrying, plus the fact that their watches were set on different times, we've got to assume that they were traveling," Sonquist speculated. He contacted both the Federal Bureau of Investigation and the Royal Canadian Mounted Police, and sent detailed teletype messages to scores of law enforcement agencies throughout the Midwest seeking clues to the pair's identity.

"Somewhere, somebody has got to know that these people are missing," the sheriff said. "Whoever they were, they really went first class—the best of clothes and jewelry, and plenty of dough. People like this just don't disappear unnoticed."

The Canadian money in the man's back pocket included a dozen $100 bills, nine in numerical sequence. From the Mounties, Sonquist learned the nine bills were part of a cash shipment delivered late the previous year to a Toronto bank from one in Ottawa. The Mounties went to work on the money angle, theorizing the cash might have been proceeds of a bank robbery.

The victims' clothing, most of it foreign made, was sent to the FBI lab in Washington for analysis.

"This case is a real blockbuster, like something out of an 007 novel, with characters to match," the puzzled sheriff told inquisitive reporters. "The man looks every inch to be a successful businessman, tanned and wealthy. And the woman is very pretty, like a model. Motive? I've got eighty deputies and each one of them has a reason of his own on how he thinks it went down, and why."

The thirty-one-year police veteran enlisted the aid of twenty Explorer Scouts to pick their way on hands and knees through a quarter-mile square area of prairie grass around where the bodies were found, in a futile search for shell casings or other evidence.

By the end of the week Detectives Hubbard and Crichton had filled a seventeen-inch file case with data and notes of conferences with lawmen from throughout the Midwest and Canada, where it was felt the couple might have resided.

"We just have to keep plugging away. I don't like to guess. I'd rather work it out doggedly," said Sonquist, a man not known for shooting from the hip. "Right now we're just chasing rainbows, with people calling in missing persons reports from all over the U.S. Until we find out who the heck these people were, there just isn't much we can do."

While it was suspected the couple came from Canada, Sonquist did not overlook the possibility that the Canadian bills had been planted on the man's body to throw police off the track. Another theory was that the two were from somewhere else, possibly Europe, and had recently traveled through Canada.

"We've got to get pictures of these people circulated. That's the only way anyone is going to tell us who they are," Sonquist asserted. For awhile he toyed with the grisly idea of photographing the dead faces and sending pictures of the bodies throughout the country. Then he came up with a better idea.

George Pollard, a nationally-known artist who had made lifelike sketches of prominent personalities from sports heroes to presidents, lived in Kenosha. The sheriff picked up the phone and gave the artist a call.

"Tell me, George. Would it be possible to draw a likeness of a dead person as though that person were alive?" he inquired. "You know, with the eyes open, and with a natural facial expression?"

"Oh, yeah. No reason why not, Gerry," the artist responded. "Tell me. Do you have in mind what I think you do? I read about the couple in the papers."

"We need help, George, Could you do it?"

"Just tell me when and where you want me."

Pollard met the sheriff at a downtown funeral parlor where the bodies were being kept on hold in a basement room. There, in the eerie surroundings of death, he expertly sketched both victims, front and side views—minus the awful bullet wounds—with their eyes open as they would have appeared in life.

The artist's likenesses were published in the local press, without result. Nobody in Kenosha had ever seen the couple. The pictures were also mailed to the wire services, but were generally overlooked in the mountain of impersonal press releases the news agencies are deluged with from day to day.

Nine days passed since the discovery of the bodies and the investigation appeared at a standstill when, at five o'clock in the morning on Friday, March 27, *Chicago Tribune* reporter Ed Baumann walked into the sheriff's office and requested copies of Pollard's drawings. He and fellow crime writer, John O'Brien, prepared a story that ran with the sketches in the Sunday *Tribune* under the headline: "DOUBLE MURDER BAFFLES COPS OF 2 NATIONS."

The article, which was distributed from coast to coast via the *Tribune's* syndicated wire service, drew immediate response in more ways than one.

First Coroner Dorff, whose phone was listed in the Kenosha directory, was awakened in the middle of the night by a male caller who warned gruffly, "You'd better keep a close watch on those bodies."

"I'd better what?" Dorff asked, stalling for time.

"Who is it?" asked his wife, Vi, a Kenosha police officer.

"The son of a bitch hung up," the coroner replied, relaying the message. "It could be a hoax, but I'm not taking any chances, Vi. We already know for sure that somebody doesn't want those bodies identified."

"What are you going to do, Tommy?" she asked as he rolled out of bed.

"Vi, I've got a brainstorm. I'm gonna kidnap the corpses."

"You're what?"

"I'm gonna move the bodies. Hide 'em, so nobody but I will know where they are."

Dorff phoned a private ambulance service and secretly removed the two murder victims from the local funeral home and transported them to a mortuary in Racine, ten miles away. The ambulance drivers were told not to identify their ghostly cargo, and Dorff informed no one of the clandestine body-snatching episode.

Mission accomplished, he returned home and told his wife, "It's cheaper to quietly move the bodies to a secure location than to have to provide officers to guard them at the funeral home tomorrow."

Then, on Tuesday, March 31, two days after the drawings appeared in the *Tribune*, Kenosha authorities received a telephone call from Thomas Nelligan, night manager of the swank Continental Plaza Hotel on Chicago's Gold Coast. Nelligan had seen the lifelike drawings in the *Tribune* and recognized them as a couple who had stayed at the posh Michigan Avenue hotel.

"The drawings in the newspaper were very good. I recognized Mr. and Mrs. Crane right away," he told Sonquist.

"Crane, you say?" the sheriff asked.

"Oh, yes. They were friendly and polite when they checked in, and we talked from time to time. They checked into a $125-a-day room on March 5. They disappeared, leaving their luggage behind, on St. Patrick's Day."

"That would have been the day before the bodies were found," Sonquist said. "This could be the break we've been waiting for. Sit tight Mr. Nelligan. I'm sending two of our detectives down to talk to you. They should be there in a little over an hour."

When Sonquist's men arrived in Chicago, Nelligan showed them the hotel's register, listing the couple in question as Mr. and Mrs. Walter Crane of Seattle. "Come with me," he said. "I'll take you to their room."

If the detectives thought they now knew whose bullet-riddled bodies had been found in the Chiwaukee Prairie they were mistaken. In the couple's room they found luggage with Toronto baggage tags listing two different names. This established the Canada connection, all right, but it only added fuel to the mystery. And there was more to come. Prescription medicine bottles in the room bore yet two other names on the labels—Walter Callahan and Rose DeCarolis.

"It's beginning to look like these people had more names than a telephone directory," Sonquist was advised by phone.

"I'd go with the names on the medicine bottles," the sheriff suggested. "A doctor usually knows who his patients are if he's prescribing medication for them. One more thing: How did they pay their bills at the hotel? Check out the names on their credit cards while you're at it."

Easier said than done. "He, the man, said he never carried credit cards," Nelligan explained. "Everything was cash. He reached into his side pocket and pulled out a roll of bills large enough to hold a Chicago election. He deposited $300 or $400 in his account for a three-day stay and said he'd get a receipt when he checked out. Then, every two or three days, he'd come down, whip out more $100 bills, and tell me they were staying longer."

Nelligan said that on March 17 the man known to him as Walter Crane came down to announce the couple would not be returning that evening. "We're going on a sleep-out," he told the hotelman. "He didn't explain the meaning of 'sleep-out' but I took it to mean they were going somewhere with friends," Nelligan opined.

The sleep-out reference indicated the couple might not have been ambushed, but possibly had scheduled a meeting of some kind with someone they knew and presumably trusted.

Said person or persons, of course, could have been used to set them up for an eternal sleep.

"After several days when they weren't seen around the hotel, I sent an assistant to their room to leave a note asking the Cranes to stop at the front desk to settle their account," Nelligan continued. "But there was no response."

Ten days later, on Friday, the twenty-seventh, Nelligan figured the couple might have skipped, so he sent a bellhop up to check out the room.

"Their luggage was still there, and the closet was crammed with new items of clothing from some of Michigan Avenue's finest stores—Lord & Taylor, Gucci, Saks Fifth Avenue, and Marshall Field's on State Street," Nelligan explained. Whoever the couple had been, there was nothing cheap about their lifestyle.

The detectives returned to Kenosha with two good clues to their identity—the names of Rose DeCarolis and Walter Callahan on the medicine bottles. They lost no time in contacting Dr. Ivan M. Spear of Worcester, Massachusetts, the physician whose name was on the prescription label for Rose DeCarolis. The doctor provided his patient's address, and from "information" the detectives were able to secure her telephone number in Worcester. They put in a call to the DeCarolis home. Instead of being able to establish the identity of the dead woman, however, they got another surprise. Rose DeCarolis, a middle-aged housewife, answered the phone in the flesh.

"My God! I have no idea how my medicine bottle could have possibly gotten in that Chicago hotel room," she gasped, when the detectives explained why they were calling. "No, I've never heard of anyone named Crane or Callahan. I'm as mystified by this as you are."

Certain that the couple who had stayed in the luxury hotel for two weeks before disappearing were the murder victims, Kenosha deputies huddled with Chicago homicide investigators under Belmont Area Commander Kenneth Curin, whose district included the Continental Plaza. Since it now appeared the pair had been abducted in Chicago, driven across the state line, and slain in America's Dairyland, the Chicago detectives offered their expertise in helping Kenosha authorities to identify the gunshot victims.

The deeper investigators dug, the greater the mystery. Why the couple had tried so hard to keep their true identities a secret only heightened the intrigue surrounding their violent deaths. Sonquist facetiously told reporters, "Fictitious names and addresses—you wouldn't have enough room on your front page to print all the names these people used. They traveled, skipping around from one country to another. And everywhere they went, they seemed to be somebody else."

The implement that finally solved the puzzle was the telephone. In going over hotel records, detectives checked long-distance phone calls made from the couple's Chicago hotel room to New York, and methodically placed calls of their own to those numbers.

Of the parties reached, many seemed vague or hesitant to cooperate with authorities. Not Marie Ann Barker, however. The attractive blonde dancer from New York City told investigators she had received a number of calls from her close friend, Wendy McDade, a twenty-nine-year-old chorus girl from Manhattan. Wendy told her she had been honeymooning in the Windy City with a wealthy stage-door Johnny named Bill Callahan.

"Now we're getting somewhere," Sonquist said triumphantly. "That was the name on one of the medicine bottles—Callahan!"

Barker was able to provide the names of Wendy's parents, Gordon and Willa Schmeer, of Seattle. The sheriff and coroner contacted the Schmeers and made arrangements for them to fly to Kenosha, where Dorff had them register in a local motel under assumed names. On Thursday, April 2, the coroner accompanied them to the funeral home where they positively identified the slain woman as their daughter. They also tentatively identified the dead man as fifty-four-year-old William Callahan, whom they described as a New York business executive.

Sonquist's men had already been in touch with New York authorities, and on that same day Detective Robert Keane, assigned to the office of Manhattan District Attorney Robert Morgenthau, arrived in Kenosha with a photo of Callahan.

He was accompanied by Assistant District Attorney Seth Rosenberg, Morgenthau's top aide in the fraud division.

They took one look at the murder victim and agreed that the mystery of his identity was over. "We've been looking for Mr. Callahan for a long time," Rosenberg said.

"Just who the hell is he?" Sonquist asked.

"Was," Rosenberg corrected. "William Callahan was the vice president and treasurer of Arc Electrical Construction Company, one of New York's biggest outfits, with 600 employees and annual sales of $25 million. For the last twenty-nine years Mr. Callahan had been—and still is—married to the boss' daughter, Eleanor Rao."

"He was married to two women at once? Is that why you guys were looking for him?" Sonquist asked incredulously.

"Hardly," answered Keane. "We didn't even know about this wife, although we're not overly surprised. We've been on this guy's tail since October, when he disappeared at just about the same time the IRS discovered a shortage of $10 million in his company's books."

Keane and Rosenberg explained to Sonquist that his murder victim was really two different personalities. The highly respected William H. Callahan, a top business executive with a family and three expensive homes, was also an ex-hoofer known as Broadway Bill—a scoundrel, bigamist, philanderer, womanizer, and free-spending bon vivant.

"There are a hell of a lot of people who would have liked to see him dead," Sonquist was advised.

Broadway Bill! The sophisticated New York press, which originally took a pass on the double homicide as just another Midwest prairie shoot, suddenly jumped into the fray with four-inch headlines. Under the banner "X-rated life wins an A from his guys 'n' dolls" the *New York Daily News* proclaimed:

William Callahan arranged secret trysts with beautiful lovers, bankrolled a porno movie for a girlfriend, beat his wife, and carried on a brazen affair with yet another woman in the same Hawaii hotel where he and his wife were staying.

There seemed little doubt that Callahan was the target of assassins, and Wendy McDade took three bullets in the head because she just happened to be at his side when fate caught up with him.

From Wendy's parents authorities learned she was born in Portland, Oregon, and grew up in the upper-middle class Seattle suburb of Normand Park, overlooking Puget Sound. A year after graduating from high school in 1970 she met Scott McDade and they were married.

The two went off to Ohio State University and, after graduating, sought their fortunes in New York where the leggy Wendy launched her career as a dancer while her husband became a film writer. Wendy performed with Manhattan's prestigious Pearl Lang Dance Company, and then landed a spot in the Rainbow Grill chorus line atop the RCA Building in Rockefeller Center.

"Wendy was a wonderful, beautiful, young, and gorgeous girl, dedicated to her art," recalled her father-in-law, Edwin E. McDade.

Her dedication began to wane, however, once Broadway Bill waltzed into the picture. It was in 1978, while dancing at the Rainbow, that she first spied him. He would reserve the center table at each and every performance, and would toast the lithe young dancer with Dom Perignon champagne.

The debonair Callahan began to lavish Wendy with expensive gifts and attention. In September she finally told her stunned husband, "Scott, I've fallen in love with an older man." All Wendy knew about Callahan at the time was that he said he was "in the real estate business." But she left her husband for him, and moved into an apartment he set up for her on Eighth Avenue. She divorced McDade in March of 1980—exactly one year before her murder.

If anything was going to provide investigators with a solution to the slayings, they felt they would find it somewhere in Callahan's multi-colored background.

Callahan was born in New York, and broke into show business in 1940 at the age of thirteen in a musical comedy, *Western Union, Please.* He made his Broadway debut three years later in Cole Porter's *Something for the Boys,* starring Ethel Merman. The following year he landed in a Mike Todd production, *Mexican Hayride,* with Bobby Clark and June Havoc.

As soon as he reached eighteen, Callahan patriotically joined the Merchant Marine. After World War II he went on to Fordham University, but succumbed to the seduction of the stage before he graduated. He had parts in *Call Me Mister* and *As the Girls Go* before he took a westbound train to Hollywood in 1948, under contract to Twentieth Century Fox.

Poring over old newspaper files, investigators dug out publicity shots of Callahan in the 1949 movie, *Chicken Every Sunday,* with Dan Dailey, Colleen Townsend, Celeste Holm, and Alan Young. He left Tinseltown in 1951 to return to Broadway, where he appeared in *Top Banana* and *Two's Company,* with Bette Davis.

From the Manhattan prosecutors, detectives learned that Callahan left the stage to marry Eleanor Rao of New Rochelle, the daughter of prominent businessman Charles Rao. He joined his father-in-law's electrical firm and rose rapidly to a top corporate position.

Bill and Eleanor, an enviable couple to all outward appearances, had three children, William, Jr., born in 1955; Eleanor, in 1956; and Charles, in 1960.

Callahan flaunted his newfound wealth with a $500,000 estate in New Rochelle, ostentatious summer homes at East Hampton and Montauk, and a cozy retreat at Lake Placid. A friend who knew him recalled, "He gave parties like Ziegfeld. His driveway looked like a Mercedes showroom. They owned at least four Mercedes-Benzes and several motorcycles. Bill gave their daughter a silver Mercedes for her sixteenth birthday."

Meanwhile the devil-may-care Callahan's marriage was festering from within, and it all came to a head the day the Internal Revenue Service audit turned up the multi-million dollar shortage—and Broadway Bill took a duck without so much as a curtain call.

In February, one month before her errant husband's body was found, Eleanor Callahan filed for divorce in Westchester County Supreme Court, charging that he had been blatantly cheating on her for six years. The divorce action charged Callahan had boasted about affairs with other women, "flaunted such affairs in her face, and bragged about his sexual prowess and achievements with other women."

And while Eleanor was home rearing their children, Callahan was out seeding more of his own. His wife charged in her divorce petition that he boasted of fathering two illegitimate girls with a woman identified as Aulette Concia.

The court papers also charged he had conducted a lengthy affair with a model by the name of Renata Boeck, for whom he even built a home on Long Island; also had an affair with a woman identified as Kathryn Phillipe; and bankrolled a pornographic film for actress Nai Bonet, whom he put up in the same Hawaiian hotel where he was vacationing with his wife.

Bonet—the only one to publicly refute the charges at the time—admitted knowing Callahan but denied going to Hawaii with him or appearing in a porn flick.

The distraught Mrs. Callahan further charged that when she confronted her husband about the affairs in September, "He severely beat me and threatened to set goons and henchmen after me."

A former neighbor recalled that Eleanor's father once appeared at the Montauk home on Long Island, apparently to confront Callahan about his philandering—"But Callahan hid in the trees all day until old man Rao left."

Two months after Callahan disappeared, Arc Electrical filed suit in New York State Supreme Court charging he had embezzled from $3 million to $5 million of the firm's money over a two-year period from 1977 to 1979. On December 26, the high court ordered an attachment of Callahan's assets—an order that was still pending on the day Broadway Bill turned up in the Wisconsin weeds with three bullets in the head.

As the embezzlement probe widened the suspected loss approached the $10 million figure, authorities said. What Callahan had not spent on lavish living and lady friends was believed stashed in secret Swiss-type bank accounts on Grand Cayman Island in the Caribbean. Only $2,000 was found in Callahan's U.S. bank accounts according to the Rao family attorney, James Maloney.

Meanwhile the nationwide publicity over the identification of Callahan as one of the murder victims triggered the memory of Rose DeCarolis, the Worcester housewife who had not been able to explain how her pill bottle got into the couple's Chicago hotel room.

In February Mrs. DeCarolis had vacationed on St. Vincent, one of the Windward Islands in the British West Indies, where she stayed at the Sunset Shores, a small twenty-room facility catering mostly to retirees.

Because most of the hotel guests were her own age, Mrs. DeCarolis said she couldn't help but notice the shapely, young redhead in the bikini sunning herself at poolside.

"We struck up a conversation and she introduced herself as Wendy McDade," she recalled. "That evening, at dinner, she introduced me to her husband, 'William McDade.' She said they'd just been married on Barbados and were honeymooning." That explained why the name "Callahan" had meant nothing to Mrs. DeCarolis.

The man she knew as McDade had complained of a back problem, which he attributed to a water skiing injury. Mrs. DeCarolis said that she, too, had trouble with her back and took a muscle relaxant called Norflex. "I had my pills with me and offered several of them to Bill," she recalled. "The next morning he raved about the results and said he had to get some of those pills for himself. He asked me if he could have the bottle so he wouldn't forget the name."

The May-September couple and the Massachusetts housewife enjoyed one another's company and spent much of their time together. When it was time to leave their island paradise "Bill" chartered a private plane to take the three of them to nearby Barbados. There Mrs. DeCarolis made a February 20 commercial airline connection for the United States, and the "McDades" hopped a flight to Canada.

"The next time I heard from them was March 10," she said. "Bill telephoned me at home in Worcester, just to extend his and Wendy's regards. He said he was calling from Toronto."

It was a lie, but why? In checking hotel phone records detectives determined the call had been made from Chicago. Why would Callahan go to such length to conceal his whereabouts from a woman he had met only casually on vacation, after going to the trouble of telephoning her in the first place?

With the help of Mrs. DeCarolis and others, authorities in Kenosha and New York were able to trace Callahan's movements since he dropped from sight the previous October. He and Wendy spent four months on Barbados and St. Vincent, which accounted for their deep tans.

They had, indeed, flown from the West Indies to Toronto on February 20, but less than two weeks later checked into the Continental Plaza in Chicago. How whoever wanted Callahan dead was able to track the couple to Illinois became apparent in a lengthy interview police had with Wendy's friend, Marie Ann Barker. It is quit possible that she unwittingly fingered the pair in their hiding place.

Wendy disappeared from the New York social scene about the same time as her lover, and anyone who knew Wendy had to know that Marie Ann Barker was her best friend. It would have been a simple matter to put a tail on her. Authorities learned that she visited the doomed couple twice in Toronto and flew to Chicago to be with them only days before they were shot to death.

After getting a phone call from Wendy, Barker said she took a plane to Chicago on Saturday, March 14, bringing some clothing that Wendy had asked for. She told New York detectives and FBI agents that she spent the night in the Continental Plaza at Callahan's expense, and the next day the two women went on a shopping spree. They toured the swank shops in Water Tower Place and then went sightseeing. Callahan, who wed the flaming-haired dancer while still married to his wife in New York, joined Wendy and Marie for meals at several top flight restaurants, but otherwise seemed preoccupied with business of some kind.

Barker said Wendy complained of being "lonesome," but otherwise neither she nor Callahan gave any indication of trouble, or of being in fear for their lives. "If I was followed to Chicago, I certainly wasn't aware of it," she assured investigators.

Two days after she returned to New York the couple disappeared, and on the third day they were found dead.

Now that identification had been established, Wendy's parents had her body cremated and the remains returned to Seattle. But Callahan's body, which had been returned from Racine to Hansen's Funeral Home in Kenosha, remained unclaimed. The flamboyant Broadway Bill—once so popular in life—lay unwanted in death.

Paul Rao, Jr., a former assistant district attorney and cousin of Callahan's legal wife, Eleanor, even questioned whether the body on the slab was actually that of Callahan—or was yet another trick in his lifetime of deceit.

"I feel like St. Thomas right now," he said. "I want to put my fingers where the wounds are before I'll believe that's Callahan's body. There was a man who stole from his father-in-law who gave him his bread and butter, and he cheated on his wife, who gave him three children."

Coroner Dorff insisted that formal identification of Callahan be made by a member of his family, and pleaded for one of them to get it over with. "The guy's been laying there for so long he's starting to turn black," he complained.

"This is not a case of a devoted father killed in an accident," an attorney for the Rao firm advised Dorff. "Under the circumstances of the case, the family is not anxious to go out there to Kenosha." Finally, on April 9, Callahan's twenty-four-year-old daughter, Eleanor, agreed to fly to Kenosha, accompanied by Maloney, the Rao family lawyer.

"This is my father," she softly told Dorff after viewing the body.

Deputy Coroner Matthew Kulbiski then signed a cremation order and Kenosha authorities disposed of the body.

The mystery of who was shot to death that chilly March morning on the Chiwaukee Prairie along the Lake Michigan shore had been solved. But who pulled the trigger might never be known.

Motives? Sonquist and his detectives had a file cabinet full of them. Here was a man who shamed his good wife and blackened his family name; an adulterer who moved from one girl friend to another before discarding them like worn gloves; a bigamist who never told his bride or her family he was already married; a man suspected of stealing as much as $10 million from his father-in-law's business; a man so insensitive to those who once loved him that his own family turned their backs on his body.

And what of Callahan's later-day life, after he assumed the identity of McDade? Could he have become involved in a shady business deal that led to his being taken for a Chicago-style "one way ride?" Wendy's parents told Sonquist that, just before the murders, Callahan telephoned them to say that Wendy would be flying out to visit them in Seattle on March 19—alone. He told them, "I've got business to attend to."

What kind of business? One of the many theories is that Callahan had become involved in narcotics, but no evidence of that was ever uncovered. Yet it was the style of murder, more than anything else, that pointed to a drug or money deal gone awry.

"There's no question about it. It was a highly professional execution," Sheriff Sonquist said.

Authorities in Wisconsin and New York believe a murder contract was probably let on Callahan from the East Coast, and carried out by professional hit-men from one of Chicago's Mafia street crews. No one from New York, or anywhere else for that matter, could possibly have known about the sparsely populated prairie where the bodies were dumped, a good seven miles off the Interstate Expressway.

"No outsider could have found that place," Kulbiski, the deputy coroner agreed. "You have to know that territory, and whoever did it was no stranger—he had to have been there before."

And beautiful Wendy McDade, who had so much to live for? All agree she had to be killed, plain and simple. With professional killers, murder is a matter of survival. One or two, it doesn't matter to them.

If only she hadn't looked back at the handsome Don Juan who toasted her with Dom Perignon from the center table at the Rainbow Grill back in 1978, she might still be dancing.

UPDATE

Despite Callahan's murder, the Manhattan district attorney's investigation into the multi-million dollar embezzlement remains "open, but inactive." It will never be closed, said former Manhattan Assistant D.A. Seth Rosenberg, now in private law practice, until authorities can trace the missing money. And if they do, they might also clear up a double homicide that started in the hustle and bustle of Chicago's "Magnificent Mile," and ended in the awesome stillness of a Wisconsin prairie.

BOOK VI

NOT SAFE AT HOME

SUNDAY MORNING MASSACRE

With so many witnesses to the awful bloodletting on West Greenwood, in northwest suburban Woodstock, Illinois, it seemed a "given" that solving the homicide would be just a matter of routine legwork. Yet the person identified as the killer, a high school football star and former altar boy, has managed to elude police at every turn.

The nightmare began shortly before 5:30 A.M. Sunday, Aug. 21, 1988. According to any number of witnesses, nineteen-year-old Richard "Rick" Church, a handsome, dark-haired six-footer, broke into the Raymond Ritter home at 209 West Greenwood. Within a matter of minutes the interior of the comfortable Cape Cod style bungalow had become an abattoir.

Raymond Ritter, forty-three, and his forty-five-year-old wife, Ruth Ann, lay dead of knife wounds, a few feet from one another. Their seventeen-year-old daughter, Colleen, young Rick's high school sweetheart, and her ten-year-old brother, Matthew, had also been stabbed and were fighting for their lives as the crimson fluid oozed from their bodies.

A friend of Colleen's, Amy Quinlan, who was sleeping over, saw it all. Utterly terrified, she cowered under a bed, unnoticed in the carnage around her.

The first the outside world knew of it was when Colleen, wearing only her T-shirt and panties, burst out of the house barefoot and screaming, and collapsed in the street.

"It was like a nightmare. I said to myself, 'Is this really true?'" said Chris Gehrke, who was in his home across the street watching early morning television when he heard the screams outside.

"The guy was right there in the street. The girl was on her back. I thought he was beating her. It sounded like he was hitting her with a club. He was going so fast. He was like a maniac, just hitting her until she stopped moving. It was so still you could hear everything—really bad screams. The last one, she gave it all she had."

Gehrke and his roommate, Ronald Abt, instinctively ran to the fallen neighbor girl's aid. As they drew near, Church rose to his full six feet, stared eye-to-eye at Gehrke for several moments, then turned tail and ran, disappearing between two neighboring homes.

Abt dropped to his knees to minister to Colleen. "I wiped her off. She was all covered with blood," he would relate to police afterward. "She was laying in the middle of the highway with nobody around her. Her face was all cut up. The middle of her back was cut real bad. Blood was pouring out. He really laid into her."

Abt was covering her with his shirt as the door of the Ritter home burst open again, and ten-year-old Matthew staggered out, bleeding from a knife wound under his left arm, dangerously near the heart.

Woodstock police, who were on the scene within minutes after being alerted by neighbors, went into the Ritter home, where they found both of the children's parents dead, and the visiting schoolgirl hiding under a bed.

An all-points bulletin was put out for young Church, a husky 185-pounder, who neighbors said drove off in his mother's two-tone blue 1981 Dodge pickup truck with Illinois license plate number 746 849 B. It should have been easy to spot on the little-traveled roads on a Sunday morning but, incredibly, the youth and his pickup seemed to have vanished into thin air.

And what had precipitated the bloody massacre was even harder to comprehend. Rick Church just didn't fit into the mold.

A 1987 graduate of Marian Central, a private catholic high school, he was extremely well liked. He was the starting center on the school's football team when Marian Central won the state championship. From high school he went on to Northern Illinois University, where he was described as "a bright young man with a high intelligence quotient . . . a bright student and a good athlete."

The wall of his dormitory room at NIU was plastered with photographs of Colleen, including a poster-sized depiction of her dressed as rock star Cyndi Lauper.

Colleen, a high school cheerleader, worked as a waitress at the Woodstock Ice Cream Company, a local hot dog and fries hangout for teen-agers. She had been dating Rick for two and one half years, but she broke off the affair at the request of her parents, who feared Rick was partying too much since arriving at college.

On the night before the massacre, Rick had called the Ritter home and threatened to commit suicide.

With Rick still on the loose, Police Chief Herbert J. Pitzman ordered a police guard placed over Colleen, who was in intensive care after undergoing seven hours of surgery at Northern Illinois Medical Center in nearby McHenry, and her brother, who had been taken to Woodstock Memorial Hospital. The chief also put a police guard on the sleep-over friend who had witnessed the massacre.

A nationwide alert was put out for Church and a warrant was issued for his arrest. All twenty-five Woodstock police officers, plus a dozen auxiliary officers, worked virtually around the clock on the case, and overtime costs were running the small department $1,800 a day. Police distributed pictures of the handsome athlete to the press, in the hope that someone from the general public might have seen him.

More than sixty reports came in from all over. A motorist phoned Illinois State Police to say he spotted Church driving his pickup south on Interstate 294 near the Willow Road exit at Northbrook. Trooper Howard Kimbel cruised the area, but found nothing.

An airplane donated by Galt Airport north of town was brought into play to fly over Woodstock and the surrounding area in an effort to spot the blue pickup truck, but the hunters came up with nothing.

"He could be anywhere," Chief Pitzman said. "We have determined, in talking to his family, that he had about $700 on him when he took off."

Police also canvassed the campuses at NIU and at Southern Illinois University in Carbondale, suspecting he might have tried to blend in with the student population.

A preliminary report by Coroner Alvin J. Querhammer indicated the slain couple died of blows to the head inflicted by a "blunt instrument," as well as stab wounds. He said they died within a minute of one another.

Three days after the double slaying the search for the suspect shifted to the Wisconsin Dells, where a motel clerk reported a man matching Church's description had stayed overnight.

"I saw this guy's picture on the TV newscast. The same person checked into the motel Sunday afternoon," the clerk related. "When he left Monday morning, he took a blanket, some towels, soap, and a drinking glass with him."

A check of motel records disclosed the man identified as Church had used an assumed name when he registered at 1:30 P.M., and paid cash for the room.

An airplane search was conducted over the sprawling Dells resort and recreation area, on the theory that Church might have pulled into one of the many campgrounds after taking the blanket, towels, and soap from the motel, or might have decided to try to lose himself in the wilderness.

"If he intends to disappear into the wilderness, I think the chances of finding this kid are very good," Bob Fletcher of the

Illinois State Police Department of Criminal Investigation suggested. "It's a romantic notion for a young person to think he can survive in the wild for a long period of time. You can't do it."

Chief Pitzman agreed. "Even an experienced woodsman needs supplies to survive," he said. "If Church tries to buy them, he'll run the risk of being recognized. If he tries to steal them, it'll attract too much attention. Hopefully, if he's still out there, he'll want to turn himself in."

Faced with the certainty that young Church had fled across the state line, the FBI issued a fugitive warrant for the suspect and joined in the search. Interpol, the international criminal investigation organization, distributed copies of a wanted poster to the Royal Canadian Mounted Police.

On Tuesday, September 27, Woodstock police learned that the blue Dodge pickup truck had been found abandoned outside a 7-Eleven store in West Hollywood, California, more than two weeks earlier. When Woodstock police put out the original wanted bulletin for Church, they had not included a description of the get-away vehicle, unfortunately. Thus California police were unaware that the abandoned truck belonged to a murder suspect. They routinely had it towed away, ran a license plate check, and notified the Church family in Woodstock by mail.

Woodstock police did not know the truck had been found until Church's family passed the information on to them.

Due to that oversight, two valuable weeks had been lost. Woodstock authorities notified the FBI of the location of the truck. FBI agents in California who went over the vehicle established that the suspect's fingerprints were all over it. He had indeed been there, but was obviously long gone. The trail had grown stone cold.

The discovery of the truck, all the way across the country in California, caused surviving members of the Ritter family to breath a sigh of relief. "Since it's way out there, at least he can't walk back here to threaten the rest of us," said Colleen, who had recovered from her wounds and returned to school, where she was voted homecoming queen by her classmates.

Shortly after finding the abandoned truck, members of the Los Angeles County Sheriff's West Hollywood division brought in a suspect who clearly resembled Church. A check revealed that he was not the suspect, but a look-alike, thus complicating the search. "We've received a number of reports that Church has been seen in the Los Angeles area, but we can't be sure whether it's him or the look-alike," Sheriff's Lieutenant Gary Stephens explained.

Back in Woodstock the case took a bizarre turn when insurance investigators attempted to determine who died first, Ritter or his wife. At stake was a payment of $360,000.

The question was not who was stabbed first, but who clung to life the longest afterward. If Mrs. Ritter survived her husband by as little as an instant, the $360,000 in life insurance would go to the couple's three surviving children, Colleen, Matthew, and another son, Steven, fifteen, who was staying with friends on the morning of the bloodletting. If Raymond Ritter lived longer than his dying wife, the insurance money would go to his seventy-five-year-old father.

The McHenry County coroner's office listed Ruth Ritter's time of death as 6:00 A.M. and her husband's as 6:01 A.M. However George Mueller, an attorney representing the couple's estate, pointed out that the established times were merely arbitrary, entered on records by police who were called at 5:30 A.M.

"By the time the coroner's office was called at 6:01 A.M. they were both already dead," Mueller pointed out. "I don't think they were lingering in that room before the coroner's people got there."

The lawyer pointed out that eighteen years earlier Ritter had taken out two insurance policies, with a double indemnity death benefit of $360,000. The couple had no children at the time. He listed his wife as the first beneficiary, and his father, Henry, as the second. If Ritter died as little as one second ahead of his wife, the money would have legally gone to her, and thus become a part of the couple's estate, which included a house and a two-flat valued at $150,000. But if

Mrs. Ritter died first, the insurance would have gone to the second beneficiary.

After a year-long investigation, and lengthy consultations with Dr. Robert J. Stein, the Cook County medical examiner, the McHenry County coroner's office ruled that Raymond Ritter had lived one minute longer than his wife. This made Henry Ritter the beneficiary of his son's insurance. He had died during the interim, however, making his estate the beneficiary. After prolonged legal negotiations between lawyers for Raymond Ritter's children and Harry Ritter's survivors, an agreement was reached for the disbursement of the $360,000.

"That's settled," declared Thomas F. Loizzo, one of the lawyers involved in the negotiations. "Now what's left is for Church to be brought to justice."

UPDATE

Richard Church, still facing charges of murder, attempted murder, and home invasion, remains at large.

"We continue to get leads," Chief Pitzman said. "Most of them now come from well-intentioned viewers of television mystery and talk shows, which mention the case from time to time."

The discovery of the fugitive's abandoned truck outside the California convenience store in the fall of 1988 was the last positive lead authorities had, according to FBI Agent Robert Long.

Although investigators are convinced Church is alive, they searched for him among the exhumed bodies of victims who fell prey to a satanic cult in Matamoros, Mexico, and also compare his fingerprints to those of any unidentified male of his age who is found dead, Long said.

"Unfortunately, he's still out there somewhere."

WHO POPPED THE PIZZA MAN?

At 4:30 P.M. on Saturday, Nov. 18, 1989, forty-four-year-old Karen Canzoneri and her two teen-aged daughters went to a bar mitzvah in their North Shore suburb of Highland Park. Her sixty-one-year-old husband, Salvatore "Sam" Canzoneri, the owner of two local pizza businesses, was not enthused about sitting through the long Jewish coming-of-age ceremony. "I'll see you at the reception afterward," he said.

Sam should have gone to the bar mitzvah. When Mrs. Canzoneri and her daughters returned to the family's $800,000 home around midnight he was waiting for them in a pool of blood on the laundry room floor.

It was Mrs. Canzoneri who found the body, while looking for Sam to give him a piece of her mind. She was fuming because he had failed to show up at the reception as promised. The minute she and the girls got into the house she told Jamie, fourteen, and Cori, thirteen, "Go to your rooms. Your father and I are going to have a big argument."

It was then that she noticed the overturned tables and chairs. Something was terribly wrong. It was as though a tornado had whipped through the luxurious home. "Sam, where are you?" Mrs. Canzoneri called out, going from room to room. "What's going on here?" When she reached the utility room she found the door smashed. Peering inside, she could only gasp in horror.

Highland Park paramedics got the emergency call at 12:10 A.M., but there was nothing they could do for the man on the bloodstained floor. He had three bullet holes in him.

Canzoneri was no stranger to guns. He was an ex-Chicago cop who went on to greater things. He owned Pizza Crisp International and Panhandle Pizza, Inc., and held several patents in the food industry. His plush home on Tennyson Lane was in a new section of town where lot sizes started at about an acre. In addition to the two girls living at home, Canzoneri had two grown sons and four married daughters.

Highland Park Police Chief Robert Rash, along with Deputy Chief William Donnelly and Lieutenant Daniel Rottman, could tell at a glance that Canzoneri had not given up his life without a fight. The overturned furniture clearly indicated that a scuffle had taken place. Also scattered about were pizza product samples and Canzoneri's business cards.

From all appearances, Canzoneri had opened the front door and admitted his killer or killers, thinking they were potential business customers. He then went out to his car and brought in some of his sample wares, along with his business cards. Once he realized his peril, Canzoneri tried to flee, knocking over furniture in a frenzied flight to get out of the way. He was able to scramble to the utility room, where he slammed the door shut and tried to barricade himself inside.

His assailants fired a volley of shots through the door, hitting him three times, including once in the chest. They then forced open the door, apparently to make sure the bullets had struck their mark.

Lake County Coroner Barbara Richardson told investigators it was a .38-caliber wound near the heart that did Canzoneri in.

Apparently no one heard the gunshots. There were three vacant lots on one side of the house, and the nearest neighbor was some distance away on the other.

In an effort to establish a motive for the slaying, High-land Park police delved into the pizza firms' books to deter-mine whether the victim owed any large sums of money, or whether there might have been a dispute over a bill.

Meanwhile, a routine background check to see whether there might have been anything in the victim's past that could have led to his murder turned up a lot of information Highland Park police did not know about the local pizza king.

Canzoneri, a one-time merchant seaman, was a former Chicago narcotics detective and ex-night club owner, with some rather questionable associates. He served on the Windy City police force for twelve years, from 1954 to 1966, before resigning for "personal reasons." That was the year his former partner, Police Sergeant Sheldon Teller, was convicted on federal drug charges.

In the late 1960s Canzoneri and Teller were partners in the Rivoli Ballroom, a Northwest Side nightclub that intro-duced many top country headliners to Chicago, including Willie Nelson and Merle Haggard. Teller, who later went into business in Phoenix, was named to the Chicago Crime Commission's list of organized crime figures after he and his wife, Leah Joyce, were convicted of being ring leaders of a major narcotics ring.

Canzoneri, himself, had several brushes with the law after leaving the force. The Police Internal Affairs Division advised Highland Park authorities that he had been under investigation for associating with crime syndicate figures while an officer.

Police records also indicated he was arrested in Chicago in 1969 on gambling charges, in Skokie in 1970 for unlawful use of a weapon, and again in Skokie in 1976 for attempting to pose as a Chicago Police Department Intelligence agent. He was not convicted of any of the charges.

Because of Canzoneri's checkered past, officials of the federal Task Force on Organized Crime—including the FBI, the IRS, and the Chicago Police Department—offered to assist in the investigation of his murder.

In addition to going over the books of his pizza companies, investigators checked phone company records in an effort to determine who might have made an appointment with him on the night of his death.

In a search for a motive for the slaying, police also checked out reports that a late-model Cadillac, similar to Canzoneri's car, was often seen parked outside the home of Salvatore "Sollie D" De Laurentis, forty-one-year-old gambling figure, in Inverness.

One theory was that the killing was a warning from organized crime to potential witnesses not to cooperate with a federal gambling investigation.

It was in the Lake County courthouse in Waukegan, however, that investigators found out the most about Canzoneri, and the fact that his marriage was anything but a Garden of Eden.

According to a divorce action filed earlier in the year, both he and his wife had accused one another of threatening to kill each other.

Mrs. Canzoneri filed suit on February 28, claiming her husband had tried to choke her and physically threw her against the fireplace in their Highland Park home. "He has an uncontrollable temper and on repeated occasions has struck me and caused me great bodily harm," she said. "Salvatore Canzoneri has firearms in the house and has repeatedly threatened to kill me. I do believe in fact that Salvatore Canzoneri will kill me or cause me great bodily harm."

She asked the court to dissolve the twenty-year marriage, and give her custody of their two daughters.

Canzoneri, however, filed counter charges claiming that it was Karen who had repeatedly threatened to kill him, and on one occasion waved "a large carving knife at me."

The suit also contained a sworn affidavit from Mrs. Canzoneri's father, Jerome Sultan, of Ft. Lauderdale, Florida, who said Canzoneri told him in a telephone conversation, "She had better watch out or you will find her in a cast or a casket."

The divorce action was pending before Judge Jane Waller for only two weeks, before it was voluntarily dismissed on March 14.

Police questioned Mrs. Canzoneri at length. They determined that she was actually the family breadwinner, operating a market research business known as Car-Lene Research, Inc., in Highland Park. Canzoneri, it appeared, needed financial support from his wife because his new pizza businesses were "not yet generating income."

No charges were ever filed in connection with the homicide. After more than 100 interviews of family members, neighbors, and business associates, Highland Park police said they were unable to even pin down a motive for the slaying.

UPDATE

In March 1990, Canzoneri's six adult children from a previous marriage offered a $10,000 reward to anyone providing information leading to the arrest and conviction of their father's killer. The offer brought no response.

On Sept. 8, 1990, the victim's two sons, Thomas and Robert, and his four daughters, Patricia Galuski, Linda Liebach, Marlene Colby, and Shelley Cummings, made the game a little more interesting. They upped the ante to $75,000.

"We are convinced that our father knew the person who shot him," Thomas' wife, Linda Canzoneri, declared. "We will pay $75,000 to whoever can tell us who that person is."

NO SIGN OF FORCED ENTRY

Concepcion "Connie" Reyes had dedicated her life to helping others, and it was probably someone she was trying to help who took that life away from her.

In her early years she was a teacher and Girl Scout leader in her native Philippines, and later at an American school in Laos. By 1969 her travels had brought her to Kenosha, Wisconsin, where she became a caseworker for the Kenosha County Department of Social Services. She held a master's degree, and specialized in helping foster children, some of whom had been victims of sexual assaults.

Reyes, a diabetic, left work early on Thursday, April 12, 1990, explaining that she did not feel well. She did not attend Lenten services that evening at Our Lady of Mt. Carmel Catholic Church, as she usually did. The next day was Good Friday, and nobody saw her around the neat bungalow on Kenosha's West Side.

A friend from work phoned on Saturday, the day before Easter, to see how she was feeling. When she received no answer she and her husband stopped by the house to make sure everything was all right.

Letting themselves into the locked home with a key they had been entrusted with, they found Connie's partly nude body lying face down on the kitchen floor. Thinking she had suffered a diabetic attack, they notified authorities.

But when Dr. Robert Bjork, a coroner's pathologist, performed an autopsy at St. Catherine's Hospital, he discovered that Concepcion Reyes had been strangled. He estimated she had been dead since Thursday afternoon. Her mail, which had been delivered at 12:30 P.M., was still in the box.

Police, under the direction of Assistant Chief Robert Carney and Lieutenant Michael Bostetter, found evidence of a struggle in the living and bathroom of the victim's home. There was no sign of a forced entry, however, and the killer had apparently locked the door behind him when he left.

Neighbors told police the victim, who lived alone, had a very close circle of friends, and was always cautious. "I don't think she would have opened her door to a stranger," a next door resident opined.

Police Captain Robert Young agreed. "From all appearances, she knew her assailant," he said. "We haven't focused on any one person, or ruled out any possibilities, but we believe the culprit is someone known to her. There is some connection, whether it be through a personal relationship, a past client, some work associate."

As the months passed, however, the identity of the killer remained a mystery.

"The whole thing is very mysterious," Young said. "We're not any closer today to deciphering what occurred than we were shortly after her body was found. We've left no stone unturned. We've even consulted psychics. But the more people we talk to the more the mystery deepens. The problem is, there weren't a lot of people to talk to."

UPDATE

The Kenosha Area Crime Stoppers program posted a $1,000 reward for Connie Reyes' killer. In August 1990, four months after the murder, the slain woman's friends and co-workers in

Boys playing on a winter's day froze in horror upon finding the body of Mary Ellen Kaldenberg in an abandoned hearse. She had been stabbed to death.

Body of slain mobster Anthony Spilotro lying face down in an Indiana cornfield grave. The burial had been intended as a mob secret, concealing forever his disappearance and murder.

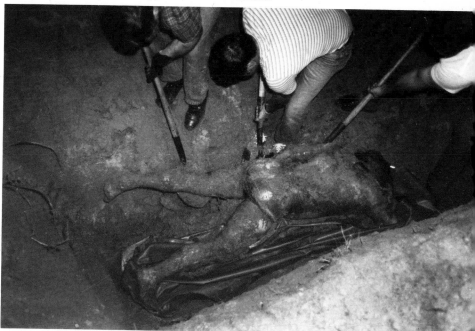

Photo courtesy Indiana State Police

Above. Evelyn Hartley was snatched out of the home where she was baby-sitting, subdued, and pulled through a basement window before forever vanishing into darkness. *Below.* The house in La Crosse, Wisconsin, from which Evelyn Hartley was abducted in 1953. Police found footprints outside the basement window (1), and bloodstains on the lawn (2).

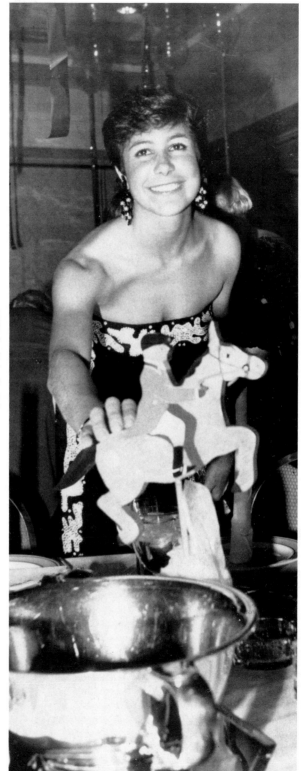

Equestrian and University of Illinois scholar Maria Caleel was alone in her off-campus apartment when she was fatally stabbed.

Above. Charles Percy and his daughter, Valerie, in 1964, two years before she was slain by an intruder who invaded the Percy home located north of Chicago.

Right. Actress Karyn Kupcinet shown here with actor boyfriend Andrew Prine. Police said both had received threatening letters, with words cut from magazines which were found in Kupcinet's apartment.

Chicago school teacher Dorothy Tapper was stuck with surgical needles and tortured before she was killed and her body dismembered. Parts of her body were found in Indiana.

Oil company executive Charles E. "Chuck" Merriam was shot dead in the foyer of his home. Merriam's secretary and the killer were the last people to see him alive.

$50,000 REWARD

FOR INFORMATION LEADING TO THE ARREST AND CONVICTION OF THE MURDERERS IN THIS CASE

DONNA LYNN HARTWELL
DONNA LYNN HARTWELL   **&**   FRANK A. MATOUS
FRANK A. MATOUS

WHITE FEMALE
AGE: 23
EYES: Hazel-Green
WEIGHT: 135 lbs.
HAIR: Blonde
HEIGHT: 5'5''

WHITE MALE
AGE: 39
EYES: Brown
WEIGHT: 190 lbs
HAIR: Dark Brown
    & Beard
HEIGHT: 5'7''

On September 5th, 1987 the body of Frank A. Matous was found in his burning car in McHenry County. He had been shot to death. A short time later the body of Donna Lynn Hartwell was found at his appartment in River Grove, IL. She had been dead over 24 hours. The circumstances surrounding her death are suspicious.

The Cook County Medical Examiner's Office ruled that Miss Hartwell had died of a drug overdose, but there were suspicious marks on her body and police believe the overdose was induced by Matous' killers to eliminate witnesses.

If you have any information related to this case, please contact:

The McHenry County Sheriffs Police
1-815-338-2144 ext.751
or
River Grove Police Department
Investigation Division
1-708-453-2123 or 1-708-453-3830
or
CRIME STOPPER'S
1-800-535-STOP

Police circulated this $50,000 reward poster in an effort to flush out clues to the murders of Donna Hartwell and Frank Matous.

Opposite page, top. Special agent Julie Cross: while surveilling a counterfeit money operation in Los Angeles, she and her partner were shot by a would-be robber. Her partner survived his head wounds.

Opposite page, bottom. Rogue cop Richard Cain was blown away by masked men in a sandwich shop in 1973, and there was no shortage of motives.

Opposite page. Artist's drawings of William Callahan and Wendy McDade, whose bodies were found next to each other. They had been shot.

Left. New York chorus girl Wendy McDade danced her way into the heart of her married lover, William Callahan. His cheating ways resulted in murder for himself and McDade.

Below. Wisconsin murder victim William Callahan was a charmer, all right. And a philanderer and embezzler, too. Here the former dancer is shown with Celeste Holm (right) in the movie, "Chicken Every Sunday."

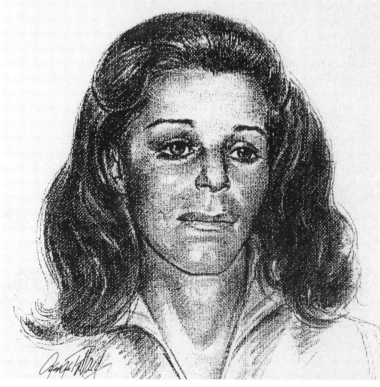

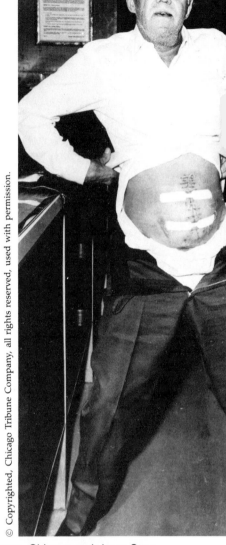

Left. Singer Phyllis McGuire and her beau, Chicago mob boss Sam "Momo" Giancana, shared more than a glass of wine. G-men and heartaches were just as plentiful. *Right.* Mobster madman Sam DeStefano bared his scarred abdomen to photographers after his arrest for, of all things, illegal voting. Shotgun blasts ended his life in 1973.

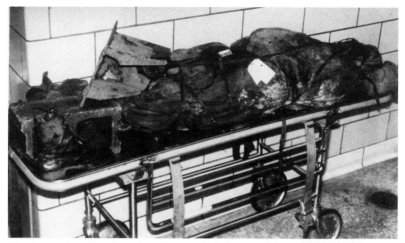

The bagged body of unidentified adult male murder victim, complete with angle iron and cement block which were used to weight down the victim in Chicago's Calumet River. Violent crimes detectives appeal for information about the man, who was shot in his right kneecap and spine, had his head crushed, and then was fatally shot point-blank in the back of his skull.

Lake County (Ill.) Coroner Robert H. "Mickey" Babcox has taken no shortcuts while investigating such cases as the shotgun killings of Bruce and Darlene Rouse.

ATTENTION

Representative of the 15th Senatorial District of the
nois, was abducted at 9:55 P.M., Thursday June 11th, 195

CLEM GRAVER

rs of age, 5 ft. 7 in. in height, weighing about 180 lb:
a suit, light Panama straw hat and black and white shoe:
976 W. 18th Place, Chicago, Illinois. State Representa
Republican Ward Committeeman of the 21st Ward, Chicago,

a men encountered victim as he placed his automobile in
of 1824 S. Morgan St., Chicago, 22nd Police District,
date, and forcibly placed him in a 1950 or 1951 black l
icense number unknown, driving south on Morgan St. from

1 perpetrators described as follows:

Above. Illinois legislator Clem Graver was last seen outside his Chicago
home in 1953. Witnesses said several men in a car abducted Graver just
as he reached the would-be safety of his home.

Opposite page. Chicago police left no manhole cover unopened in their
search for Clem Graver. Here they pry open a sewer lid in an industrial
section.

Charles "Chuckie" English (right) was high up in the mob in 1963, when this photo was snapped. But after Sam Giancana was murdered, English fell out of favor—so far out of favor that he was murdered in 1985.

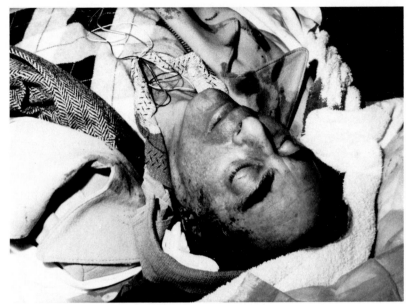

Millionaire mob insurance executive Allen Dorfman was intercepted by hitmen and shot to death outside a hotel in Lincolnwood, Illinois, in 1983. Dorfman was slain after he and others were convicted in a mob bribery plot, and some of the *boys* feared he might talk rather than go to prison. The murder guaranteed his silence.

Candy heiress Helen Brach disappeared leaving a vast estate but no clues of her fate.

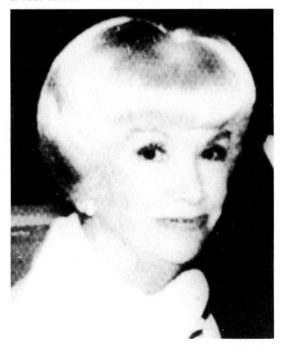

Above. Just after political kingmaker Jay Given won a door prize at a political fund-raiser, he was fatally shot. Though there were 400 people attending the party, no one saw what happened. *Right.* The end view of this .45-caliber shell casing shows how the slug was defaced in an obvious attempt to prevent the identification of the murder weapon in the Given slaying.

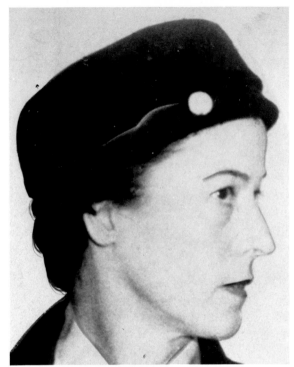

Above. Crusading newspaper editor Amelia J. "Molly" Zelko wasn't afraid to take on anyone— including the mob. This could be why she was never seen again after leaving her office on Sept. 25, 1957. *Below.* Molly Zelko's second floor apartment (arrow). Parked at the curb is her Chrysler, next to which her shoes were found.

the Kenosha County Courthouse and Social Services Department chipped in and raised another $1,000, doubling the reward to $2,000. The reward fund continues to grow through public contributions, but the killer remains at large.

ALL FOR ONE AND
ONE FOR ALL

Coroner Robert H. "Mickey" Babcox knew from the day it happened that the killer of Bruce and Darlene Rouse had to be one of three people. Eeny, meeny, miney, moe . . .

Rouse, forty-four, a wealthy gas station chain owner, and his thirty-eight-year-old wife were slain by shotgun blasts fired at point-blank range as a thunderstorm raged outside their luxurious home in the Bull Creek subdivision just north of Libertyville. Their bodies, dressed in nightclothes, were found in their bed on the ground floor of their thirteen-room colonial mansion.

Babcox, one of the first lawmen at the scene, observed that Rouse had been shot in the lower jaw. He had also been beaten about the head, apparently with the gun butt, and stabbed six times in the heart. Mrs. Rouse had been shot between the eyes.

"Whoever did this was a person with a lot of hatred," Lake County Sheriff Thomas Brown commented, in calling the coroner's attention to powder burns on Mrs. Rouse's forehead. "He pressed the shotgun right against her head and pulled the trigger."

She had died instantly. The explosion apparently awakened Rouse, who lurched upright momentarily before a second blast from the same weapon took away the left side of his face, splattering blood and flesh on the bedroom wall. The blast hit no vital organs, however, and the killer moved around the bed and finished him off with the butt of the gun, then plunged a knife into his heart again and again, just to make sure.

Two of the Rouses' children were in the home when the slaying occurred. Their son, Billy, fifteen, and his sixteen-year-old sister, Robin, had rooms directly overhead on the second floor. Another son, Kurt, twenty, lived in an old servant's cottage about 100 yards from the main house on the seven and one half acre estate.

The discovery of the bodies was reported by Robin at 8:30 A.M. She had gone to her parents' bedroom after an employee of one of her father's gas stations telephoned to get the combination of a safe. Rouse normally opened the station himself, but had failed to show up that Friday morning, June 6, 1980. After peering through the bedroom door at the carnage she awakened Billy, who telephoned police.

Upon arriving at the home police found Robin in a state of hysteria, but noted that both Billy and Kurt, an unemployed musician, seemed unusually calm in view of the circumstances. They told Sheriff's Investigator Kurt Proschwitz that they heard nothing unusual during the night.

Babcox estimated the couple had met death somewhere between 2:00 and 3:00 A.M. Robbery was ruled out as a motive, since $300 in Rouse's wallet and valuable jewelry in the bedroom remained untouched.

No weapon of any kind was found in a search of the Rouses' $300,000 home, although it was known that Rouse had kept several shotguns and rifles in the house for hunting.

Curiously, bloodstains were found in the dead man's car, which was parked outside the home. The windshield wiper switch was in the full-speed position, indicating the auto had been driven during the storm that swept through the area during the night. "The father wouldn't have had the wipers on because, when he drove home from work, it wasn't raining yet," Sheriff Brown observed.

Divers searched area creeks, a pond near the Rouse home, several gravel pits, and the nearby Des Plaines River in an unsuccessful effort to come up with the murder weapon and other guns missing from Rouse's collection. Sheriff's investigators, meanwhile, took a long look into the victims' backgrounds in an effort to establish a motive for the double slaying.

The Rouse family, which consisted of numerous branches, had been around the Libertyville-Mundelein area since the 1880s, and the slain man's grandfather had once served as mayor of Mundelein. Darlene Rouse, who was born in Chicago, had lived in Libertyville since childhood.

Rouse got his first job pumping gas in a family-owned filling station. He ached to be on his own, however, and broke with the rest of his kin, opening his first station before he was twenty-one. He had the foresight early on to set up facilities in the corner of his garage for installing air conditioning units in automobiles before they became standard equipment. Motorists from throughout the Chicago area brought their cars to him to have them air conditioned, and he made nearly $80,000 during his first year in business. By the time he was forty Rouse owned several service stations, had extensive real estate holdings, was a partner in a cable television station, had interests in a concrete ready-mix firm and a used car business, and had a personal fortune of around $3 million.

Yet he continued to roll out of bed before dawn and regularly put in fourteen hours a day getting his hands dirty at the station nearest his home in Libertyville.

He and his wife also found time to become deeply involved in community activities, including Condell Memorial Hospital, service clubs, a bowling league, and the Chambers of Commerce in Libertyville, Mundelein, and Vernon Hills.

Police were immediately curious about three things: How was it that the two younger children, who slept immediately above their parents' bedroom, failed to hear the shotgun blasts? If the murders were committed by an intruder, why didn't the family dog, a black Labrador, bark and awaken the children? And why were all of Rouse's weapons missing?

The fact that his gun collection had disappeared certainly indicated that one of his own shotguns had been used to kill him.

Before authorities got around to question Robin, Billy, and Kurt, all three of the children hired attorneys. The lawyers advised them not to talk to investigators. The sheriff's office asked them to take lie tests, and they refused.

Meanwhile the slain couple's wills, filed in Lake County Circuit Court in Waukegan, left the entire $3 million estate to the three children. The wills placed the estate in trust with a Lake Forest bank, to be divided equally between them when they reached the age of twenty-one. They were also the sole beneficiaries of $900,000 in life insurance on their parents.

Unable to question the three surviving children, the sheriff's investigators turned to other sources—friends, acquaintances, fellow club members, and business associates. What they learned was not pretty. Even before the double murder things were far from tranquil beneath the sweeping roof of the rambling Rouse home hard by the Des Plaines River.

"The whole family didn't get along with one another. There was trouble among everyone. The parents didn't get along. The kids didn't get along," a sheriff's investigator reported.

Members of Darlene Rouse's coffee club recalled the day she displayed pictures of herself showing bruises that she said her husband had given her.

Robin, on the other hand, was the apple of her father's eye. "He'd do anything for her," a family friend told investigators. "When she wanted a horse, he bought her two. Then he built the stables for her and bought her saddles. When she turned sixteen, he bought her a car."

But neither Robin nor her parents got on well with Kurt, who never held a steady job and wasted his days sitting in

Cook Park smoking pot and drinking with his buddies. Robin still resented a time when she was younger, when her older brother got her drunk and kept her out all night with his friends.

On the day before their bodies were found Bruce Rouse and his wife had both exchanged angry word with Kurt over his leonine mane of long, stringy hair and scruffy beard. They were after him to join the army and get his act together. At one point, friends said, Kurt agreed to go into the army if his parents would make it worth his while. They offered him a cash payment up front, plus $500 for each month he served, but he reneged on the deal.

"When they found out he had changed his mind, they became absolutely incensed," a family friend told police. "It had gotten to the point where parent and child couldn't stand one another. They had become completely alienated."

Kurt was a powerful youth, who had been a guard on his high school football team and was runner-up state champion wrestler at 167 pounds while attending Lake Forest Academy. His father had sent him to the private school because he had trouble getting along with his classmates at Libertyville High.

Two days after the murders, before his parents were even in their graves, Kurt called the sheriff's office in Waukegan to ask if he could have his mother's 1973 Cadillac, which police had impounded. He also inquired about a possible increase in his allowance, and asked whether it would be okay if he moved to California.

Billy, the youngest of the children, had been having ongoing psychological problems, the sheriff's investigators learned. While in the sixth grade he had been sent to the principal's office for setting off a false fire alarm, and his parents were notified. His father was furious. He showed up at school with a police officer and told his young son, "The policeman is going to put you in jail."

A person familiar with the incident told investigators, "Billy was absolutely terrified, white as a ghost. They took him to the police station and he became absolutely hysterical, screaming and crying. His bowels moved uncontrollably. The fact that he had soiled his pants in public had a terrifying, humiliating impact on him."

Billy was subsequently placed in a special school for children with behavior and learning problems, but he never forgot the humiliation he had endured while in the public school, the friend said. He and several friends later went on a rampage of vandalism at three Libertyville schools, where he reportedly took "vicious glee" in trashing a principal's office.

Following the murders of their parents, the three children moved out of the home and went to stay with relatives. An insurance company, which held policies on the property, hired a private security firm to post guards outside the vacant house. On the morning of Tuesday, June 24, one of the guards was clubbed unconscious by someone who sneaked up behind him as he patrolled the yard.

Had the killer returned to retrieve something he had forgotten? Police went over the house, but could find nothing amiss.

All three of the Rouse children invoked their Fifth Amendment rights against self-incrimination and refused to testify before a grand jury looking into the killings on July 21. They also refused to testify at a coroner's inquest into their parents' death, called by Babcox on August 8.

Only one witness was called at the inquest, Detective Proschwitz. He testified that Robin Rouse told him right after her parents' bodies were discovered that she believed one of her brothers had committed the murders. Before she could say anything more a relative told her to keep quiet.

The investigation into the slayings continued through the summer and into autumn, without the cooperation of the heirs to the murdered couple's estate.

In early October surveyors working near an isolated spot along the Des Plaines River came upon two plastic bags containing bloody clothing, four shotguns, and a rifle. The bags had been thrown into three feet of water about thirty feet from shore. Ten divers from the sheriff's department, using a magnet, shovels, and sifting baskets, found half a dozen unfired shotgun shells, clothing, a woman's watch, Darlene Rouse's purse containing her driver's license, and costume jewelry bearing the murdered woman's initials.

Sheriff Brown turned the weapons over to the Northern Illinois Crime Laboratory in Highland Park for analysis. Investigators determined that one of the weapons belonged to Billy Rouse, and the other four had belonged to his father. All of the items, including the shotgun believed to have been the murder weapon, had been wiped clean of fingerprints.

The site where the items were found was about four miles from the Rouse home, and about 900 feet from a bridge crossing the river at Ill. Hwy. 60.

Brown's deputies uncovered a witness who had seen Rouse's car on the bridge the night of the murders. The witness said someone got out in the darkness and tossed something into the water. The plastic bags apparently drifted downstream to where they were found by the surveying team.

With the discovery of the items, Sheriff Brown huddled with State's Attorney Dennis Ryan and Undersheriff James Donaldson, to discuss their next move. The best chance of getting an indictment, they decided, was to call Robin Rouse to testify before the grand jury under a grant of immunity, to force her to tell what she knew about the slaying of her parents.

It would be just a matter of time, they figured, before her conscience would get the best of her, or a rift developed between her and her brothers, and she would tell authorities what she had been on the verge of blurting out right after the slayings. Getting at Robin, they agreed, was the most likely way of breaking the code of silence among the three musketeers.

Their hope of solving the homicide was dashed to pieces on a Friday afternoon in August 1983, when Robin Rouse, alone in her car, was killed when it slammed into a utility pole near Racine, Wisconsin. She was nineteen years old at the time.

UPDATE

The Rouse home, known locally as "Murder Mansion," was subsequently sold and turned into an illicit gambling casino catering to underworld figures from throughout the Chicago area. It was closed down after Robert Plummer, a Lake County mob gambling figure, was bludgeoned to death on a stairway, according to government documents. His decomposing body was later found in the trunk of his wife's Lincoln Continental in nearby Mundelein.

Kurt Rouse left the area after his sister's death, married, and moved to California, where he purchased property with his two-way split of his parents' life insurance.

Billy Rouse drifted down to Key West, Florida, where he became known as a "big spender" attracting a questionable circle of friends who found they could live high on the hog off him. In 1984 he was arrested for stabbing a twenty-six-year-old man in the belly during a quarrel over a chess game. He was sentenced to sixty days in jail, fined $1,000, and ordered to pay the victim's $1,585 hospital bill.

Coroner Babcox succeeded Brown as sheriff of Lake County, where he made the Rouse case the number one item on his agenda. He was never able to make an arrest, however, and said nobody ever would until one of the two brothers decides to talk.

"The cops really screwed this one up," Babcox told the authors just before cancer took his life in 1988. "They should have separated the three kids right away—before they got a chance to get together. Now the big-time lawyers have moved in. There's $3 million here and everybody wants a piece of it. This thing could drag on for years."

BOOK VII

GOOD COP-BAD COP

STAKEOUT TO MURDER

British born Julie Cross had been a San Diego police officer for four years when, at age twenty-six, she realized a far loftier ambition. In October 1979 she became a U.S. Secret Service agent—one of only twenty-one female agents in the federal department.

Described as "sinewy, competitive, and upbeat," she was originally assigned to the Secret Service staff in San Diego, where she grew up. On June 1, 1980, after separating from her husband, a San Diego police detective, she transferred to the agency's anti-counterfeit squad in Los Angeles.

"The day before she left she spoke of a premonition," recalled San Diego Police Sergeant Cheryl Meyers. "She said she was excited, but said she felt that something bad was going to happen. I told her everything would be fine."

Less than a week later she and her partner, agent Lloyd Bulman, found themselves hot on the trail of a band of counterfeiters in Los Angeles.

Their investigation led them to a house on Belford Avenue in Westchester, near Los Angeles International Airport, and they decided to place the building under surveillance.

On Wednesday night, June 4, the two of them were sitting in an unmarked Buick sedan near the intersection of Belford

Avenue and Interceptor Street, staking out the suspect's address while waiting for other agents to arrive with a search warrant. Bulman was seated behind the wheel, and Cross was on the passenger side. They had a twelve-gauge shotgun in the front seat with them, in case anybody objected when they went to serve the warrant.

As the two of them idly chatted, two muscular black men, seemingly bent on robbery, sneaked up on the couple in the darkness. One of them stood six feet two inches tall, weighed 190 pounds, and wore a black double-breasted coat. The other was about five feet eleven inches tall, weighed about 185 pounds, and had a stocking cap pulled down over his face.

One of them leaned down, stuck his head into the car window, and announced a stickup. When Bulman identified himself as a police officer, the gunman said, "Oh, yeah? Well I'm a cop, too."

Bulman pushed his way out of the car and began to struggle with one of the men in the street, while the other ran around to the passenger side of the auto and grabbed the shotgun. As Cross shouted a warning to Bulman the assailant turned the shotgun on her as she sat in the car and squeezed the trigger. She was hit full force in the abdomen at point-blank range, and died instantly.

The killer then ran back around to the other side of the car and fired at Bulman, who had fallen to the street while wrestling with the other man. The charge ricochetted off the pavement, showering his head with bits of stone and dirt, drawing blood and leaving him stunned but otherwise unhurt.

The assailants, apparently thinking he, too, was dead, jumped into a two-tone brown 1971 Buick or Pontiac and sped off into the night, taking Cross' .357 Magnum service revolver and the shotgun with them.

The shooting brought out a virtual army of investigators, determined to solve the first slaying ever of a female Secret Service agent in the line of duty.

Primary jurisdiction in the case fell to the Los Angeles Police Department's major crimes investigation unit, headed by Lieutenant Ed Henderson. Working with him were teams of Secret Service investigators brought in from throughout the country by Larry Sheafe, head of the Los Angeles Secret Service field office.

Giving the case number one priority, Robert E. Powis, assistant director of the Secret Service, declared flatly, "These killers will be apprehended and prosecuted."

Thousands of leads were checked out, and memos relating to the investigation would eventually fill a four-drawer filing cabinet. One tip police received was that Cross was killed because she had knowledge of Cuban involvement in the assassination of President John F. Kennedy.

Investigators are satisfied, however, that the slaying had nothing to do with that, or the counterfeit house stakeout. They are convinced that the killers were simple street-thugs who spotted the couple sitting in the darkened car and decided on the spur of the moment to rob them, having no inkling as to their true identities.

UPDATE

The Secret Service posted a $25,000 reward for the killers of Agent Cross, and "anonymous donors" added an additional $75,000, bringing the total reward to $100,000—the largest ever offered by any U.S. Treasury agency. "We are still confident that this case will be solved," said Richard J. Griffin, who subsequently took over as special agent in charge of the Los Angeles Secret Service office. "There are things happening even now that lead me to believe arrests will be made." Julie Cross was only the fourth agent to die in the line of duty since the Secret Service was established in 1865 by Allan Pinkerton, America's first "private eye." Her murder remains unsolved, and still carries a number one priority rating in the Treasury department.

The home that she and her partner had staked out was, indeed, a counterfeiting plant. Secret Service agents raided the house after the shooting, arrested a twenty-four-year-old man, and confiscated $7,000 in bogus $20 bills.

HELP WANTED—ONE KILLER

In February 1987 the following ad appeared in a Chicago newspaper:

> Unsolved homicide. Anyone having information on the murder of Cook County Sheriff's Police Officer Ralph Probst on April 10, 1967, please write: P.O. Box 56035, Harwood Heights, Ill. 60656.

The ad is no longer running. It was just a shot in the dark anyway, but after twenty long years of wondering, Sheriff's Deputy Bob Borowski was willing to try anything to find out who killed his partner, and why.

Probst, a thirty-year-old father of three, was spending a quiet evening at home with his family on April 10, 1967. It was a rare treat for a member of Sheriff Joe Woods' Special Task Force, but for the past two weeks Probst had been taking training classes for the canine unit, which gave him his nights off.

He and his wife, Marlene, were watching the Academy Awards on TV in their duplex in southwest suburban Hometown at around ten o'clock, when Probst got up and went into the kitchen for a glass of water. His wife was on the couch in the front room, and for the second night in a row the deputy's German shepherd was acting restless, as though disturbed by something in the yard.

As Probst entered the kitchen a gunman who had been lurking in the darkness outside drew a bead on the unsuspecting lawman with a powerful .41-caliber Magnum handgun and pulled the trigger. The bullet smashed through the kitchen window, ripped through Probst, and dropped into a burner on the stove as he fell to the floor, dead.

In the nearly quarter of a century since that shot was fired, police have been unable to solve the murder of one of their own.

In the weeks before he was slain Probst had boasted to his partner and to friends on the Hometown Police Department, where he had worked before becoming a sheriff's investigator three years earlier, "I'm working on something really big. When this breaks I'll make sergeant, watch and see." In fact he was so sure of the promotion that he confided in Hometown Police Chief Nick Kolbasuk that he had already ordered a new car.

Whatever it was, the tight-lipped Probst kept it to himself. He never discussed the case with his partner, Chief Kolbasuk, or even his wife. He kept his records of the investigation in his car, rather than leave them back at headquarters. But when detectives searched the auto after the murder, his files were missing.

What had Probst been working on, and why did his reports on the case disappear?

"We did everything we could to try to elaborate on that," said Jerry Harmon, a former sheriff's lieutenant, now retired from the force. "Our investigators reviewed all his arrests over three years, even the traffic citations he had issued. We also looked for a safety deposit box, but if he had one we couldn't find it. The best lead we had involved a stranger who visited the house across the street."

Harmon said the home directly across from Probst's was up for sale, and in the weeks before the fatal shooting a man who claimed he was a prospective buyer visited the property on several occasions. "He thoroughly familiarized himself with the house that was for sale, and then he pointed across to the Probst house and asked the owner if both houses had the same general floor plan." The owner advised him that the homes' interiors were identical.

At about that same time Harmon received a phone call from John Gallagher, a federal narcotics agent. "Jerry, I think we might have something that you can use," Gallagher told him. "One of our informants tipped us that he overheard a hood named Frank Calvise bragging that he killed a county cop. This might tie in with the Probst shooting."

The owner of the home across the street from Probst had already given police a description of the suspect and his car. The description matched that of the fifty-two-year-old Calvise, an ex-convict cartage thief. Harmon's detectives obtained a mug shot of Calvise and showed it to the home owner. "Have you ever seen this person before?" he was asked. "Yes, I sure have," the property owner replied. "That's the guy. He's the one who was so interested in the floor plan of Ralph Probst's house."

Calvise was picked up and put into a police lineup, so the neighbor could view him in the flesh. No identification was made, however. The neighbor took one look at Calvise and broke out in a cold sweat.

"I've got my family's safety to think about," he stuttered. With that he fairly ran from the police station. Harmon's men questioned Calvise, but he was not cooperative. Calvise died of natural causes several years later, without ever disclosing what he might have known about the deputy's murder.

The same can be said for Roger Douglas, a twenty-five-year-old burglary suspect from Summit. On Dec. 27, 1968, police broke up an attempted burglary of a liquor store on South Pulaski Road, and shot Douglas when he raised an object they thought was a gun—but which turned out to be a hammer. Douglas was taken to Von Solbrig Hospital, where he was questioned on his deathbed by Harmon's partner,

Sheriff's Detective Chris Fosco. Douglas was believed to have been privy to a number of gangland secrets, and Fosco was giving him an opportunity to clean the slate before he crossed the river Styx.

Fosco bent over the dying man, listening intently as Douglas slowly formed his words, mentioning a number of criminal matters. "What about Ralph Probst, Roger? Who knocked him off?" Fosco asked gently.

Douglas began to speak, but suddenly clammed up and stared toward the door of his hospital room. Fosco turned his gaze from Douglas to see what had distracted him. There, in the doorway of the hospital room, stood Sheriff's Sergeant James Keating. His mere presence was enough to end the conversation, and Douglas died shortly thereafter.

Keating, who authorities later determined had been a mole for the mob, was subsequently convicted of conspiracy to commit murder and extortion in connection with another case, and is now in a federal prison.

Police also considered the possibility that loudmouthed mob figure Sam DeStefano, with whom Probst had had a recent run-in, might have been involved in the slaying.

DeStefano was confined to the Cook County Jail hospital on Jan. 23, 1967, when Probst and Borowski discovered he was enjoying lavish treatment and special privileges. They put a stop to it, and had DeStefano shackled to his bed. As Probst herded members of the mobster's family out of the hospital room, DeStefano raged at him, "You'll be sorry you treated me this way!"

Harmon questioned DeStefano, who denied threatening the lawman. DeStefano, who was utterly mad, was a known killer who often threatened police and newspaper reporters, but he never carried out those threats.

He, himself, was murdered in April 1973, probably by fellow mobsters who felt they had to shut his big mouth for their own safety.

"We have always felt that the person who shot Probst was qualified to use a handgun," Harmon said. "What puzzled us was the murder weapon. A .41 Magnum was unusual in those days. It had just been marketed and only about 100 had been sold in the United States. It was the type of handgun that only a gun enthusiast—or a police officer—would have used."

Long after sheriff's investigators and Hometown police gave up on trying to find Probst's killer his partner, Borowski, continued to devote every hour of his free time to the case. Placing the newspaper ad was just another thought he had—anything to keep the investigation alive. Solving Probst's murder had become an obsession with him.

"I just can't fathom it—a policeman dead and nobody doing anything about it," he said. "I want it solved. Probably, till the day I die, I'm going to work on this case."

UPDATE

While no one was ever charged in the Probst slaying, and no sure motive established, Harmon and other investigators are convinced that Frank Calvise either pulled the trigger himself or set up the ambush slaying. If so, he took his secret to the grave.

THE COP WHO MADE HIS OWN RULES

Police Officer Mark Thanasouras started his career on an upbeat, he rose with the speed of light, and he fell as hard as any meteor plummeting to earth. The last sound to ever echo off his eardrums was the deafening blast of a shotgun as it went off in his face.

The popular Chicago lawman made his first arrest in 1956 when he nabbed a suspected sex offender while still a trainee at the police academy. His aggressiveness captured the eye of Orlando W. Wilson, the reform police superintendent who was brought in to shake out the bad guys and shape up the department.

It was soon Sergeant Thanasouras, then lieutenant, and within six years after he had joined the force Wilson elevated him to the rank of captain. In 1966, at the age of thirty-seven, he was promoted to commander of the West Side Austin District.

With "O.W." as his "Chinaman," Thanasouras could do no wrong. He quickly gained the reputation of being a ramrod commander, expecting every one of his troops to give as much of themselves as their leader.

In 1968 the North Austin Boys Club honored Thanasouras as "Man of the Year." In accepting the award he declared:

"Austin youngsters are learning that policemen are no different from other people who serve the community. This award is not mine, it belongs to the men of the district who have volunteered hundreds of hours of service to coaching teams and taking part in youth activities."

Wilson, meanwhile, stepped down as police superintendent, feeling that he had achieved what he set out to accomplish. And with his "Chinaman" gone, so went Thanasouras' clout.

Underneath the slick veneer of his office there had, for some time, been troublesome rumbles of corruption and shakedowns within the district. There were reports of a "$100-a-month club" in which saloonkeepers were muscled into paying monthly tribute in exchange for promises of immunity from police harassment.

Wilson's successor as police superintendent, James B. Conlisk, lost no time of relieving Thanasouras of his command and demoting him to his civil service rank of captain, with a $1,600-a-year cut in pay.

The resulting investigation uncovered one of the biggest police scandals in the city's checkered history, and Thanasouras was fired when he refused to testify before a federal grand jury looking into charges of police corruption.

In 1973 the federal panel indicted Thanasouras and thirteen of his men for extortion. On the day he was scheduled to go on trial Thanasouras pled guilty to extorting $275,000 from thirty tavern owners over a four-year period, and cut a deal with the prosecution to testify against his men.

The former high-riding police commander was sentenced to three and a half years in prison and fined $20,000. He was initially confined to the federal prison at Terminal Island, California, but abruptly moved to a jail in Arizona after authorities learned he had been marked for death by imprisoned members of the Black Panthers gang.

He was brought back to Chicago in 1974 to testify before a federal grand jury investigating gambling payoffs to high level police officials. He finished out his term in the Federal

Correctional Center in Lexington, Kentucky. In exchange for his cooperation with authorities, he was released in the fall of 1975 after serving only eighteen months.

The man who went to jail for shaking down tavern owners then took a job—of all things—as a bartender. He went to work for an old friend whom he had helped set up in the business, George Christofalos, operator of the L & L No. 2, a roadhouse featuring nude female dancers on U.S. Hwy. 41 in the suburb of North Chicago.

In the early morning hours of Friday, July 22, 1977, Mark Thanasouras, then forty-nine and suffering from diabetes and failing vision, washed all his glasses at the girlie night club and lined them up on the shelves. He checked out the cash register receipts with Christofalos, locked the whisky cabinets, and called it a night.

He got into his car and headed south, down Hwy. 41 and the Edens Expressway, going straight to Chicago's Northwest Side. The sun was already coming up over Lake Michigan as he pulled up to the curb outside his girlfriend's house at Campbell and Catalpa avenues and got out of the car.

It was just about 5:00 A.M. when neighbors were startled from their beds by two loud shotgun blasts. Peeking through their blinds they saw a man run from the scene, and heard an auto speeding away.

Thanasouras lay dead in the bloody street. He had caught both blasts head-on, fired from only a few feet away.

Citywide Homicide Commander Joseph DiLeonardi dismissed robbery as a motive for the killing. No effort had been made to lift Thanasouras' watch or his wallet.

"We don't know who was out to get him, but it was a professional job," DiLeonardi declared.

The ex-police commander's girlfriend, Joan Baum, a strikingly beautiful woman who worked in the John Hancock Center on North Michigan Avenue, could shed no light on the killing.

The elusive Thanasouras stopped by regularly to pick up his mail, which he had delivered to her address so no one would know where he really lived, she said.

Who would have wanted Thanasouras dead? Between the people he shook down, the underworld characters he associated with, the bad guys he had sent to jail as a cop, and the fellow lawmen he had finked on as a stool pigeon, DiLeonardi could have rounded up enough suspects to fill a small stadium.

The only clue police had was that the murder weapon was a twelve-gauge shotgun. The pellets taken from Thanasouras' body told them that.

"Mark just had a propensity to pick up enemies because he burned people rather often," said a federal investigator who had helped send him to prison. "He was always getting involved in unsavory transactions."

Samuel Skinner, the U.S. attorney for northern Illinois, who went on to become a member of President George Bush's cabinet in Washington, said, "Any time you associate with people in organized crime, you take the risk that your former friends may become your enemies."

Mark Thanasouras took the risk, and paid with his life.

On Sunday, March 11, 1979, Thanasouras' friend and former employer, Christofalos, was ambushed and cut down by shotgun blasts as he was leaving his L & L No. 2 nightclub at 4:30 A.M.

A club employee who witnessed the assassination, said the forty-two-year-old Christofalos was seated behind the wheel of his 1976 Cadillac Eldorado convertible, warming up the engine, when two men wearing ski masks appeared brandishing shotguns.

While one of the gunmen pinned the employee against the club's front door, the other man fired three shotgun blasts through the window of the Caddy, striking Christofalos in the left side and chest.

"There is no question but that this was a professional hit job," said Coroner Robert H. "Mickey" Babcox, a former sheriff's policeman, as he surveyed the body at the scene.

The similarities in the ambush slayings of Christofalos and Thanasouras fairly leaped out at investigators:

1. Both murders appeared to have been carried out by professional hit men.

2. Both men were gunned down by twelve-gauge shotgun blasts in the early morning hours after a night's work at the L & L club.

3. Thanasouras worked for Christofalos, and while still a police captain had interceded in his behalf with the Lake County Liquor Commission to help him get a liquor license.

DiLeonardi sent homicide detectives to North Chicago to work with Lake County lawmen in the wake of the Christofalos shooting, in an effort to establish whether the two slayings were connected. They couldn't prove that they were—and they couldn't prove that they weren't.

UPDATE

In 1989 Gerald Scarpelli, a fifty-one-year-old mob hit man, turned federal informant. He told authorities that he was the "back-up man" in the Christofalos murder and several other killings, in which he implicated mobster William "Butch" Petrocelli. Petrocelli was himself tortured and slain in 1980.

Scarpelli was also implicated in the Thanasouras hit, which police linked to a "porn war" between the crime syndicate and independent pornographic shop and strip joint operators.

Before federal agents could verify the information, Scarpelli committed suicide while in protective custody in Chicago's Metropolitan Correctional Center.

THE WALKIE-TALKIE MOB HIT

Everything about Richard Cain was a lie, except, perhaps, his final breath. That, for sure, came a millisecond before someone took off his head with a shotgun blast that decorated the walls of a North Side sandwich shop with his gray matter.

The high point of Cain's roller-coaster life probably came when he was revered as the chief investigator for the highly respected sheriff of Cook County, Richard Ogilvie, who went on to become governor of Illinois. The nadir, no doubt, was the miserable time he spent as chauffeur for Sam "Momo" Giancana, the one-time Chicago mob chief who had been exiled to Mexico.

In between, it seemed, the dapper Cain tried to be all things to all men, especially himself.

A native Chicagoan who was reared in Owosso, Michigan, he variously insisted that his last name was Cain or Scalzetti. The truth of the matter is that his maternal grandfather, Ole Scully, a wealthy Sicilian sewer contractor, had been born Scalzetti but had Americanized his name upon coming to Chicago.

Scully, a staunch believer in law and order, was beaten with baseball bats and shot to death by Mafia thugs on Dec. 17, 1928, the night before he was to testify as the state's star witness in a Black Hand kidnap-extortion trial.

Cain, a self-styled soldier of fortune, quit high school at seventeen to enter the army on a forged birth certificate. He boasted of having been a cloak-and-dagger officer with American underground forces in China, blowing up railway stations during World War II. He still carried shell fragments in his head as a reminder, he added. Army records showed he was nothing more than a clerk, serving in the Virgin Islands from 1947 to 1950.

He put his time there to good use, however, becoming proficient in Spanish and picking up the first of at least three wives. After his discharge he went to work as an investigator for the William J. Burns Detective Agency in Dallas. He came back to Chicago in 1951 and enrolled in a polygraph operator school run by police Captain John H. Scherping.

Although he was one-fourth of an inch short of the five feet nine inch height requirement for the Chicago police department, Cain became a cop four years later thanks to Scherping's clout, and an $800 bribe, he told friends.

When he joined the Chicago force, Cain listed his date and place of birth on police records as Oct. 4, 1924, in Owosso, Michigan. That was a lie by at least six years and 200 miles. Paul D. Newey, former chief investigator for State's Attorney Benjamin S. Adamowski, dug out Cain's birth certificate which showed he was born in 1930 in Chicago. The natal document also proves that he was not born Richard Scalzetti, as he often claimed.

His career as a lawman was a stormy and well publicized one. In April 1959 Cain and his partner, while working as vice detectives, fatally shot an ex-convict extortionist named Harry Feigel in what they claimed was a gun battle behind the Greyhound Bus depot in the Loop.

Newey said he has information, however, that the shooting actually took place on the South Side, around 63rd Street, and that the two vice dicks hauled the wretched corpse downtown and dumped it in the alley. Furthermore, according to Newey, the "drop gun" that had been planted on Feigel's body didn't even have a firing pin.

"The police wanted to indict Cain and his partner for Feigel's killing, but they had too much clout," Newey said. A coroner's jury ruled the shooting "justifiable homicide."

Several weeks earlier Cain and his partner made news when they seized $60,000 in cash during a raid on a sixty-eight-year-old prostitute's apartment on the South Side. The two vice cops were publicly lauded for turning in the cash hoard, but actually they had no choice, since a policewoman had been along on the raid. And the elderly hooker subsequently beefed that $1,500 was missing from her purse after the cops left, and another $30,000 to $40,000 stashed in a lock box also disappeared.

Cain quit the force in 1960 after it was discovered that he and his partner, while on leave of absence and working for the state's attorney's office, had "bugged" the office of Mayor Richard J. Daley's commissioner of investigations.

Cain spent the next two years in Mexico. He told associates he was working with the Central Intelligence Agency training Cubans for the Bay of Pigs invasion. What he was really doing there is anybody's guess.

Meanwhile Ogilvie, a top federal prosecutor, ran for Cook County sheriff on the Republican ticket and was elected. Cain, who had returned to Chicago in 1962 to campaign for Ogilvie, was appointed the sheriff's chief investigator. He got the coveted job after assuring the future governor, "I know the hoods, I'm not afraid of the hoods, and I hate the hoods."

While he was Ogilvie's chief investigator, Cain forced suspected informants to undergo lie detector tests at the public's expense to determine whether they were giving away mob secrets. Authorities did not learn until years later that Cain was a double agent, relaying the information he learned through the polygraph tests to mob bosses, who were thus able to identify any stool pigeons in their midst and deal with them accordingly.

Cain's career as a supercop took a dive after he raided a suburban motel in January 1964 and "recovered" $43,000 worth of drugs that had been part of a $240,000 theft from the Louis Zahn Drug Company warehouse in Melrose Park. The state's attorney's office exposed the raid as a phony, masterminded by Cain to make himself look good, after he planted the drugs in the motel himself.

Ogilvie fired Cain two weeks later. The Cook County grand jury indicted him for his role in the Zahn caper, and he was found guilty.

He served six months in jail for perjury, concurrent with a four-year prison sentence handed down in 1968 as an accessory to bank robbery, conspiracy, and concealment of evidence in connection with the $43,000 robbery of the Franklin Park Bank in 1963.

After he was paroled from federal prison in 1971, Cain went to Mexico where he worked as a driver for Giancana. He eventually became a courier and financial adviser to the mob boss, making numerous trips between Chicago and Mexico, when not cabareting in the Rush Street bistros with a different blonde almost every night. So highly thought of was Cain in his new capacity, that he toured Europe with Giancana, looking for investment opportunities.

Cain returned to Chicago in December 1973 to spend the Christmas holidays. His double-dealing past caught up with him on a bitterly cold Thursday, December 20, as the temperature dropped to two degrees above zero after a massive snowstorm snarled traffic.

Cain had gone to Rose's Poor Boy sandwich shop at 1117 West Grand Avenue to meet four other men. It was an obvious setup.

Fifteen minutes into the meeting two gunmen wearing ski masks entered the restaurant, and Cain's four companions hurriedly took a duck. The masked men, armed with a shotgun, a pistol, and a two-way radio, lined everybody else in the restaurant up against the wall

While Cain, Sam "Jelly Belly" Cozzo, the owner, a waitress, and three patrons stood facing the wall, one of the gunmen chatted on the walkie-talkie with an outside accomplice, who kept them advised about the approach of pass-ersby. "Someone is coming . . . all right, it's clear now," the lookout reported.

With the all clear signal, one of the men told Cain to turn around. Without saying another word he raised the shotgun to Cain's lower jaw and pulled the trigger twice in rapid succession, killing him instantly.

As the sound of the shotgun blasts died with Cain, the voice on the walkie-talkie was heard to say, "Make sure you get the package."

Because his face had been completely blown away, it was several hours before Cain's body could be positively identified. He carried no ID papers in his pockets according to Michael Spiotto, deputy police superintendent, who raced to the scene to supervise the homicide investigation. The body was taken to the county morgue as a "John Doe" murder victim.

In stripping the body at the morgue, homicide detectives found seventeen dollars in the dead man's pockets, his eyeglasses, a house key, and a scrap of paper bearing an address on Lunt Avenue. While examining his expensive gray slacks, which had come from an exclusive Michigan Avenue men's shop, they discovered Cain's name imprinted in the waistband. His identification was then confirmed through fingerprints.

Police believe he went to the sandwich shop to meet someone, and that he was carrying a package, although none was found at the scene.

Shortly before Cain arrived at the shop, mobster Mar-shall Caifano and two unidentified male companions were seen loitering inside the place. Minutes before the shooting the two unidentified men stepped outside through a back door and, standing in a gangway, were seen pulling on the ski masks. Where Caifano vanished to was never established. Was he the outside man with the walkie-talkie?

The investigation into Cain's murder never got off the ground. "We didn't see nothin'," the witnesses inside the restaurant insisted. "We don't know nothin'."

A coroner's jury heard only one witness, Homicide Investigator John Philbin, who described the blood-spattered crime scene. The jurors then deliberated for eight minutes before returning a verdict of "murder by persons unknown."

UPDATE

There were a variety of theories as to why Cain had to be eradicated. The onetime supercop had garnered an array of enemies on both sides of the law, and it was hard to find anybody who shed a tear at his abrupt passing. When one knowledgeable lawman was asked who he thought killed the rogue cop he quipped, "Take your pick."

If there was a package, police speculate it might have contained incriminating tape recordings, or possibly photographs, that would have been of interest to law enforcement officials. Cain was known to be financially strapped. Had he brought the package to "sell" to someone who didn't want its contents made public, or was he hoping to use it to buy his way up in the ranks of the mob?

Shortly after his return to Chicago from Mexico, Cain commenced boasting of a grandiose scheme to install himself as Chicago Mafia chief. "I am going to become Chicago's Godfather," he declared with authority.

The best bet is that the then reigning underworld bosses were not yet ready to relinquish the throne, and settled the matter out of court, in a manner of speaking. Or, if Cain was trying to blackmail someone, he was paid off in a manner he hadn't expected.

Chicago police say they suspect the killer with the shotgun was Harry Aleman, a professional hit man for the mob. If it was Harry, he got away with murder, because he was never indicted for the crime.

BOOK VIII

MOB JUSTICE

MURDER ON A MEAT HOOK

The unconscionably vicious murder of forty-year-old William "Action" Jackson was without a doubt one of the most hideous ever carried out by the Chicago crime syndicate in its perverse history of depravity.

The naked body of the 300-pound "juice man" for Mob loan sharks was found festering in the oven-like trunk of his own Cadillac, parked in the lower level of Wacker Drive between Franklin and Wells streets in the summer heat.

Patrolman George Petyo, who was cruising the lower level on the night of Aug. 11, 1961, noticed the two-tone green 1957 Caddy with a flat tire, and stopped to investigate. As Petyo approached the auto he nearly gagged at the overpowering odor that hung around it like an aura of death. Petyo called his sergeant, John Costas, who took one whiff and agreed that someone was using the Cadillac as a mausoleum.

Holding handkerchiefs over their faces, they circled the car, which proved to be unlocked. Whoever had driven it to Lower Wacker had conveniently left the keys in the ignition. Costas opened the door on the driver's side, leaned in, pulled the keys, and went back and unlocked the trunk.

Costas and Petyo had expected to find a body when they raised the lid, but they were hardly prepared for the sight that greeted them—300 pounds of stinking, bleeding, burned, cut, bruised, and beaten feces-covered human meat. There were rope marks around the midsection and ankles, indicating the victim had been tied up before being tortured to death.

The car was registered to William Kearney of Cicero. Jackson, who often used that alias, lived at the Cicero address. Coroner Andrew J. Toman ordered the body removed to the Cook County morgue where fingerprints were taken to confirm the victim's identity.

Action Jackson, an ex-convict who had done jail time for robbery, assault, and rape, was a muscle man and "juice" loan collector for Sam DeStefano, West Side syndicate boss and "Mad Hatter" of the mob, and William "Willie Potatoes" Daddano, rackets boss for Kane, Du Page, and McHenry counties. He was known as "a sadist with an apologetic tone" in his role as a collector of overdue accounts for the underworld loan sharks.

At the time of his death he was under a federal indictment with three other men for hijacking a $70,000 interstate shipment of electrical appliances from the Burlington rail yards. Jackson was known to have demanded, and received, lawyers and cash from DeStefano and Daddano to fight the case. The matter was due up in court the following month.

A postmortem examination by Dr. Toman revealed that Jackson's chest was crushed, and that he had been shot in the knee, stabbed, beaten, and tortured mercilessly before he died.

His pubic hairs were singed and his testicles, which had swollen to the size of grapefruits, were cherry-red from having been burned with a blowtorch.

The excruciatingly painful damage to his genitals indicated a sexual motive, perhaps revenge. Authorities knew that a year earlier Jackson had broken into the flat of a jailed burglar, raped his wife, and committed other brutalities. A check of prison records, however, showed that the burglar was still behind bars and could not be considered a suspect in Jackson's murder.

Jackson was involved in so many illicit activities that police had no shortage of motives behind his death. They eventually narrowed them down to a handful:

1. His free-lance hijacking of trucks had incurred the wrath of syndicate authorized hijackers.

2. He had run afoul of mob bosses by shortchanging them on money he had collected from "juice" loans.

3. Fellow hoods feared Jackson might tell too much when he went on trial for the latest hijacking bust.

4. Burglars, whose loot he had disposed of, might have killed him because he cheated them.

5. He ignored syndicate warnings to stop stealing from other thieves.

6. None of the above.

The fact that the car with the body in the trunk was left in a public place, with the keys in the ignition, told authorities whoever killed Jackson wanted his tortured body to be found, as a lesson to others.

One underworld informant told police the murder took place in the basement of Mad Sam DeStefano's home at 1656 North Sayre Avenue, on Chicago's West Side. Other sources, however, said it happened in the basement of a building owned by Sam's brother, Mario.

It was quite by accident that federal authorities heard the awful truth of how Jackson met his demise. In February 1962, FBI agents were tuned in to a bug that had been planted in a Florida home rented by Chicago mobster Jackie "The Lackey" Cerone. As the agents eavesdropped, Cerone, Fiore "FiFi" Buccieri, and several of their underworld cohorts regaled one another with lighthearted stories about some of the more memorable murders they had been in on.

Buccieri soon got around to Action Jackson. He said Jackson, who was suspected of being a federal informant, was taken to the basement of a Mob-owned building on Chicago's West Side and tied hand and foot. "Then we decided to have a little fun with the son of a bitch."

The "fun," as Buccieri described it, consisted of hoisting the ponderous juice man up onto a meat hook, beating him with a baseball bat, and jabbing him with an ice pick as he bellowed in pain. Then, to increase the "fun," Jackson's tormenters pulled off his pants, shot him in one of his knees, and applied a fiery blowtorch to his testicles.

But the "fun" wasn't over yet. Someone produced an electric cattle prod. They poured water on it, shoved it up Jackson's rectum, and turned on the juice. Jackson, who was barely conscious, writhed and quivered on the hook as he lost control of his bowels. "Boy, did he stink!" Buccieri guffawed.

Jackson remained suspended on the hook for two days before he finally died. His torturers busied themselves taking pictures of his mutilated body, to be kept on file as a reminder to others what can happen to any misguided insider who might decide to talk to the feds. Afterwards his body was hefted into the trunk of his car and transported downtown, where it rotted in the August heat for four days before the passing patrol officer was attracted by the sickening stench.

That was the sad part, according to Buccieri. "I was sorry the big slob died so soon."

UPDATE

Years later federal authorities were filled in on the details of Jackson's torture-murder by Charles "Chuck" Crimaldi, a mob hit man in the employ of Sam DeStefano. Crimaldi had been granted immunity from prosecution for giving information in another murder, and threw in the Jackson killing as a gesture of his sincerity.

"Action was supposedly meeting with government agents. He had gotten nailed on a hijacking beef, and he was going to give them information. He was going to sacrifice a few people," Crimaldi explained. He went on to say that Lou Fazio, a convicted murderer, had seen Jackson meeting with federal agents in a Milwaukee restaurant and passed the information on to DeStefano.

"So Sam set Jackson up to go to Sam's house one night. When Jackson got there, Sam wasn't home. His wife, Anita, told Action that Sam would be home later and asked if he was hungry. He said he hadn't eaten all day, so Anita cooked him a steak and gave him a real nice dinner," Crimaldi continued. He said DeStefano later telephoned his home, and told Jackson to meet him at his brother Mario's restaurant, where he was playing cards. "Then Action got whacked!"

Crimaldi said Jackson was "whacked" in the basement by "Sam and Mario and two other people" whom he did not name. "He was put on a block and tackle and hoisted on a meat hook. They used an ice pick and a cattle prod and a blow torch. They shot him, and they beat him with a baseball bat. Then they dumped him in the trunk of his car and he was taken to the lower level of Wacker Drive with a tow truck."

All of which proved that Sam DeStefano wasn't such a bad guy after all. He did see to it that his obedient wife cooked up a hearty meal for the condemned man, didn't he?

THE MADMAN OF THE MAFIA

Sam DeStefano was a definite embarrassment to organized crime. He was never tried for Action Jackson's brutal murder, but the winds of justice caught up with him just the same.

FBI Agent William F. Roemer, Jr., called him "the worst torture-murderer in the history of Chicago . . . a sadistic, arrogant, swaggering thug of the worst order."

He even had a torture chamber in the basement of his home on Sayre Avenue, in a quiet residential neighborhood on the city's West Side. Among the unsuspecting who visited DeStefano's basement and never came out alive was Artie Adler, a local restaurant owner, who had been a witness before a federal grand jury investigating the mob. Adler's naked, frozen body was found clogging a sewer near DeStefano's home in the spring of 1959.

Roemer, who called at the DeStefano home to accuse Sam to his face of being Adler's killer, said Mad Sam met him at the door in his pajamas, "fly open, his dingus hanging out."

The two sat down over coffee as DeStefano swore "to God above" that he had nothing to do with Adler's death. The FBI man later learned that DeStefano had peed in his coffee.

On another occasion, DeStefano and his brother, Mario, literally exacted the proverbial "pound of flesh" from an unfortunate borrower who didn't pay back.

According to Sam's paid triggerman, Charles "Chuck" Crimaldi, who later flipped (turned government informant), Sam DeStefano received Mob Boss Sam "Momo" Giancana's blessing to do away with Leo Foreman, who owed DeStefano $5,000. Foreman's mutilated body was found in the trunk of his own car on Nov. 18, 1963.

Crimaldi said the forty-two-year-old Foreman, a loan collector for the mob, was lured to the basement bomb shelter of Mario's home in suburban Westchester on the pretense he would be given a batch of stolen diamonds to fence. Crimaldi and Anthony "Tony" Spilotro, another mob gunsel, were lying in wait for him.

"When he walked in Mario pulled a gun, I pulled my gun. We fired. Tony was in there too, and he fired. We fired together," Crimaldi related. "Then Mario took a knife and cut Leo's belt and took his gun and holster off, and pulled his pants down. Mario stabbed him a few times and Tony kicked him and I kicked him. Leo kept moaning and I asked Mario, 'Why can't we put a bullet behind his ear and get him out of his misery?'"

At that point Sam DeStefano, attired in pajamas, walked in, pressed a gun to Foreman's genital area and threatened to blow his testicles off. Foreman, who had affectionately known Sam DeStefano as "Uncle," pleaded, "Please, Unc. Oh, my God. Please Unc . . ." The pleas worked. Instead of shooting Foreman in the groin, Sam rolled him over with his foot and shot him in the buttocks.

"Then Tony stabbed him a few times. Mario stabbed him a few times, and Leo kind of stopped moving," Crimaldi continued. "Mario took a knife and cut some flesh from his arm . . . He just gouged a piece of flesh out."

"I told you I'd get you for this," Crimaldi quoted Sam as gloating while his brother carved out the pound of flesh. As the killers prepared to carry Foreman's body out and dump it into the trunk of his car, they looked down at the dead man and noticed a smile on his face. "Look at him. He's laughing at us," Sam declared.

There once was a third DeStefano brother, Michael, but Sam killed him, too. Michael, a.k.a. Buster, was a drug addict, and Sam wouldn't stand for that. After all, he had his principles.

Detective Bernie Brown was working narcotics out of the old Maxwell Street station (the one used on the "Hill Street Blues" TV show), when an anonymous caller said there was a dead man in a car at Laflin and Flournoy streets. The location was a block from the DeStefano family home, and across the street from an elementary school.

"I went over there with other detectives and we pried up the trunk lid. There was this guy lying in the trunk, all dressed up in a shirt and tie. His head was resting on a pillow. And there was something else—somebody had given him a bath. Under the clothing he was still wet. Oh, yeah. He'd also been shot," Brown recalled. "I recognized him on sight as Sam's brother, Buster. He had only recently gotten out of the government hospital at Lexington, and before that I had talked to him."

Moments after police popped open the trunk and found Buster laid out within, Sam DeStefano himself walked up and announced that he wanted to view the body.

"So we let him," Brown said. "Then he just walked away. He never said, 'Oh, my God, that's my brother,' or gave any hint that he was shocked. That told me he probably killed him. I figure two guys had to be in on it to give him a bath and dress him up and all. It had to be a family affair."

Police later learned that Sam was concerned that Buster might get high on drugs and blab family secrets. After killing his brother, Sam bathed him to "cleanse his soul" of all impurities.

DeStefano's antics were fast becoming legendary, and the local Mafia didn't need all the attention he was generating.

Acting as his own attorney, he once appeared in court

wearing pajamas and shouting through a bull horn. When he lost his case he sent a funeral wreath to the judge. When not haranguing police, politicians, his own lawyer, or fellow mobsters, he often telephoned the downtown newspapers and harangued the press. Woe be unto the unfortunate city desk man who picked up the phone and discovered he had Mad Sam on the other end of the line. The conversation would begin with four-letter words and quickly blossom into four-syllable expletives.

The quickest way to get him off the line was to lay the phone down, let him rave his brains out, and then say, "Thanks for calling."

The bizarre madness that was Sam DeStefano ended on April 14, 1973. At 10:30 that morning neighbors in the 1600 block of North Sayre Avenue heard two bangs that sounded like a car backfiring. They were used to such noises coming from the DeStefano property, and didn't even look up. If you lived around Sam DeStefano you soon learned to mind your own goddam business.

A half hour later Detectives Thomas Spanos and James Turney of the Shakespeare District burglary unit stopped by to talk to DeStefano about an attempted break-in at his home a week earlier.

A business associate of Sam's, who was supposed to meet him at 11:00 A.M., was standing in the driveway. "Sam's been killed," he yelled, pointing to the open garage door.

Sam had been lying dead on the concrete floor for a half hour, in full view of the entire neighborhood, except nobody bothered to look. He had only one arm. His left arm had been ripped off just below the shoulder by a shotgun blast. Another blast caught him right in the heart, if he had one, and knocked him backward with such force that his eyeglasses flew off. He was sixty-four years old.

Who killed Sam DeStefano? "He had a bottomless pit of enemies who would have waited years to get him, if necessary," said one investigator, who really didn't care, just as long as the job was done.

Police learned that Mad Sam had apparently been the victim of a gangland double cross. According to underworld informants, DeStefano was waiting in the garage for two henchmen to join him, so they could go out and slip the bump to Chuck Crimaldi, to keep him from testifying at Sam's upcoming trial for killing Leo Foreman.

DeStefano was attired in a zipper-jacket and slacks when he died. "Sam was dressed for a hit," an informant told Chief of Detectives John Killackey. "He was waiting to be picked up, and then he and the guys who were supposed to pick him up were going to knock off Crimaldi. Only they whacked Sam instead."

UPDATE

They can't prove it, but police think one of DeStefano's killers was Richard Cain, the rogue cop turned gangster. Cain, known to have been a messenger for Momo Giancana, was seen in Chicago a week before Mad Sam was murdered. He dropped from sight immediately afterward, and didn't come back to Chicago until the Christmas holidays. And that's when he found himself looking down the barrel of somebody else's shotgun from the wrong end—just as it went off.

ADIOS, GODFATHER

Salvatore (Sam) "Momo" Giancana has been described as the leading crime figure in Chicago since Alphonse Capone. The major difference between the two was that Capone died of syphilis of the brain, and Giancana succumbed to lead in the head.

During Giancana's reign as boss of all bosses of the Chicago crime syndicate from 1957 to 1966 there were seventy-nine mob murders, all of which needed his malevolent nod of approval. Not that he wasn't involved in more than that. He was indicted for his first killing at the age of eighteen, and was the subject of countless homicide investigations during most of his sixty-seven years, including three before he reached the age of twenty. He was rejected for military service during World War II as a psychopath.

All this qualified him as a leader of men. The thing the rest of the outfit didn't appreciate about Giancana was that he failed to keep the traditionally low profile.

He liked to travel with the show biz crowd, had his picture in the papers with his girlfriend, Phyllis McGuire, and hobnobbed with Frank Sinatra's "Rat Pack." What he didn't know was what some of them said behind his back. Actor Peter Lawford referred to him as "an awful guy with a gargoyle face and weasel nose."

Sinatra absolutely fawned over the real life Godfather, and once exchanged rings with him. Author Kitty Kelley, in *His Way: The Unauthorized Biography of Frank Sinatra*, quotes Joseph Shimon in describing a meeting between Frank and Momo at the bar in the Fontainebleau. Sinatra had phoned Giancana's room twenty times, and Sam finally slipped on the ring Frank had given him and went downstairs to see what he wanted:

"I was sitting next to Sam when Sinatra walked over. 'I can't even keep up with you,' Sinatra said. 'Where you been keeping yourself?'

"Sam said, 'Look, I'm busy. You know I got to keep moving around.'

"Frank looked down at Sam's hand. 'I see you're wearing the ring.' Sam said he always wore it.

"'Oh, no, you don't,' said Sinatra, 'I heard you hadn't been wearing the ring. I heard you never wore it.'

"He was talking like some frustrated little girl with a broken heart. Finally, I couldn't help it. I said, 'What is this? Are you two bastards queer for each other or what?' Sam fell off his chair laughing, but Sinatra was very embarrassed and turned his back on me."

Sinatra sued to keep Kelley's book out of print, but lost. Giancana, on the other hand, didn't care what anybody wrote about him, as long as they spelled his name right—which wasn't always easy.

Born Gilormo Giangono and baptised Momo Salvatore Giangono, he was variously known as Momo, Moe, The Cigar, Mooney, Sam Mooney, Sam Moonie, J. Mooney, Sam Gincani, Giancaco, Giacana, Gianenna, Gianeana, Giancane, Gincanna, Gincanni, Ginncana, Giancano, Giancona, Albert Mancuso, Albert Masusco, Michael Mancuso, G. Stanley, P. Rosie, Sam Flood, and Sam Volpe.

Whoever he was, he was attracting too much attention to be ignored. In 1965 Giancana, who earlier had taken the Fifth thirty-five times before the McClellan Senate Rackets Committee, was hailed before a federal grand jury in Chicago. He refused to answer any questions, even under a grant of immunity, and was slapped into Cook County Jail for contempt of court until he decided to change his mind. True to the Mafia's code of silence, he languished in his cell for one full year.

Upon his release in 1966 Giancana, his power greatly diminished, went into self-imposed exile in Mexico until the government heat died down. He hardly led the life of a recluse, however. He commuted between two posh villas in Cuernavaca and a lavish penthouse in Mexico City, spending pesos like they were going out of style. Rogue cop Richard Cain, former chief investigator for the Cook County Sheriff, turned up South of the Border shortly thereafter as Sam's chauffeur and personal henchman. Cain was shotgunned to death in 1973 while back in Chicago on a presumed mission for Momo.

Giancana was deported from Mexico the following year and returned to Chicago, where he set out to regain his former standing in the mob. The new regime, headed by Joseph "Doves" Aiuppa, did not look with enthusiasm on Giancana's return. Fearing they might have a loose cannon on their hands, they put out a contract on their onetime chief.

Word that Momo had been tagged for a bump filtered down to the feds, and they put him under surveillance. Not that anyone would go into mourning if something happened to the "guy with the gargoyle face and the weasel nose."

But wouldn't it be nice, just once, to catch someone in the act of carrying out a gangland hit?

On June 19, 1975, Giancana, suffering from blood clots and barely able to walk, stepped feebly off a plane from Houston, where he had gone for medical treatment. If the mob was going to make an example of him, it had better be soon, before nature took its course.

That night Giancana had three visitors to his home at 1147 South Wenonah Avenue in Oak Park. Detectives Howard McBride and Kenneth Hauser of the police Organized Crime Unit's intelligence division, who had the home under surveillance, identified the callers as mobster Charles "Chuckie" English, attorney Jerome DePalma, who was Giancana's son-in-law, and Dominick "Butch" Blasi, who had replaced Cain as Giancana's chauffeur, gofer, and bodyguard.

The trio left around ten o'clock. Blasi returned a short time later, presumably to tuck his boss in for the night. After waiting a reasonable length of time, McBride and Hauser left their unmarked car and circled Giancana's house to make sure there was no further activity. As they walked around the rear of the building they heard several muffled pops.

"Sounds like someone's popping open a couple cans of beer," McBride commented. "The house is dark as a graveyard. Let's call it a night." They hiked back to their car and returned to their base to make out their report.

What they didn't know was that Giancana, a widower, had decided to make himself a late night snack. He had gone down to a basement kitchen, turned on the stove, and set about preparing a dish of sausage and spinach.

A caretaker found Momo lying dead on the basement floor when he went to check on him at midnight. He had been shot once in the back of the head, and six more times in the mouth and chin as he fell, landing on his back. Six .22-caliber shell casings were on the floor around the body.

Police turned off the gas flame on the stove. The sausages in the pan were not burned, however, indicating the shooting had taken place only a short time earlier. McBride, who is now retired and living in Door County, Wisconsin, thinks he and his partner actually heard the fatal shots, which they mistook for beer cans being popped open.

Two months later, on August 19, the murder weapon—a .22-caliber automatic pistol with a silencer—was found in a ditch in River Forest. Agents of the Treasury Department's Bureau of Alcohol, Tobacco and Firearms subsequently traced the weapon to two Chicago police officers who had been manufacturing and selling illegal silencers for the underworld.

In trying to establish a motive for the slaying, police came up with the several that seemed logical: Momo wanted his old boss job back, and had refused to share profits of his foreign operations, including Europe and Cuba, with the rest of the mob; old and sick, the mob was afraid he might go soft in the head and start spilling their secrets; he was killed to keep him from being called before a congressional committee, about to open hearings into Giancana's dealings with the CIA in an abortive plot to assassinate Fidel Castro; he was fooling around with other hoods' wives.

Giancana could have been killed for any or all of the reasons listed above. The best guess was that the mob feared the short-tempered Momo, miffed at being dethroned, might start blabbing to the feds. He was the highest ranking Chicago mobster ever executed by his own kind. It was a hit the killers wanted the world to see. A lesson to everyone in the mob to "know your place."

UPDATE

In an affidavit filed in federal court in Kansas City on Jan. 21, 1986, FBI agents accused Giancana's successor, Aiuppa, of "recommending" the ex-Godfather's execution. Aiuppa, never charged in the Giancana killing, was sentenced to a federal prison instead for conspiring to secretly own and steal $2 million from the Stardust Casino in Las Vegas.

Detective McBride, who was outside Giancana's home that night, is "absolutely convinced" that the actual executioner was Momo's trusted friend and compadre, Chuckie English, who had called at the house to welcome Giancana back. Federal agents, on the other hand, lean toward Blasi as the likely killer.

All of which means that the brazen execution was carried off so swiftly and efficiently, right under the noses of the law, that to this day nobody in authority can declare for certain who pulled the trigger, or why.

ENGLISH WASN'T ENGLISH ANY MORE

Charles "Chuckie" English (nee Inglese), who had been Momo Giancana's second in command, was the Mob overseer of all gambling operations in the North Side Twenty-Ninth Ward, as well as handbook, vending machines, and loan sharking in Cicero.

He had an arrest record going back to 1933 for robbery, extortion, highjacking and conspiracy, loan sharking, counterfeiting phonograph record trademarks, and murder.

He fell out of favor with Mob leaders after Giancana's sudden demise, and was stripped of his ownership of Lormar Distributing, a jukebox and record company at 2311 North Western Avenue. The reason, according to one group of Chicago police mob watchers, was his refusal to "set up" Giancana for the bump. This, of course, contradicts other police, who are convinced it was English who acted as executioner.

English reportedly went into semiretirement and moved to Florida, leaving behind $2,090 in delinquent real estate taxes on his home in River Forest. Unfortunately for him he returned to Chicago from time to time to keep up his old contacts.

On Feb. 9, 1985, as the seventy-year-old English prepared to get into a Cadillac in the parking lot of Horwath's Restaurant at 1850 North Harlem Avenue in Elmwood Park, two men wearing ski masks walked up and shot him between the eyes.

UPDATE

English's slayers were never identified. Former FBI Agent William F. Roemer, Jr., said his sources told him that "Chuckie was murdered for continuing to bad mouth the successors to his buddy, Giancana, even after repeated warnings." Police learned that several months before his murder he had switched allegiance from Joseph "Joey the Clown" Lombardo to Joseph "Joe Nagaul" Ferriola, and he thus could have become the victim of a power struggle between the two mob factions.

Unless, of course, you subscribe to the theory that English killed Giancana, in which case, perhaps, one of Momo's loyal subjects evened the score.

THE MAN WHO KNEW TOO MUCH

Mothers tell their children, "If you play with fire, you might get burned." It was a warning that Allen Dorfman failed to heed in his adult years. The multimillionaire Chicago insurance magnate and union financial wizard made the fatal mistake of playing footsie with the mob.

Danger was no stranger to Dorfman. He served with valor in the Marine Corps during World War II, where he won the Purple Heart medal for wounds suffered in combat. In those days, when a man's only thought was staying alive until tomorrow, he never dreamed that his future would lie in insurance.

Upon returning from the military service Dorfman, a handsome, well-built man, landed a $4,000-a-year job as a physical education instructor at the University of Illinois' branch at Navy Pier. He might still be doing calisthenics were it not for the fact that his stepfather, Paul "Red" Dorfman, president of the Chicago Waste Handlers Union, had greater things in mind for his wife's son from a previous marriage.

Red Dorfman, a onetime prizefighter with underworld cronies, struck a deal with Jimmy Hoffa, the ambitious head of the Teamsters Union in Michigan, who was casting around for ways to expand his base of power. "I can get you an 'in' with the 'boys' if you'll throw some union insurance business my son's way," he told Hoffa. Hoffa agreed, and Red Dorfman introduced him to mob boss Tony Accardo and other crime syndicate figures. Allen dutifully quit his PT job and set up the Union Insurance Agency. In 1950 Hoffa handed him his first lucrative contract for Teamster insurance. Within five years Allen was a millionaire.

As Hoffa rose in power to take the reins of the massive International Brotherhood of Teamsters coast-to-coast, Dorfman ascended with him and began to wield tremendous influence over the union's financial affairs. He and Hoffa hit the jackpot when they combined the pension and welfare funds of dozens of local unions to create the giant Central States Pension Fund and the Central States Health and Welfare Fund. It was a deal through which Dorfman, serving as consultant to the funds, would reap millions.

The suave, suntanned Dorfman, meanwhile, was actually leading two lives. While wheeling and dealing with Hoffa and his sleazy underworld sidekicks on one hand, he was establishing himself as a benevolent philanthropist on the other. There were awards and plaques and testimonials in his honor. In 1977 the Little City Foundation for the retarded in Palatine honored him as its "Man of the Year" at a gala banquet where he was hailed by Chicago Mayor Michael Bilandic and scores of business and civic leaders.

Dorfman and his wife, Lynn, lived the lifestyle of the rich, without being famous. They shuttled between a $750,000 home in the northern Chicago suburb of Riverwoods, a plush condo in Miami, a $350,000 home at the swank La Costa Hotel and Country Club in Southern California, and their 167-acre Jack O'Lantern lodge and horse farm at Eagle River, Wisconsin.

With help from his Teamster properties, Dorfman's financial empire grew like Topsy, until he controlled fourteen companies ranging from the giant Amalgamated Insurance Agency Services in Chicago to an apartment complex in Las Vegas and a nursery in Florida.

But Dorfman's highly profitable relationship with Hoffa was also his downfall. The two of them were indicted in 1964 for jury tampering in Tennessee. Dorfman got off, but Hoffa got a guilty verdict. In 1971 Dorfman served nine months in prison after being convicted of accepting a $55,000 kickback to arrange a loan from the Teamsters pension fund.

Three years later Dorfman was indicted for fraud in connection with another loan from the $4.5 billion fund, along with bail bondsman Irwin Weiner and crime syndicate figures Anthony Spilotro and Joseph "Joey the Clown" Lombardo. Spilotro, the Chicago mob's overseer in Las Vegas, was known as a frequent house guest of Dorfman's whenever he came back to the Windy City for instructions. Lombardo, according to FBI Agent Peter Wacks, was the mob's liaison man with the Teamsters. "His most important assignment as a member of the Chicago outfit was to ensure that Allen Dorfman carried out La Cosa Nostra's wishes concerning pension fund matters," Wacks declared in an affidavit filed in U.S. District Court in Chicago on March 22, 1990.

As to the charges against Dorfman and his codefendants, all were acquitted after the government's star witness, Daniel Seifert, was shot to death by four gunmen at his place of business in suburban Bensenville.

Dorfman's "Chinaman," Hoffa, dropped from sight the following year. His body was never found. There has been no shortage of rumors over the past fifteen years as to Hoffa's fate, including the widely accepted suggestion that he was driven down to the Everglades and fed to the alligators. Dorfman quickly fell in tight with Hoffa's ultimate successor, Roy Williams.

They were so tight, in fact, that they were indicted together, along with Lombardo and Spilotro, for conspiring to bribe U.S. Senator Howard Cannon of Nevada to scuttle legislation to deregulate the trucking industry. This time the four defendants were convicted, and Dorfman, who had just turned sixty, found himself staring a possible 110-year prison sentence in the face.

There were rumors among members of the mob that Dorfman couldn't sit out another prison sentence and might 'flip'—turn government informer—in exchange for leniency. This could be dangerous. Dorfman for years had been privy to the mob's innermost secrets. He even knew, federal authorities believed, what happened to Hoffa.

On Thursday, Jan. 20, 1983—while free on bond awaiting sentencing—Dorfman slid behind the wheel of his Cadillac Fleetwood Brougham and drove over to Tessy's Restaurant in north suburban Lincolnwood, to keep a luncheon date with his old pal, Irv Weiner. As they walked single file between two cars in the restaurant parking lot, with Weiner in the lead, they were accosted by two men, one of whom raised a pistol and pumped eight bullets into the back of Dorfman's head.

It was a classic gangland execution—number 1,081 in Chicago's turbulent history of organized crime. When Lincolnwood Patrol Officer John Janecek arrived moments later Dorfman lay dead between two parked cars, his $1,000 suit and camel's hair coat covered with blood, and his cheeks still rosy from the winter cold. He had $1,000 in cash in his pants pocket.

Several witnesses, who had seen the gunman and his accomplice run from the scene and jump into a waiting car, described the killer as a tall heavyset man with a beard. Little else could be seen of the slayer, who was bundled up due to the cold.

Weiner, of course, didn't see anything. How the hit men knew to be waiting for Dorfman in the restaurant parking lot was a mystery to him. "We had planned to go somewhere else, but it was too crowded, and decided to come here on the spur of the moment," he explained.

Since Dorfman was a convicted federal prisoner, the FBI put an unprecedented seventy-five agents on the case, the largest number ever assigned to a gangland assassination in Chicago. And there was no question that it was a gangland killing. "It's part and parcel of life in the United States that association with the Cosa Nostra often leads to a sudden death," observed Chicago FBI Chief Edward D. Hegarty.

"Allen Dorfman was an absolute encyclopedia of knowledge about the crime syndicate. He could have given up the whole Chicago organized crime hierarchy and their political cronies on a platter. He knew that much," added Patrick Healy, executive director of the Chicago Crime Commission.

Was Dorfman's killer ever brought before the bar of justice? Are you kidding? "We haven't had a very good success rate over the last sixty years solving gangland killings," noted Chicago Police Superintendent Richard Brzeczek, who assigned his top investigators to work with FBI agents and Lincolnwood police on the case.

Healy was even less optimistic. "I'd say the chances are zilch," he said. "Approval for a hit like this one—a hit that they knew would generate tremendous publicity—had to come from the top [of the mob]. More likely than not the killer and his accomplices were from out of town, and are long gone by now."

The federal investigation into Dorfman's death led to an ex-con from Chicago, Raymond P. Spencer, who had been living in Coral Springs, Florida.

FBI agents established that Spencer had flown up from Florida and was definitely in Lincolnwood on the day of the ambush. Spencer, who stood six feet one inch tall, weighed 260 pounds and had a beard, furnished an alibi for his whereabouts at the time of the shooting, however. Several of his friends, all known mobsters, said, "Ray was with us."

Dorfman used to like to tell friends. "My dad always told me, when you're going up the ladder, remember who's coming up behind you. Because if you ever fall down, he'll be waiting for you."

During that frigid January lunch hour in 1983, in Tessy's parking lot, somebody was.

UPDATE

Raymond Spencer, the prime suspect in the Dorfman slaying, was found dead of mysterious causes on Aug. 31, 1984, in his Coral Springs apartment. He was forty-four.

Joseph "Pops" Panczko, an ex-convict and career thief who was paroled from federal prison in January 1990, told the authors that it was common knowledge in the underworld that Spencer was, indeed, Dorfman's executioner. "Ray was poisoned," Panczko related. "The mob, they wanted to shut Ray up because he knew too much. So they fed Ray an Italian beef sandwich spread with rat poison and Ray croaked."

PLANTED IN AN INDIANA CORNFIELD

Allen Dorfman's codefendant in various courtroom episodes, forty-eight-year-old Anthony Spilotro, never made it to prison for his role in bribing the United States senator either. It would have been better for him if he had. But he remained free through the high priced legal hocus-pocus that keeps a lot of bad guys out on the street after they've been arrested, tried, and convicted in a court of law.

Spilotro, meanwhile, ran afoul of authorities in Las Vegas, where he was employed since 1971 as overseer of the Chicago crime syndicate's illicit operations. A federal grand jury in 1986 indicted him on racketeering charges in connection with directing a Las Vegas burglary ring. This put him in hot water with the mob bosses back home, who complained that he had become so engrossed in preparing for his trial that he was letting the once lucrative Nevada mob operations go to pot. Spilotro, while free on bond, received federal court permission to fly back to Chicago to visit his mother before his trial, scheduled for June 30 (although the real reason was to try to square things with his bosses).

He had risen through the mob ranks as a protege of crime chief Joseph "Doves" Aiuppa, and once bragged to an FBI agent, "I'm gonna be the next capo [boss], just you wait and see." But when Aiuppa landed in the "joint" for skimming untaxed profits from Las Vegas casinos and Joseph Ferriola took over the "Outfit," Spilotro's position became a bit sphincter-tightening to say the least. In 1971, according to federal authorities, Spilotro had killed Ferriola's brother-in-law, Sam "Sambo" Cesaro on orders of imprisoned mob boss Felix "Milwaukee Phil" Alderisio, because Sambo had stolen Milwaukee Phil's girlfriend.

Back in Chicago Spilotro huddled with his younger brother, Michael, who had his own problems. He was under indictment on federal extortion charges. Then, when Anthony set up a Saturday afternoon meet with the boys, Michael unfortunately decided to go along in case Tony needed moral support.

The brothers were last seen driving away from Michael's Oak Park home in his 1986 Lincoln on June 14. They had told Michael's wife, Ann, "If we're not back by nine o'clock, we're in big trouble." The car was found abandoned two days later in a motel parking lot near O'Hare International Airport in Schiller Park. Police popped open the trunk, expecting to find you-know-who, but were surprised to discover nothing but the spare tire.

Where were Anthony and Michael?

On Sunday afternoon, June 22, farmer Michael Kinz was spreading weed-killing chemicals over the cornfield he leased on the edge of the 12,000-acre Willow Slough wildlife preserve in Newton County, Indiana, about fifty miles south of Chicago. Strange. As Kinz rounded the southwest corner of the field he noted markings on the ground as though something had been dragged from the nearby road, and freshly turned soil that had not yet dried to assume the color of the dirt around it.

Kinz phoned his friend Dick Hudson, a biologist for the Indiana Fish and Wildlife Division. "Dick, it looks like maybe some poacher killed a deer out of season and buried the remains on my property after gutting it and taking off the edible meat," he suggested. "I thought you might want to come over and take a look."

Hudson and a friend, Deland Szczepanski, drove to the scene, just off County Road 100 North about two miles east of the Indiana-Illinois state line. They arrived at 6:30 P.M., got a pair of shovels out of the trunk, and started digging into the wet, sandy soil. About three feet below the surface Hudson's shovel met some resistance, and he carefully scooped the sand away to expose a human midsection. Aghast, he turned to Szczepanski and said, "Stop digging Del, this isn't a deer, it's a person. We'd better call the sheriff."

Newton County Sheriff Charles "Pat" Mullen pulled up with a team of deputies a short time later and continued the dig. Sure enough, they unearthed the partly decomposed body of a middle-aged man, clad only in his undershorts. As they were pulling the corpse out of the hole they noted that the surrounding soil was only loosely packed. A little more digging produced a second body, buried under the first. It, too, was a white male, also in his underwear.

Mullen sealed off the cornfield gravesite and notified state and federal authorities. Agent E. Michael Kahoe, head of the Gary FBI office, was among the first federal officials to arrive. FBI agents working under his direction scooped up sandy soil around the grave to be analyzed at a laboratory for any "trace evidence" that might have been dropped by whoever disposed of the bodies.

On Monday the two corpses were taken to Indianapolis, where autopsies were performed by Dr. John Pless, director of forensic pathology at Indiana University. He advised Dr. David Dennis, Newton County coroner, that fluid in the victims' lungs and other evidence indicated the two men may have been buried alive.

Before being thrown into the grave they had been severely beaten about the head, neck, and chest, causing them to bleed profusely. But it wasn't the beatings that killed them. They had literally gagged to death on their own blood while in a state of unconsciousness, apparently as the dirt was being shoveled back onto them.

"Death was due to asphyxiation," Pless told Dennis. "But both of them have defensive wounds on their hands and arms, as though they tried to shield themselves while being kicked and beaten."

Authorities had been looking for the missing Spilotro brothers for a week, and Edward Hegarty, agent in charge of the Chicago FBI office, had a pretty good idea now where they were. He obtained their dental charts from yet another brother, Dr. Patrick Spilotro, a dentist, and passed them on to the coroner—also a dentist—who was able to make positive identification.

Hegarty said there was little doubt that the Spilotros had been killed by their crime syndicate cronies. Unlike the public execution of Dorfman, which was interpreted as a warning to others facing jail not to tell what they knew, it appeared that the bodies of Anthony and Michael Spilotro were never intended to be found.

"They wanted this to be just like Hoffa," Hegarty said. "The disposal was botched in that the grave was dug inside a newly planted cornfield. The shoots of corn weren't high enough to hide the site."

A car stolen on Chicago's South Side on June 15, the day after the brothers disappeared, had been found burning the following day on the county road near the gravesite. Hegarty said the auto had apparently been used to transport the victims to what their abductors had figured would be their final resting place.

The mob often burns cars used in killings to prevent crime lab technicians from uncovering microscopic but incriminating fibers, hairs, or other trace evidence.

The burial site was about twelve miles east of St. Anne, Illinois, where imprisoned mob boss Aiuppa once had a hunting club frequented by underworld figures driving down from Chicago. This fact did not escape FBI agents, who speculated that the Willow Slough dumping ground might have been chosen by someone familiar with the area. The name of Albert "Caesar" Tocco came to mind in particular. Tocco, a protege of Ferriola, was known to frequent the area, and was suspected of using western Indiana chop-shops to dismantle stolen cars before selling the parts.

Newton County, only an hour from Chicago by expressway, had become a disposal station for murder victims in recent years. Since 1980 no less than ten bodies had been found discarded in ditches, rivers, and cornfields. "There's liable to be many more we haven't found," remarked Sheriff Mullen, a twenty-seven-year police veteran. "They blast them, bring them down here, throw them out, and bury them."

Authorities suspected that Anthony Spilotro was slain because he had allowed the Las Vegas operation to fall apart, while at the same time his organization had become honey-combed with federal informers. Furthermore, he'd skimmed some $10 million from casino, extortion, and fencing operations and had hidden it for his own use. Michael, they theorized, had to be removed simply because he made the mistake of being with his brother at the wrong time.

A second theory was that Anthony's death could have been a revenge killing by friends or relatives of someone he had caused to be murdered during his thirty-year rise in the Chicago mob. Authorities had implicated him in seven homicides over the years, and suspected his involvement in as many as twenty-five.

The bodies of the murder victims were returned to Chicago, meanwhile, where the Roman Catholic Archdiocese denied them a public church funeral because of their links to organized crime. They were buried in the family plot at Queen of Heaven Cemetery in west suburban Hillside after a brief private service in the cemetery chapel.

Police in Phoenix were watching developments in the Spilotro case with interest. They had a body on their hands, too, and were looking for another. Former Chicagoan Emil "Mal" Vaci, seventy-three, a close associate of Anthony Spilotro's in Vegas, had been found shot to death in a drainage ditch. Meanwhile an associate of both men, mob figure Jay

Vandermark, had disappeared from his Las Vegas home and was presumed dead. It looked like somebody was cleaning house.

While local police and the FBI investigated the Spilotro deaths, the murders sparked a bit of down-home Indiana humor. At summer festivals in the nearby towns of Kentland and Roseland, hucksters did a brisk business selling T-shirts emblazoned with two mounds of dirt among cornstalks, and the legend: "Spilotro Brothers Fertilizer—We Grow Corn Deeper in Newton County." And a deputy sheriff who was in on the shovel detail turned up wearing a baseball cap saying, "I dug up the Spilotro Brothers."

Meanwhile the Newton County Ambulance Service which had transported the bodies to Indianapolis for the autopsies billed Michael Spilotro's family $575 for the service. Brother Anthony had no known mailing address, so Ann Spilotro got stuck with the tab for the both of them.

UPDATE

About 300 years ago English dramatist William Congreve wrote in The Mourning Bride, "Heaven has no rage like love to hatred turned, Nor hell a fury like a woman scorned." It is doubtful that south suburban crime boss Albert "Caesar" Tocco ever read those lines, but he can sure tell you what they mean. Oh, boy, can he!

In the fall of 1989, while Tocco sat fuming behind bars in Chicago's Metropolitan Correctional Center, his raven-haired wife, Betty, a former lingerie model half his age, decided to let it all hang out. It was Albert, she told federal authorities, who headed the ill-fated Spilotro burial detail.

In an affidavit filed in U.S. District Court, FBI agents said Mrs. Tocco told of driving to the cornfield near Enos, Indiana, in the early morning hours of June 15, 1986, to pick up her husband, who had been on an all-night mission. Tocco, his clothing covered with sand and dirt, told her he had just buried the Spilotro brothers, and complained that he might have left his fingerprints on one of the shovels. He needed a lift back to Chicago because he'd gotten separated from the people he came down with and they drove back without him. The affidavit quoted Mrs. Tocco as identifying her husband's associates on the venture as Dominick Palermo, a Chicago Heights union official; Albert John Roviaro, a beverage distributor; and Nicholas Guzzino, a Tocco cohort.

After the bodies were found Betty said Albert flew into a panic, fearful that he would be killed by mob higher-ups for bungling what no one was ever supposed to find.

Another federal informant subsequently told authorities that the Spilotro brothers were actually stripped of their clothing and beaten in a Chinatown garage.

He said Tocco later boasted of the enjoyment he got out of kicking and punching the Spilotros before they were driven to Indiana and tossed, unconscious but still breathing, into the cornfield grave.

No one has ever been charged with the Spilotro murders. Federal authorities said they have all the time in the world to consider what action, if any, should be brought against the sixty-two-year-old Tocco.

On May 14, 1990, the sausage maker turned mobster, convicted of thirty-four counts of racketeering, extortion conspiracy, and tax fraud, was fined $2 million and sentenced to 200 years in prison.

HIT MAN WITH AN EMPTY GUN

John Fecarotta, who outlived the Spilotro brothers by three months, had not expected to die on the night he kept an appointment with several unidentified associates. In fact Fecarotta, a reputed mob assassin, had every reason to believe he was going out on a "hit." Strictly business. The only thing his companions didn't tell him was that *he* was the target. You can't trust anybody anymore.

Fecarotta, an ex-convict and longtime friend of Anthony Spilotro, had a police record going back to 1944 as a burglar and a collector for mob loan shark Fiore "Fifi" Buccieri. He owned no credit cards, and paid cash for everything. He drove a flashy Mercedes Benz and flaunted a stunning mistress while his wife drove a station wagon around west suburban Riverside where they made their home.

In 1985, after being ousted as business agent for the Chicago local of the Industrial Workers Union, he refused to testify before the President's Commission on Organized Crime which was investigating labor racketeering. When a federal judge ordered him to testify or go to jail for contempt, he checked into a Washington hospital with a sudden heart ailment.

James Harmon, executive director of the commission

and a former federal prosecutor in New York City, described Fecarotta as "an underboss of La Cosa Nostra in Chicago." The union's president, John Serpico, could not think of a single thing Fecarotta had done for the union during his seven years as business agent, while drawing a fat salary and driving a union car.

It was all too clear that he was a "ghost" employee using his union position as a cover for his underworld activities.

They included moonlighting as a mob assassin. In recent years Fecarotta had been questioned in at least two gangland killings and a major drug hijacking. Ken Eto, a mobster turned informant after an attempt on his life backfired, told authorities that Fecarotta had helped him set up the 1958 slaying of bolita operator Santiago Rosa Gonzales, who was resisting mob efforts to take over his gambling empire.

On Sunday night, Sept. 14, 1986, by all accounts, the fifty-eight-year-old Fecarotta went out on another hit—not realizing it was his own. Despite the late summer warm weather, he was wearing gloves so as not to leave any prints on the murder weapon, that would later be ditched. His own gun was tucked into the waistband of his trousers as a security measure. Never leave home without it.

Police sources said Fecarotta may have been led to believe that the intended victim was Al Brown, a bingo operator who ran a game out of a hall at 6050 West Belmont Avenue. Fecarotta drove to the scene with two other men in a stolen 1986 Buick Century.

The auto had been rigged as a hit car, with stolen license plates from another vehicle fore and aft—part of the sham to lure the unsuspecting victim to his death.

As the trio pulled up behind a building across the street from the bingo hall, one of his accomplices handed Fecarotta a .38-caliber revolver—the hit gun—with any incriminating identification removed. It was then and there that something went awry. Possibly Fecarotta, always a careful man, discovered that the would-be murder weapon did not have any bullets in it.

One of the men got off a quick shot, hitting Fecarotta in the stomach as he burst out of the car and split down the alley for the protection of the crowded bingo hall. The other two men were in hot pursuit, firing as they ran, to the astonishment of wide-eyed bingo players arriving to play their favorite game. Fecarotta, already bleeding from the belly wound, took three more slugs in the side, back, and right arm as he ran.

He made it right up to the door of the bingo parlor before one of his assailants caught up with him, grabbed him by the scruff of the neck, and put a final bullet into the back of his head. The killers then doubled back down the alley, where they jumped into a waiting car and sped off into the night.

Homicide Sergeant Lee Epplen, one of the first police officers at the scene, called the slaying "a classic hit." Fecarotta was still holding the empty .38 when he died. His regular gun was still tucked into his waistband.

Police found blood on the driver's seat of the stolen Buick from which Fecarotta had fled. The car was still parked behind the building across the street, its doors open, the lights turned on, and the motor running. Five rounds of live .38-caliber ammunition, apparently removed from the revolver before it was given to Fecarotta, were also found on the front seat of the car.

Elsewhere in the Buick police found a two-way radio and a package first thought to have been a dynamite bomb. On closer examination it turned out to be a bundle of road flares taped together. Sergeant Epplen surmised that the killers probably planned to burn the car after slaying Fecarotta, just as the Spilotro killers had done.

Witnesses, who got a clear look at the gunmen, told police the man who delivered the *coup de grace* to the back of Fecarotta's head was in his early or mid thirties, about five feet seven inches tall, and wore a black suit with a white shirt and white necktie. The second gunman was in his late thirties, five feet five inches tall, and wore dark clothing and a white shirt. They said the driver of the getaway car appeared to be in his late forties. But wait, other witnesses said the killer was much taller—six feet two, and was carrying a black jacket draped over his arm to hide the gun he used to shoot Fecarotta in the head. And, they said, he was in his late thirties. Other witnesses saw no second man. There was just one killer, they insisted.

So who were police looking for? A tall-short killer in his early or late thirties wearing a black suit while carrying a black jacket over his arm, with or without an accomplice. Good luck, detectives.

For the record, Fecarotta became Chicago's 1,091st gangland murder victim since authorities started keeping score after the end of World War I.

Citing the Spilotro slayings three months earlier—to the very day—Patrick Healy, executive director of the Chicago Crime Commission, attributed the killing to efforts by mob boss Joe Ferriola to "tighten up" control of the syndicate. "I see this homicide as but another move to put the Chicago house in order again," he said.

UPDATE

Investigators learned that about a year before he was gunned down, Fecarotta had confided to a federal agent that he had no known enemies "except my wife." "Who else?" he was asked. "I don't think I have too many enemies. If I do, I don't know them," he replied.

Fecarotta's wife was never a suspect in his assassination. But his comments confirmed the theory that he was killed by someone he knew. "The elaborate ruse used to lure him to his death was probably the only way he could have been killed," suggested Commander Earl Johnson, head of the Grand-Central Area detective unit, which investigated the slaying. "He was comfortable and with someone he trusted; so he never suspected that he was the intended victim."

Until it was too late.

NO DINNER FOR SIX, AT SEVEN

On Monday, Nov. 21, 1988, Philip "Philly" Goodman, a seventy-eight-year-old Las Vegas mob associate and onetime front man for the slain Anthony Spilotro, telephoned Myron & Phil's Steak, Seafood and Piano Bar at 3900 West Devon Avenue in north suburban Lincolnwood and made a 7:00 P.M. dinner reservation for a party of six.

The table was set and the head waiter was poised to direct Goodman and his party to their seats, but they never showed up. It was a case of rigor mortis, rather than bad manners, that prevented him from keeping the appointment.

At eleven o'clock Tuesday morning a maid in the Admiral Oasis Motel at 9353 Waukegan Road, Morton Grove, let herself into the room to make the bed, and found his body. There was so much blood that Morton Grove police, working under the direction of Deputy Chief George Incledon, first assumed that Goodman had been shot. An autopsy by the Cook County Medical Examiner's office, however, showed he had died of massive head injuries, including three fractures of the skull, inflicted by a blunt instrument.

"From the severity of the beating, it looks like someone was trying to send a message," Incledon said. "The motive sure wasn't robbery. He had seven $100 bills in his pocket, along with wads of $10s and $20s, plus an airline ticket back to Las Vegas." And there was more—$6,700 in cash found stuffed into a suitcase in the trunk of the rented car Goodman had parked outside.

Curiously, Goodman had checked into the motel at just about the same time he was supposed to have been dining with friends at Myron & Phil's. None of his friends showed up at the restaurant either, indicating they all knew the dinner had been called off. But why? And what had drawn Goodman to the Oasis at that particular time?

The state of rigor mortis indicated he had been murdered shortly after checking into the room for a one night stand. Yet the condition of the room showed no sign of a break-in or a struggle, indicating he had gone there at the last minute to meet someone he knew.

The names and phone numbers of 136 people were found in Goodman's address book in the motel room. Over the next few months police went down the list, checking out every one of the people they could locate. None could shed any light on the murder. Some of them, in fact, said they had never heard of Goodman and had no idea why he would have been carrying around their phone numbers.

Furthermore, none of the people on the list, including the victim's son and daughter in Chicago, had any plans to dine with Goodman on that fatal night.

The thrice divorced Goodman had spent most of his life on the periphery of the underworld, working as a bookie, oddsmaker, loan shark, and casino host at the Stardust in Las Vegas. He worked for North Side gambling boss Lenny Patrick in Chicago before moving to Las Vegas in the 1970s, and joining the underworld crew headed by Anthony Spilotro.

According to Preston Hubbs, chief of the Las Vegas Metro Police Intelligence Unit, Spilotro used Goodman as a front for several mob-run "legitimate" business operations in Nevada. Among them were a car rental agency and a travel bureau, both of which were suspected of laundering mob skim money from the casinos. Goodman's stature among the high rollers of the underworld took a sharp dive after Spilotro was dug up in the Indiana cornfield, however, and he returned to Chicago, either to explore new avenues of employment or perhaps to improve his relations with the outfit. In any event, the airline ticket to Vegas found in his pocket indicated he expected to go back out there.

FBI agents and Las Vegas police worked with Morton Grove authorities in investigating the murder, but could come up with nothing in the way of a suspect.

They even checked out mobster Lenny Patrick, for whom Philly once worked. Patrick, who seemed to enjoy almost a magical immunity from the law, had been arrested the day before Goodman's murder on gambling charges for the first time in nineteen years.

Investigators speculated that if the mob had suspected a tip by Goodman led to the bust, he would certainly have been marked for death. They didn't have to know for sure. Only suspect. As Mafia Chief Sam "Momo" Giancana once explained to a fellow mobster, "Seven out of ten times when we hit a guy, we're wrong. But the other three guys we hit, we make up for it." After all, why take chances?

UPDATE

The murder of Goodman remains unsolved. Police and the FBI don't even have a suspect. The best guess as to "why" was the Spilotro connection. Everybody who was getting knocked off at that time seemed to have been associated in one way or another with Anthony Spilotro. From all appearances the "new" mob, under Ferriola, really was cleaning house.

YOU'RE NEVER TOO OLD TO DIE

Some people don't know the meaning of retirement. Take Victor Lazarus. A tall, thin, handsome devil who affected a walking stick, he was still going strong at the age of eighty-nine. A bookie since Chicago's bawdy Prohibition Era, he had stuck with his chosen profession through the Great Depression, World War II, Korea, Elvis, the Beatles, and right on into the computer age.

The only time the feds ever laid a glove on him was when they nailed him for income tax evasion in 1936 and 1937, when he operated the Jackson Club at 328 West Van Buren Street on the edge of the Loop. According to Uncle Sam, Vic had neglected to declare a gambling income of $745,800 over the two-year period. Not bad in a day when most men were either in the bread lines or the WPA. He didn't go to jail like Al Capone, though. Lazarus struck a deal with the U.S. Attorney's office to pay the taxes he owed at thirty-three and a half cents on the dollar, at the rate of fifty dollars a month for two and a half years.

Assistant U.S. Attorney John M. Kiely advised the court, "This arrangement is acceptable to the government. After all, Mr. Lazarus has an uncertain income."

Lazarus, like his good friend, the late Phil Goodman, was

a longtime member of the so-called "Jewish faction" of the Chicago crime syndicate. These were mob-sanctioned bookies who paid protection, or street taxes, to the local Mafia which government officials insisted didn't exist.

With the coming of the 1970s, Lazarus, like his pal, Philly, migrated west and went to work for Anthony Spilotro in Las Vegas. He came back to Chicago at about the same time Goodman did, and took a room in the North Shore Hotel, 1611 Chicago Avenue, Evanston, after staying briefly with a granddaughter in Skokie. Fellow residents of the retirement hotel knew him as a "wonderful, lovable old man . . . a real gentleman" in the tradition of con man Joseph "Yellow Kid" Weil.

The last time anyone could remember seeing Lazarus around was Tuesday, June 26, 1990. A friend reported him missing the following Sunday, July 1. Later that same day a security guard spotted blood dripping from the trunk of a black 1975 Lincoln Continental that have overstayed its welcome in the Venture department store parking lot at 2015 West Peterson Avenue, on Chicago's far Northwest Side.

The car was registered to Victor Lazarus. Police popped open the trunk and solved their latest missing person case. The octogenarian bookie had been shot twice in the back of the head. His walking cane was found under the body, where somebody had tossed it before throwing Lazarus in on top of it and slamming the lid.

Like the Philly Goodman killing, the motive was obviously not robbery. The corpse still wore valuable jewelry.

A search of the car turned up two .32-caliber shells on the front seat, indicating that the shooting had taken place somewhere else, and the killer had driven the car to the Venture lot and abandoned it.

In checking out the slain man's movements, Belmont Area Detective Commander William Callahan learned that Lazarus appeared to keep a daily regimen of being met every morning by a man in a car, and driving off somewhere with him. Police also learned that the old man had still packed a gun until only recently, when an elderly woman acquaintance took it away from him for safe keeping. In his room at the retirement house detectives found telephone numbers and a ledger book, indicating that Lazarus was still taking bets.

"He was a meticulous man who kept very thorough records," Callahan said.

Oh, yes. Detectives found something else in the old man's room—a complete set of newspaper clippings about Anthony Spilotro and his brother being beaten to death and buried alive in the Indiana cornfield.

UPDATE

The last three mob hits in a row, John Fecarotta, Philly Goodman, and the dapper Vic Lazarus were all woven together by a common thread. All had once been associated in one way or another with Tony Spilotro. It appeared that the housecleaning was still in progress, but at least the mob wasn't practicing age discrimination.

TORTURE WRAPPED IN MYSTERY

Somebody wanted someone very dead—painfully so—and then erased from the eyes of humanity forever. The last part of the plan didn't work out as intended, however, and Chicago police inherited a triple mystery: Who was he, who killed him, and why?

The mystery surfaced, literally, at 8:20 on the evening of August 10, when a worker on the bank of the Calumet River near 102nd Street on the far South Side spotted a large, ominous, six-foot package bobbing uneasily in the murky water. Police, dispatched to investigate a "possible floater," knew what it was the minute they pulled the object to shore. It was the body of a man, tightly wrapped in a tarpaulin like an Egyptian mummy.

The waterlogged bundle was taken to the West Side morgue where a postmortem examination was performed under the direction of Dr. Robert Stein, Cook County medical examiner. Detective Patrick Mokry of the Pullman Area violent crimes unit stood by awaiting the results. The contents of the tarp had been labeled No. 265 for identification purposes—the 265th murder victim to date in 1983.

"Well, here's what I can tell you so far," a coroner's pathologist advised Mokry, pulling off his rubber gloves and tossing them into a metal can. "Number 265 was a white male, between the ages of thirty-five and forty-five, six feet tall, 180 pounds."

"What else?" Mokry, a homicide detective with thirteen years experience at delving into the gruesome and macabre, asked as he jotted the info down in his notebook.

"Ahhh. Now the nasty part. This guy's death was not quick, and it was not without pain. Whoever killed him wanted to make sure he knew what was happening to him. Get this: First he was shot in the right kneecap . . ."

"Ouch!" interrupted Mokry.

"Right. Then he was shot in the spine. That certainly disabled him, but he still knew what was going on. Finally, his head was crushed, and a coup de grace—the shot that killed him was fired at point-blank range into the back of his skull."

As Mokry examined the remains of what had once been a living, breathing human being on the autopsy table, he realized that identifying the victim—the first step in solving any homicide—would not be an easy job. The coroner's physician estimated the body had been in the water for several months, possibly since early spring, and the head had been crushed so badly it was impossible to tell what the dead man had once looked like.

Whoever disposed of the body had not intended that it be found, that was certain. After being tightly wrapped in the tarp, the bundle had been weighted down with sixty-three pounds of concrete block and structural steel before it was laboriously dumped into the river. In spite of its weight, the grim parcel eventually worked its way to the surface as internal gasses formed during the decomposition process.

Police checked businesses along the river in an effort to determine whether anyone had observed any suspicious activity in the months before the body came back up. Detective David Dioguardi turned up a possible lead at a riverside fishery at 95th Street.

Pointing to a bleak, isolated area at the river's edge, fishery workers recalled that two months or so earlier they had heard a splashing sound and men's voices in the night. Somebody grumbled, "I hope it sinks to the bottom and stays there." In discussing the sighting with Dioguardi, Mokry speculated that if the 95th Street location was correct, passing river traffic and swirling currents could have dragged and pushed the body to where it was recovered seven blocks away.

Mokry was convinced that the man had been a victim of organized crime, and that his death and disappearance were meant as a message to others. "He was tortured," Mokry pointed out. "As with most organized crime killings, this was done to make an example of him, though it was never intended that his body be found. His friends would get the message, even without him ever showing up again."

In an effort to determine what the murdered man had looked like the medical examiner brought in Dr. Clyde Snow, a noted anthropologist, to attempt to reconstruct the victim's cranium with clay. But the pieces were too small, and the effort failed.

Detectives pored over lists of missing people throughout the metropolitan area, and entered the victim's description in police computers for missing people nationwide. Mokry also convinced the American Dental Association to run a story and a photograph of an unusual partial bridge worn by the man. He even contacted the FBI, asking whether a fingerprint comparison could be made and whether any underworld informants were missing. All to no avail.

There is a distinct possibility that the victim had not come from the Chicago area.

"He wore no outer clothing, yet he probably was killed when the weather was cold," Mokry pointed out. "He should have been dressed warmer, unless he came from a neighborhood near the river." The dead man wore boots made in Canada. They were of a type commonly sold in stores in this country, however. The front half of the sole of each boot was deeply worn, indicating the man had worked in a kneeling or squatting position. A welder, perhaps, or an auto body worker.

"People get married, have parties, they die. Wouldn't there be talk among loved ones whenever families get together? Wouldn't they be asking about this man? 'Where's John?' Or, 'What ever happened to Jim?' Wouldn't they ask that?" asked Mokry. "Do they care?"

Who was No. 265, why was he shot to death, and how is it that no one ever came forth to report him missing?

UPDATE

"This is an open case. I'd like to know what happened," said Mokry, who was subsequently reassigned to the crime analysis section at Central Police Headquarters. "Sure, I have other cases to keep me busy. I'm looking for a guy from Kingston, Jamaica, for example, who killed his wife in Chicago fifteen years ago. These cases are open. That's what I do. Close them."

BOOK IX

MURDER ON THE HOOF

"YA BURNT MY *!#!* SHIRT!"

Salvatore "Samoots" Amatuna, known during the Prohibition Era as "the Sicilian Beau Brummel," was the proud owner of the Bluebird Cabaret, a notorious speakeasy at Halsted and Taylor streets, to say nothing of more than 200 expensive silk shirts.

He was also the known killer of two police officers, a municipal court bailiff, and various other political and bootlegging personalities in the rum wars that kept Chicago popping. Plus one unsuspecting horse.

Samoots had sent his shirts to the laundry to have the blood and wine stains washed out, and one of them came back with scorch marks from the flat iron. That did it for the hot tempered Sicilian. He whipped out his gun and put it to the laundryman's head, called him every name in the book, and then had a better idea. Marching out into the street where the delivery wagon was waiting, he put his gun to the horse's head and shot the animal dead.

Amatuna, a free-lance gunsel, succeeded Angelo Genna as president of the Unione Siciliane when Genna was gunned down on May 26, 1925. He hardly had time to enjoy his prominence as head of the local Mafia, however.

One of the joys of the swashbuckling set that Amatuna ran with was settling comfortably into a soft barber chair and getting the full treatment—which is just what he got a few months later on November 10.

Samoots was relaxing in the chair in a crowded barber shop at 804 West Roosevelt Road, getting a shave, haircut, and massage—the works. He wore a sparkling diamond ring on his pinkie finger, had a fresh flower in his button hole, and a heavy gold chain dangled from the gold watch in his vest pocket. In his coat pocket were four tickets to the opera.

As soon as he got prettied up in the tonsorial parlor he was going to drive over to the North Side to pick up his fiancee, Rose Pecoraro, and another couple, for an evening of culture. Samoots and Rose, the sister-in-law of the late Mike Merlo, head of the Sicilian societies, were going to be married the following week. The hall had been rented, the flowers were ordered, and all arrangements made.

The barber was just about finished. He had removed the hot towel from Amatuna's face, and was brushing a few stray hairs off his shoulders. Bertha Drake, the manicurist, was holding Amatuna's gun hand as the bootblack gave Samoots' shoes one last Whap! with his cloth.

Suddenly two men with guns drawn barged into the busy shop and pumped eight bullets into Samoots, and the twenty-six-year-old toppled to the floor dead.

The two gunmen backed out the door, jumped into a waiting car, and sped away. A coroner's jury, meeting several days later in the Fred S. De Cola Undertaking Parlor on West Grand Avenue, ruled that Amatuna's death was due to "gunshot wounds inflicted by persons unknown."

UPDATE

The late Judge John H. Lyle, in his 1960 book, The Dry and Lawless Years, speculated that one of the killers was Machine-gun Jack McGurn.

McGurn's real name was James De Mora, which he later changed to Vincent Gebardi. His father, a grocer, who became the chief alcohol cooker for the Genna brothers, was murdered in 1923. Over the next five years McGurn, who was nineteen at the time of his father's death, murdered five men whom he held responsible. One of them, according to Judge Lyle, was the dapper Amatuna.

McGurn, one of the triggermen in the St. Valentine's Day Massacre of 1929, was himself shot to death in a bowling alley (now a used furniture store) at 805 Milwaukee Avenue on Feb. 15, 1936.

No one was ever arrested for that one, either.

DON'T KICK A HOOD WHEN HE'S DOWN

Samoots Amatuna wasn't the only Prohibition Era assassin to bump off a horse. On May 13, 1923, "Three Gun Louie" Alterie committed a similar act to avenge the death of his dear friend, Samuel "Nails" Morton.

Morton, a Jewish lieutenant in Dion O'Banion's North Side Irish bootleg mob, was also a known cop killer. He developed an interest in equestrianism as a frequent guest of Alterie, who owned a ranch in Colorado. Leland Varain Alterie was known as "Three Gun Louie" because he carried a pair of .38 caliber nickel plated revolvers with maplewood handles in shoulder holsters, one under each arm, and a blue steel .38 snub-nose in his car.

Morton got so hooked on horseback riding that he bought himself a bay, and stabled it in a North Clark Street riding academy.

On the Sunday morning in question Morton, nattily decked out in a green sport coat, cream colored jodhpurs, and riding boots, saddled his horse and cantered over to Lincoln Park, where he was to be joined by Dion and Mrs. O'Banion for a pre-luncheon ride.

For some reason the horse reared up unexpectedly, and Nails stood up in the saddle to get a firmer grip on the reins.

As he did so a stirrup broke and he was thrown to the ground. The wildly plunging horse kicked him in the head as he lay in the grass, and he died without ever regaining consciousness.

After Morton's funeral Alterie and two of his henchmen went to the stable, saddled up Morton's horse, and led the animal to Lincoln Park to the exact spot where Morton had died. Alterie unholstered his two .38s, his assistants drew their pieces, and they emptied their guns into the horse's head. Then they called the stable and told them where they could find the saddle.

UPDATE

Alterie, who eventually took over the Theater Janitors Union, was unceremoniously ousted from office on July 18, 1935, when twelve shotgun slugs caught him fatally as he stepped out the front door of his North Side apartment.

You guessed it. An inquest jury determined that the shotguns were fired by "person or persons unknown."

BOOK X

CANDIDATES FOR MURDER

BIG CATS DON'T HAVE NINE LIVES

In the early 1960s, when blacks were still somewhat of an oddity in Windy City politics, there was nobody who could hold a diamond-studded finger to 'The Big Cat"—otherwise known as Benjamin F. Lewis, the flamboyant alderman from the West Side Twenty-Fourth Ward. Jiving, conniving, and boldly womanizing, he was without a doubt the most powerful black politician in Chicago.

Unfortunately for him, The Big Cat simply did not have the nine lives to go with the title Lewis had immodestly bestowed upon himself. On the night of Feb. 27, 1963, just twenty-four hours after he had been reelected by a fifteen-to-one margin over a hapless Republican opponent, somebody shot him dead, right in his own office.

The saga of Ben Lewis was truly one of rags to riches—to bullets. A native of Georgia, he was brought to Chicago by his parents as a child. After graduation from Crane Junior College he found work as a clerk for the U.S. Employment Service. He served in the army as a second lieutenant during World War II. Coming home from the war Lewis joined the wave of "coloreds," as city hall called them, who were moving into the West Side ward, and took a job as a Chicago bus driver.

By the 1950s the ward, which until a decade earlier had been 100 percent Jewish, had become 90 percent black. But the Jews, who had moved into all-white neighborhoods elsewhere, continued to maintain phony voting addresses, hold elective office, and wield power in the ward. The Johnny-come-lately blacks, including Ben Lewis, highly resented it.

Pretending to go along with the system, he went to work for the Democrats, and in 1952 they made him the ward's first black precinct captain. Lewis bided his time, carefully calculating every move, all the while ingratiating himself with the white political machine downtown. Then, when Sidney Deutsch, the ward's Jewish alderman, resigned in 1958 to become city treasurer, Lewis got off the bus and ran for Sid's seat on the city council, with Mayor Richard J. Daley's Irish blessing.

The nod from the "Great Buddha" was all it took to assure Lewis of becoming the ward's first black alderman. When Deutsch died three years later, Lewis was handpicked by Daley to replace Deutsch as the area's first black ward committeeman.

Once he was in control, it was truly amazing how the Big Cat prospered. When first elected to public office Lewis had to borrow money to buy a new suit for his installation ceremony. By the time he had finished his first term the bon vivant ex-bus driver had a thriving insurance business, extensive real estate holdings, drove a flashy Buick Wildcat, had six mistresses that folks knew of, and vacationed regularly in Acapulco.

The audacious flaunting of such astonishing success on an aldermanic salary of only $8,000 a year would certainly cause a raised eyebrow or two among the electorate in some cities—but this was Chicago. When Lewis ran for a second term his constituents overwhelmingly declared their approval by reelecting him over his Republican opponent by a vote of 13,198 to 888.

After the votes were counted on the night of February 26 the fifty-three-year-old victor triumphantly left Daley's political stronghold in the old Morrison Hotel, unquestionably the most powerful black politician on Chicago's West Side.

And in twenty-four hours he would be the deadest.

For his last day on earth the impeccable, five-foot eleven-inch alderman selected a $200 suit from his extensive ward-robe. Before departing from his home on Fillmore Street that wintry morning of February 27 he paused before the mirror and tugged lightly at the knot in his cravat. The Big Cat must have smiled approvingly at the slick dude in the dark blue suit, and his mirror image smiled back at him. Lewis was still wearing the neatly-pressed suit when Joseph Brown, the janitor in the alderman's newly remodeled office building at 3604 Roosevelt Road, found him at 8:57 the following morning.

Brown had gone to check the alderman's office when he noticed the lights still burning from the night before, and heard the radio playing. The stunned janitor froze when he spotted the nattily attired corpse lying face down on the wine colored carpet alongside his massive desk. The body reposed on a sheet of heavy wrapping paper that had apparently been spread out on the rug so he wouldn't soil his shiny suit. A green leather chair cushion lay across his head.

The dead man's wrists were manacled, and his face was cradled in his outstretched arms. A burned-out filter cigarette was poised between the first and second fingers of his right hand, and a long, unbroken cigarette ash decorated the carpet. He had been shot three times in the back of the head.

Robbery was clearly not the reason behind the out-and-out execution. Lewis was still wearing an expensive diamond ring and gold wristwatch, and had cash in his billfold, along with his credit cards.

The city was aghast at the crime, and Mayor Daley was apoplectic. "Alderman Lewis' death is a tragic loss to the people of Chicago," he declared, currying the black vote. "He was a good alderman who was interested in his people and in all the people of Chicago." Vowing the killer would be brought to justice, he ordered his reform police super-intendent, Orlando W. Wilson, to give the homicide his personal attention and conduct "an exhaustive and thorough investigation."

Wilson placed Captain Frank Flanagan of the old Maxwell Street district in charge of the homicide investigation. "This was not a crime syndicate hit," Flanagan opined, in ordering his detectives to compile a complete list of city payrollers holding jobs under Lewis' sponsorship.

The police crime lab had determined that the handcuffs locked on the dead man's wrists were not the type used by lawmen, but were of a brand manufactured for the navy during World War II.

"I want every payroller from the Twenty-Fourth Ward questioned. Possibly one of them had become disenchanted, or maybe the alderman tried to extort part of the guy's pay from him if he wanted to keep his job. It happens all the time in Chicago," Flanagan suggested. "I want you to especially concentrate on people holding gun jobs—court bailiffs, or deputy sheriffs, anybody whose job might include the use of handcuffs, and give the person access to firearms."

He also told his investigators to obtain permission from the alderman's lawyer, David White, to search Lewis' home and real estate and insurance office for anything that might point to a motive.

Meanwhile investigators learned that Thomas "Shaky Tom" Anderson, South Side policy wheel operator, had been unhappy over Lewis' alleged attentions toward Anderson's wife, Frances—so unhappy, in fact, that he had threatened the alderman's life.

Lieutenant John Killackey of the Maxwell Street homicide bureau put out a pick-up order on Anderson and one of his top henchmen, Jimmy Williams, a professional boxer who fought under the name of Kid Riviera. According to information obtained by detectives, both Anderson and Williams had threatened Lewis. Just three days before the election, according to one witness, Williams told the alderman, "If you are elected, you won't live a day after the election."

Williams, a hulking 325-pounder, admitted to detectives, "Yeah, I met the alderman a couple of times, but I never threatened him."

"Our informants told us that you accused the alderman of seeing Tommy's wife," detectives pressed. "You told the alderman, 'If Tommy said to kill you, I'd kill you right now.'"

"I never threatened the alderman," Williams, a onetime protege of Heavyweight Champion Joe Louis, reiterated. He was asked to take a lie test, but refused.

The slain alderman's fifty-one-year-old wife, Ella, told detectives that on one occasion when Williams had warned Lewis to stay away from Shaky Tom's wife, Lewis fetched a rifle from a closet and pointed it at the boxer. "I wrestled the weapon away from my husband, and warned him that he could destroy his political career if he shot Kid Riviera," she related.

As for her personal relationship with the man whom she had married in 1949, Mrs. Lewis told police, "In recent years I've been little more than a house-keeper. He shut me out of his life. I asked him if he wanted a divorce, and he just walked out the door without bothering to answer. I stayed with him because I had everything to gain and nothing to lose. I worked while he was getting established in politics. My money went into his career."

"Was there any love between you?" she was asked.

"Love? Hah! That's a laugh," she said. "I just stayed on."

"Was the alderman what you might call a drinker?"

"Absolutely not," she replied. "Ben never drank anything stronger than soda pop. Never!"

That puzzled detectives, since an autopsy on the murder victim indicated the presence of about twenty-seven milligrams of alcohol, the equivalent of one or two shots of whisky, in his stomach.

With the help of Mrs. Lewis and other associates of the slain man, police were able to put together a timetable of the last hours of the West Side politician.

Lewis left his home for the last time at 3:30 P.M. "He was in a good mood," Mrs. Lewis recalled, as she watched the victorious alderman saunter down the snowy sidewalk in front of the house. He arrived at his ward office five minutes later, but stayed only a short time. "I'm going down to the

Morrison Hotel," he told his secretary, Sara Mickels. She said he left at 3:45, and headed for Democratic Party headquarters in the Loop.

Lewis strutted into the Morrison at about 4:30, and delivered the final election tally from his ward to Mary Mullen, the Democratic organization's secretary. "We chatted for a few minutes about his smashing victory over the Republican, and then he left around a quarter to five," she remembered.

Lewis returned to his flashy Buick and headed back west on Madison Street, leaving the wind-whipped downtown area in his rearview mirror. At five o'clock he stopped at a restaurant near his office at 3211 West Roosevelt Road for a quick sandwich with a political crony, Derrick Smith, former secretary of the Twenty-Fourth Ward Democratic Organization. Less than fifteen minutes later he abruptly excused himself, telling Smith, "I guess I'd better go because they are waiting for me." Who was waiting? "He didn't say," Smith told police.

At precisely 5:15 P.M. the alderman's ward secretary saw him park his sporty Wildcat in a bus stop zone, just east of Central Park Avenue. Police found it still parked there the following morning, under a half-inch of new snow. With the arrogance of most big city politicians, Lewis left his car in the illegal parking spot and walked the half a block to his office, letting himself in by the front door. He snapped on the light and climbed a short stairway to a balcony. There he unlocked the door with his name proudly lettered on the glass and entered his plush suite.

A short time later Lewis made the first of two known trips downstairs to admit callers. His first visitors were a pair of neighborhood newspapermen, Morris Williams, owner and publisher of The Enterprise, a weekly news sheet, and Roosevelt Thompson, his advertising manager. Williams wanted to run a story about the alderman's stunning reelection victory, and Thompson was hoping he'd take out some political advertising.

While they were talking the phone rang. It was the Reverend Robert Ford, pastor of Union Tabernacle Church of God in Christ over on South Hamlin Avenue. "I knocked at the door downstairs but nobody answered," the pastor explained. "I'm calling from the drugstore on the corner."

"Well, come on back Reverend, and I'll let you in," Lewis assured him.

He went downstairs and admitted the minister, but told him he'd have to wait because he still had other visitors in his office. At about 6:30 P.M., Lewis escorted the two newspapermen out. Then he took Pastor Ford on a tour of the first floor of his new headquarters before inviting him up to his office.

"I telephoned my husband shortly after six o'clock, but I didn't get any answer," Mrs. Lewis told police. This could have been while he was downstairs with the clergyman.

Reverend Ford and the alderman talked for a few minutes about the church's difficulties in meeting some notes, after which the minister made a pitch for the alderman's financial support. "He was very cheerful, and told me to come back next week," Reverend Ford would later tell police. "He let me out of the building at about twenty minutes to seven and locked the door behind me."

The next known contact Lewis had with anyone came almost an hour later. Sergeant James Gilbert, thirty-six, a Fillmore District police officer and close friend of the alderman, telephoned at 7:30 to discuss a personal matter.

"The alderman told me he was dog tired. He said he had just finished tallying the votes by precincts and he was headed home for a good night's sleep," his policeman friend told detectives. "Suddenly he stopped talking to me. I felt that his voice ended on a muffled note of surprise. His attention seemed diverted as though someone had entered his office. He said, 'I'm sorry, I have to hang up now,' and our conversation was cut off."

Was this when the killer or killers walked in? Police were pretty sure of it until a week later, when detectives came up with another witness. Ruby Wellin, a twenty-two-year-old receptionist for a neighborhood doctor, said the alderman telephoned her at her office at 8:45 P.M. "He seemed jubilant and he asked me to call him back when I got home," she said. "I did, around 9:30 P.M., but got no answer."

Police were now able to pinpoint the time of death at somewhere between 8:45 and 9:30 P.M. Two neighbor women, Pearl Sutton and Dorothy Thomas, who lived across the alley from the aldermanic headquarters, told police they thought they heard shots coming from the building some time between 9:00 and 9:30, while they were watching television.

James H. Smith, the building manager, said he left at ten o'clock after hearing sounds of conversation and the ringing of a telephone in Lewis' upstairs office through most of the evening. He did not recall hearing any shots, however. When Joe Brown, the janitor, discovered the body the next morning the radio in the alderman's office was playing loudly. This could have muffled the sound of shots within the building.

Mourners by the thousands filed past the alderman's bier in the House of Branch Mortuary, and more than 1,500 people attended his funeral March 4 in Greater Galilee Missionary Baptist Church.

Police, meanwhile, pressed their investigation under pressure from the mayor, who demanded that the murder must be solved. "Hizzoner" announced a $10,000 reward for the killer from his personal contingency fund as an incentive. Flanagan put sixty homicide investigators on the case.

The thing that mystified investigators from the very start was the presence of alcohol in the dead man's stomach. "Our guys haven't been able to come up with anyone who ever saw the alderman take a drink, even at election celebrations," Maurice Begner, chief of detectives, told Flanagan. "Could be that someone forced him to take a snort, maybe to calm him down, before they shot him."

"Did he keep any liquor in his office?"

"Not a drop. Whoever gave it to him brought it in."

Another oddity: There was no sign of a struggle at the murder scene. The alderman's slayers apparently handcuffed his wrists in front of him, and then helped him to lie face down on the floor while they engaged in a conversation. Three things bolstered this theory:

1. The alderman's expensive suit was not rumpled, as it might have been if he had been knocked to the floor during a struggle. It appeared that he had been given all the time in the world to stretch out comfortably on the wrapping paper while they talked.

2. The butt of the burned filter cigarette between the dead man's fingers indicated he had casually enjoyed a smoke during the chat. There was an unbroken ash nearly two inches long on the carpet, where it had apparently fallen from the cigarette in his handcuffed hand stretched above his head.

3. Four .32-caliber shell casings were found on the floor, but the coroner's pathologist recovered only three slugs from Lewis' head. Police later found the fourth bullet under the blood-soaked carpet where Lewis had lain. The slug had made an indentation in the floor, indicating it had been fired toward Lewis as he lay in a prone position.

Homicide Sergeant William Keating and John R. Neurauter, deputy chief of detectives, agreed that some type of talk was in progress when Lewis was executed. "The handcuffs indicate conversation. They would make it safer for the killer or killers to talk to the subject," Keating suggested.

Neurauter agreed. "About the handcuffs, they're puzzling. But to me they indicate there was some kind of a waiting period in which Lewis lay on the floor. Maybe there was a waiting period for information, or a promise, or something. The cigarette business seems to indicate this also."

The actual moment of execution came when the killer pressed the muzzle of a .32-caliber pistol against the back of the alderman's head near his right ear and pulled the trigger. The relaxed manner in which Lewis's body was found tended to indicate he might have thought it was all a bluff.

The biggest problem facing investigators was finding a motive for the murder. There were so many possibilities he could have been killed for any number of reasons. The Big Cat, in effect, led three lives—personal, political, and business, and he seemed to have made more than his share of enemies in all three. Police ran up against a blank in checking out most of the rumors about his personal life, but in probing his financial status they learned quite a bit.

The onetime bus jockey, who had to borrow money to buy a suit when elected four years earlier, now had a thriving real estate and insurance business on the side and was trying to get into the savings and loan industry. In the four short years since taking office as alderman he had acquired six buildings worth nearly a quarter of a million dollars. And he once boasted to associates that the ward committeeman job he assumed in 1961 was "good for $50,000 a year for the insurance alone."

On the other hand, Lewis was in debt to a number of people to the tune of $15,000 to $20,000—a lot of money in 1963 when $5,000 was considered a good annual salary.

Police also learned that Lewis had held out about $10,000 in insurance premiums which saloonkeepers and other businessmen had paid him, but which he never turned over to the companies he represented. This meant that those customers were not actually covered by insurance, even though they had paid for it. If any of them suffered a loss it could be catastrophic.

The alderman was playing a dangerous game.

"The trouble with this case is we've got too many suspects and too many motives," Flanagan observed. "Alderman Lewis was defrauding people right and left in the insurance company. A couple of them were forced into bankruptcy as a result. He collected premiums but he didn't turn them in.

"He was an embezzler, yet when he died he owed money. Where did it all go? Women? Who knows? The guy had a broad for every night of the week."

Indeed, the police investigation turned up information that The Big Cat was also a tomcat on the side. While he and his wife endured only a platonic relationship, he was supporting at least six mistresses.

All six admitted having affairs with Lewis. They said he paid their rent, bought them clothing, and provided them with spending money. All six of them passed lie tests showing they knew nothing about his murder, however.

Meanwhile the elusive Shaky Tom Anderson was finally tracked down. Both he and his 325-pound enforcer, Jimmy "Kid Riviera" Williams, agreed to take lie tests provided police asked them only about the murder, and not about the policy rackets. The polygraph tests showed they knew nothing about Lewis' killing.

In a bizarre sidebar to the murder investigation, Shaky Tom's young wife, Frances, also took a lie test at her husband's request, to prove to the policy king that she had never had an affair with the alderman, other than enjoying dinner with him once on a trip to Mexico.

Over the years that followed the alderman's murder, police built a two and a half foot thick file covering the ongoing investigation. Unfortunately, Mayor Daley's order that the killer be brought to justice was one of the few times he never got his way.

UPDATE

More than twenty-two years after the wheeler-dealer alderman was found shot to death in his office, a hot lead in the slaying came out of the blue. Or, more accurately, over the counter.

Patrolman Bruce Johnson of the Chicago Lawn District was having lunch in a Southwest Side restaurant when the waitress casually remarked, "Would you be interested in some information about an unsolved crime?"

"Sure, tell me about it," he smiled, thinking she was just trying to make conversation.

"Well, there's this guy who comes in here to eat named Stanley Kuczynski. He's an ex-convict and he talks a lot."

"Like what?"

"He told me, 'I killed a black alderman years ago. I shot him after he was handcuffed.'"

"Did he say who the alderman was?"

"No, and I never heard of any alderman being killed, did you?"

Johnson had a long memory. He recalled the Lewis slaying, and submitted an "information report" to his superiors, dated 31 December, 1984, in which he related his conversation with the waitress.

Suddenly the long-dormant murder investigation was on again. Records showed that the sixty-five-year-old Kuczynski was an habitual criminal with a record of twenty-six arrests over a forty-three-year period extending from 1935 to 1978. He had served twelve years in prison for various armed robbery convictions. In going over his arm-long record, police noted that he was between "habitual criminal" sentences and was out on the streets at the time Lewis was murdered. He could have done it!

"I know Kuczynski. I locked him up once or twice myself," John Stibich, commander of the Brighton Park Violent Crimes Unit, told Captain George McMahon, chief of detectives. "He's a braggart. He knows some people in the outfit [crime syndicate], but I never heard anything to tie him in with Ben Lewis."

McMahon dusted off the old homicide file. Of all the hundreds of suspects police had interviewed and ruled out over the years, the name of Kuczynski had never come up. If he was indeed the killer, he had managed to keep it a secret for more than two decades before his chin began to wag. "This whole thing is weird," he said. "Bring this bird in and let's see what he has to say."

It didn't take detectives long to find him. He was laid out under a sheet in the Cook County morgue.

On Jan. 1, 1985—the day after Patrolman Johnson had dated his "information report" on the Lewis killing—Kuczynski burned to death under mysterious circumstances when the bungalow where he lived at 3324 West 38th Street erupted into flames.

To this day the cause of the fire remains listed as "undetermined"—as does the identity of Lewis' killer.

IT'S A DANGEROUS GAME THEY PLAY

The slaying of Ben Lewis was not the first time the life of a Chicago alderman—one of the city's most powerful creatures— had been snuffed out. It happened once before, more than a hundred years ago, when James Dacey, a minor politician and all around no-gooder, murdered Alderman Michael Gaynor over a drink of whisky.

It was election night, 1884, and Gaynor had wandered into Foley's Saloon on Halsted Street where the alderman was celebrating his victory. Dacey insisted that Gaynor join him in a drink, and when the alderman said, "No thanks, I don't want to drink with the likes of you," Dacey shot him dead.

But that was an open and shut case. There Dacey stood with the smoking gun in his hand, in full view of a room full of people. Public feeling ran so high after the shooting that the sheriff had to hustle him out of town to save him from a potential lynch mob. Dacey was secreted in a basement cell in the McHenry County Courthouse in Woodstock, some fifty miles away, and there he stayed until 1886 when he was marched across the street and hanged in the village square.

The solution to a political homicide in Chicago seems to be the exception to the rule, however. Most political hit men get away with murder, and over the years there have been quite a few.

During the rat-a-tat Prohibition Era when Al Capone called the shots, political violence was so widespread that in one ward alone—the "Bloody Twentieth"—three political leaders were assassinated in a single year.

The most prominent victim was Octavius Granady, an influential black politician who was engaged in a battle for control of the Twentieth Ward, just south and west of the Loop. He was shot to death on primary election day, April 19, 1928. Several policemen were indicted for Granady's murder, but the case against them was dismissed in mid-trial.

On Dec. 29, 1935, State Representative Albert J. Prignano, a powerful Democratic committeeman, was shot to death in front of his home at 722 Bunker Street (now Grenshaw Avenue). The unsolved homicide took place after Prignano had defied an order by Frank Nitti, then head of the Capone mob, not to run for ward committeeman.

On July 9, 1936, another state representative, John H. Bolton, who was reportedly locked in a struggle with local gangsters over control of West Side gambling, was murdered by a shotgun blast as he drove down Harrison Street near Washtenaw Avenue. Nobody ever figured out who fired the fatal shot.

In yet another highly-publicized political killing, William J. Granata, Republican committeeman in the Twenty-Seventh Ward, and a candidate for clerk of circuit court, was killed by a deep knife or ax wound and left in a doorway at Randolph and Wells streets on Oct. 6, 1948. Like the others, his murder was never solved.

In February 1952, Charles Gross, the fifty-four-year-old Republican candidate for committeeman from the Thirty-first Ward, was shotgunned out of the race after ignoring a suggestion by syndicate mobsters that he withdraw his candidacy. A police officer gagging at the bloody pulp that had once been the politician's face, was quoted as saying, "Only the Mafia kills like that." Gross's file, No. 52-295, is still gathering dust in the police archives. His killer remains at large.

UPDATE

The wave of political killings in Chicago eventually touched off such an outcry for reform that a merger of neighborhood anti-crime groups was established as Citizens of Greater Chicago to exert pressure on the powers that be. To assuage the public, the city council set up a special department of investigation known as the "Big Nine" to delve into the alliance between crime and politics. The group disbanded four years later amid political bickering, after accomplishing little else than the expenditure of $220,000.

And then there was Clem Graver . . .

IS CLEM OVERPARKED IN THE GRANT PARK GARAGE?

The ruggedly handsome Celinus "Clem" Graver was some-what of an oddity in Chicago's rough-and-tumble world of wheeler-dealer politics. He was a Republican who had been elected to public office. At the age of fifty-three he held two political positions, as a matter of fact—Twenty-first Ward Republican committeeman, and a state representative from the Fifteenth District.

He held those two jobs right up to the night of June 11, 1953, which was the last anyone ever saw or heard of him.

Graver's wife, Amelia, was looking out the upstairs window of their home at 976 West 18th Place at 9:55 P.M. as her husband wheeled his new Chrysler up to the front of his garage down the block, got out, and pulled up the overhead door.

Also observing the little vignette from his porch across the street, as Graver climbed back into the Chrysler and eased it into the garage, was Republican precinct captain Walter Pikelis.

Graver, tired after a long train ride from Springfield earlier in the day and a tedious ward meeting that night, emerged from the garage just as a 1950 or 1951 black Ford four-door sedan roared onto 18th Place. The car screeched to a halt as its driver, a man wearing a baseball cap, pulled alongside Graver and hit the brakes.

As the amazed Pikelis looked on, two well-dressed men jumped out of the car, pinned Graver's arms behind his back, and dragged him kicking and struggling toward their auto. "Hey! Stop that!" Pikelis yelled, as the men forced Graver into the black Ford, slammed the doors, and sped away.

Who put the snatch on Graver?

Illinois state legislators, concerned over the welfare of one of their own, posted a $100,000 reward for the apprehension of his kidnappers, but not one tipster came forward. The abduction of a state representative right off the street in Chicago was a political hot potato. Vowing "We will work on this case until it is solved," Police Commissioner Timothy J. O'Connor formed a "Graver Detail" consisting of the city's top detectives. All were assigned full-time to the case, with every other investigation shunted to the back burner. The Graver Detail questioned more than 2,000 witnesses and possible suspects, tracked down hundreds of leads, and ended up with nothing but blind alleys.

Along the way they ascertained that Graver, whose only known income was his government salary of $5,000 a year, owned two homes, wore tailor-made suits and expensive Panama hats, never left the house with less than $500 cash in his pockets, had paid cash for his new Chrysler, and had made several incognito trips to Cuba. In fact, they discovered just about everything there was to know about Clem Graver, except who snatched him, and why.

Police thought they had the answer in 1958 when a federal prisoner in Terre Haute boasted to a fellow con, "I am the last man to see old Clem alive."

Chicago detectives and FBI agents went to the federal pen to question the inmate, thirty-five-year-old Raymond Williams, a member of the notorious West Side Frank Vito mob, who was doing a stretch for hijacking.

Williams admitted that Graver often "fronted" for him and other Vito gang members. Just a month before Graver was abducted, in fact, Williams said he paid the senator fifty dollars to put in the fix for him on an assault case.

Investigators speculated that Vito gangsters, who were being jailed one by one by federal agents for hijacking, bank robberies, and other crimes, might have suspected Graver of tipping off the feds on their activities. In fact, the Vito mobsters had killed several of their own members prior to the Graver disappearance in an effort to get rid of the "stoolie" who was betraying them.

Lieutenant Patrick Deeley, chief of detectives, had his men explore the theory that Graver was killed by the Vito gang, but they never found any definite evidence to substantiate it. Another theory, which police were also unable to pin down, was that the Vito mob had entrusted Graver with $30,000 in loot from a South Bend bank job. Members of a rival gang learned Graver was holding the money, and kidnapped and tortured him in an effort to get their hands on it.

Again, police asked all the right questions, but nobody in the gang would cooperate in the investigation.

Despite the police commissioner's vow, the Graver Detail was disbanded in 1958 after five years of wheel-spinning. Two filing cabinets of worn manila folders holding the voluminous details of their investigation are gathering dust in the basement of police headquarters at 1121 South State Street. An occasional tip—never more than one a year or so—is followed up by some young detective hoping to make a name for himself, who hadn't even been born when Graver was whisked off the street.

The case remains open, but the only real hope of solving it comes when an occasional unidentified skeleton is found and police run a routine check to see if it's Clem.

UPDATE

The sleuths from the old Graver Detail have long since died or retired. But they did come up with one intriguing theory, and a lot of old-time cops fervently believe in it. It's a scenario that makes a lot of sense to anyone who knows the working of the mind of the Chicago underworld:

The sprawling underground parking garage in Grant Park was under construction that summer, and its thick cement walls were being poured at the very time Graver vanished. Could he be entombed in them?

The next time you park your car in the Grant Park underground, honk if you think he's there. Better yet, don't walk down there alone.

ANYBODY HERE SEEN SAL?

Sal Pullia joined the list of crime statistics shortly after midnight on June 4, 1981, when he left Rocky's Italian restaurant at 2212 North Avenue, just two blocks from his comfortable home in Melrose Park. He slid behind the wheel of his silver 1981 Volvo sedan with its distinctive telephone antenna at 12:45 A.M. and drove off into the night. He left behind a worried wife and a promising political career.

A former secretary of the Proviso Township Democratic Organization, Pullia had taken over as committeeman in 1973 after his predecessor, Ralph "Babe" Serpico, was sentenced to prison for bribery and tax evasion. In 1977 he was elected Democratic state central committeeman over three other candidates, including the incumbent.

Because of the heavy political implications of Pullia's disappearance, State's Attorney Richard M. Daley (who would later succeed his father as mayor of Chicago), Sheriff Richard Elrod, and the Illinois Department of Law Enforcement joined in assigning their top investigators to the case.

Detectives discovered that Pullia had been advised not to seek reelection by none other than John D'Arco, Chicago's First Ward Democratic committeeman, who was generally regarded as the mob's connection in city hall.

Pullia refused to step down, however, and held meetings with campaign workers in outright defiance of D'Arco.

"I do not believe in smoke-filled-room politics," Pullia was quoted as saying. "I'm not a part of those people. My reputation is the only thing I truly value."

Investigators also learned that Pullia had borrowed $10,000 from Salvatore Gagliano, son of the late Joseph "Joe Gags" Gagliano, a mob loan shark. Pullia never repaid the loan. He considered it a "political contribution," he explained.

The ten grand reportedly came from John "Jackie the Lackie" Cerone, reputed number three man in the Chicago crime syndicate and Salvatore Gagliano's godfather. Coincidentally, investigators were told, Cerone was a secret owner of Rocky's restaurant, where Pullia was last seen alive.

Before quitting his $30,000-a-year job to open his own consulting firm just a month before his vanishing act, Pullia spent ten years in the office of Cook County Clerk Stanley Kusper, working as a tax extension supervisor.

On the last known day of his life, according to Robert Miller, an investigator for prosecutor Daley—himself a former Democratic committeeman—Pullia had dinner with a Chicago banker, Sam Scott, at Vic Giannotti's restaurant in Forest Park.

On the way to meet the banker, Pullia stopped at a neighborhood drugstore on an errand for his wife of twelve years, Karen. After dining at Giannotti's he drove over to Rocky's at around 11:00 P.M. One hour and fifteen minutes later he was gone forever.

In addition to the IDLE agents, sheriff's detectives, and state's attorney's men assigned to the case, Mrs. Pullia's twenty-eight-year-old brother, police detective John Carpino, waged a tireless investigation on his own time.

Carpino contacted authorities in Las Vegas, and asked them to check out a hotel Pullia favored when there. He also prevailed upon Chicago police to prowl the Rush Street cabaret area, and asked Wisconsin lawmen to check a lake resort, both among Pullia's favorite haunts.

Carpino and Pullia's younger brother, Frank, a Triton Community College student, walked the entire parking lot at Midway Airport and also prowled shopping center lots in a vain search for Sal's silver Volvo with the SPP vanity license plates.

At the same time, Chicago police examined every car in the sprawling O'Hare International Airport parking complex, also with negative results.

"I don't know where to look anymore. It has all been very frustrating," Carpino said six months after his brother-in-law vanished into the mysterious void. "There just isn't much to go on. Not even so much as a single anonymous telephone call or a letter. Nothing! Zero!"

Detective Commander Robert Banks of the Des Plaines office of the Illinois Department of Law Enforcement was equally frustrated.

"All leads have been exhausted," he said.

Gary Marinaro, a sheriff's employee who was named interim successor to Pullia said, "We all want Sal back, but it doesn't look like that is going to happen."

UPDATE

On June 6, 1988, Pullia's wife, Karen Carpino, who had resumed her maiden name, filed suit in Cook County Circuit Court to have Sal declared legally dead. Her suit pointed out that his whereabouts had been unknown for seven years, the minimum period a person must be missing before he can be declared dead under Illinois law.

The reason for the action, she explained, was that two insurance policies on Pullia's life, with a total value of $100,000, were still outstanding and could not be collected as long as he was legally alive.

THE MAYOR WAS MARKED FOR DEATH

Mayor William Hawkins of the mostly-black suburb of Phoenix, just south of Chicago, had a peculiar habit of writing notes to himself on a yellow legal pad. On or about Wednesday, Oct. 10, 1979, he took his pen and scrawled on the pad: "I was to be executed Tuesday but I got a stay of sentence and I am now on probation."

Police found the cryptic message in the mayor's briefcase a week later when going through his personal effects.

Hawkins, fifty-seven, married and the father of five grown sons, was ambushed on the night of Tuesday, October 16 as he arrived home from his full-time job as a foreman at a nearby steel plant.

As he got out of his late model Buick parked in the driveway alongside his modest home, six shots from a .233-caliber combat rifle thundered out of the darkness. Three of the slugs were on target, ripping into the mayor's left thigh, left arm, and right kidney.

His last words, as he slumped to the ground, were, "Help! Somebody, please help!"

A neighbor woman, who had heard the gunfire, cautiously opened the side door of her home and saw Hawkins lying on the ground in front of his car. She notified village police at 11:28 P.M. The mayor's son, Gerald, who lived two doors away, also heard the shots and ran to his father's aid.

No one was at the mayor's home at the time of the shooting. Hawkins' wife, Nancy, was in Ingalls Memorial Hospital in nearby Harvey being treated for diabetes and gastritis. Hawkins, still alive but unconscious, was rushed to the same hospital where he underwent five hours of surgery. Phoenix has no hospital of its own. Nor does it have a funeral home. If you get sick, or die, you have to leave town.

Back at the scene, police found six AR-15 rifle casings at the base of a tree, about seventy-five feet from the pool of blood that marked the spot where the mayor fell. "The mayor's house is well lighted. It would appear that whoever shot him hid in the darkness behind the tree across the street," observed Police Sergeant Beverly Richie.

Police were still going over the area and interrogating neighbors an hour after the shooting when the phone rang in the home of Police Commissioner Robert Howell. When the commissioner answered, a male voice uttered an obscenity and growled, "If you don't resign we're going to get you next. We got the mayor."

Less than fifteen minutes later Phoenix police radio dispatcher Michelle Harvey took a call, apparently from the same man, who told her, "Listen bitch. I missed the mayor tonight. I missed good, but, bitch, you listen, you tell that commissioner if he appears at another meeting, he is next. You hear?"

Hawkins, a fighter all his life, lost the battle at 2:00 P.M. Thursday when he succumbed to his wounds. He died before he could tell investigators who he thought was going to kill him.

At the request of Police Chief Christopher Barton, Lieutenant Howard Vanick of the Cook County Sheriff's police, sent his detectives into Phoenix to assist local authorities in what was now a homicide investigation. They needed all the help they could get.

Mile-square Phoenix, three miles south of the Chicago city limits, had just 3,700 residents, 87 percent of them black. It ranked 197 out of 205 Chicago suburbs in family income.

One focus of the investigation was the village's ragtag police department itself. Just two weeks before Hawkins was gunned down, police had staged a four-day strike, during which three shots were fired into the mayor's home.

Some members of the force had resented the mayor's efforts to professionalize the department, which consisted of only seven full-time and forty-one part-time police officers, some of whom only came to work when they felt like it. The strike had been called over Hawkins' efforts to fire six supervising officers whose salaries had been paid through federal Comprehensive Employment and Training Act (CETA) funds, after the federal grant expired.

Vandalism ran rampant during the police strike, the Town Hall was ransacked, the mayor's office was trashed and the windows broken with axes, all of the tires on the three squad cars were slashed, and the village's only ambulance was stolen. Hawkins finally capitulated. He agreed to pay the six officers out of village funds, and a truce was called, but the resentment lingered.

Sheriff's detectives interviewed more than 200 people after entering the case, but got nowhere. "We're not getting the best of cooperation from members of the police department," Sergeant Arthur Jackson complained to Lieutenant Vanick. "That's not to say they're involved in the shooting, but we're sure having difficulty getting them in for interviews."

Because official corruption has long been a way of life in some Chicago suburbs, especially the lower-income communities, investigators speculated as to whether the mayor's assassination might have related to other activities, with the killer using the police controversy to throw them off the trail.

An audit of the village's finances, however, disclosed nothing worse than sloppy bookkeeping. Nor could investigators uncover any evidence of payoffs from contractors. Speculation in the press that organized crime figures were trying to muscle in on village rackets and killed Hawkins to get him out of the way was also discounted.

Vice in Phoenix consisted of little more than a frequently-raided whorehouse and a few dice and poker games. It was too rinky-dink to even matter to the powerful crime syndicate.

Sergeant Jackson, who had known Hawkins personally, said, "I found him to be a dedicated, articulate, intelligent person who liked what he was doing. But he obviously made some enemies."

A native of Mobile, Alabama, Hawkins came to Phoenix as a young man, and had served as mayor since 1973. He regularly put in a full day at his office in the Village Hall before reporting to work at his 3:00 to 11:00 P.M. job at Interlake Steel Company, in Riverdale, where he was also a union official.

He and his wife, Nancy, sweethearts since the first grade, had been married for forty years. "Bill believed in Phoenix, and was determined to clean it up," she said. "He did not want it to become a place for wholesale illegal drugs. He told me, 'Nancy, I think I can make Phoenix a better place.'"

He died trying.

UPDATE

A dozen years after Hawkins was gunned down in the driveway outside his home, his murder remains an open file. The FBI entered the case, on the grounds that the slaying was a violation of Hawkins' civil rights. FBI agents and sheriff's detectives turned up evidence that Hawkins may have been marked for death by certain police officers whom he suspected of extorting money from a Phoenix brothel. Less than a month before he wrote the cryptic note predicting his own execution he engaged in a bitter quarrel with a police officer who acted as the bagman in collecting the pay-offs. A week before his murder Hawkins met secretly with Cook County Sheriff Richard Elrod. He asked the sheriff to investigate vice in the village because he could not trust his own police department. Sheriff's Sergeant James Houlihan, who worked with the FBI in the case, said authorities believe they know the identity of the killer. "This is a dead bang case," he said. "I can tell you that they are moving on it."

THE ELKS CLUB MURDER

Ask yourself this: How in the world could a prominent attorney get himself blown away in the midst of a crowded political fund-raiser without anyone being the wiser? Police in East Chicago, Indiana, are searching for the answer.

From the night he took a .45-caliber bullet in the head there was no shortage of suspects in the brazen assassination of Jay N. Given, political kingmaker, guardian of secrets, and onetime city attorney in the northern Indiana community. As Joseph S. Van Bokkelen, a special deputy prosecutor assigned to the case pointed out, "Keep in mind that this murder took place within thirty feet of 400 people."

One of the more bizarre homicides in northern Indiana history, it is a crime riddled with political intrigue, ethnic rivalries, and even some questions about the integrity of the police department—since vital evidence was tampered with while in the hands of the law.

Jay Given was fifty-one years old when his decade-long reign as East Chicago's Democratic powerhouse abruptly ended with the crack of a bullet on the night of May 15, 1981. The slaying took place in the Elks Club, a popular oasis for local politicians and the scene of some of Given's greatest triumphs.

Married and the father of three children, Given was known as a clever behind-the-scenes manipulator whose political influence extended throughout Lake County. His law firm handled virtually all of the city's lucrative legal work, with a Given attorney assigned to every department and bureau. More than one hint of impropriety was raised over the years before he and eight of his law partners withdrew from the city's legal practice in 1974 in the midst of a conflict of interest scandal.

On his last night on earth Given drove to the Elks Club on Magoun Avenue to attend a Las Vegas-style fund-raiser for County Commissioner N. Atterson Spann, Jr., the city's leading black politician. By the time he arrived at 9:00 P.M., some 300 celebrants had gathered to pay homage to Spann on the club's second floor. Downstairs, in the Jockey Club restaurant and lounge, another 100 people were enjoying the popular Friday night fish fry.

Given spent about two hours at the Spann salute, and early on that evening it appeared that luck was on his side. His name was the first one drawn in an elimination raffle for a $5,000 grand prize, and he won $300. Well-wishers crowded around to clasp his hand or pat him on the back over his good fortune.

At precisely 11:14 P.M. his luck ran out. Given had said his good-byes and was striding through the ground floor vestibule toward the outer door, his car keys in his hand, when a single shot echoed through the building. The slug, fired at close range into the back of his head, tore through his brain and exited through the forehead, smashing into the plate glass door.

The impact of the bullet propelled Given forward, and he was dead before his body lurched to the floor.

Although hundreds of party goers on both floors of the Elks Club heard the fatal shot, police could find no one who actually witnessed the murder or saw the killer flee. Several late arrivals who were approaching the building at the moment said nobody came out the front way and brushed past them. Nor was anyone seen bucking the flow of curiosity seekers who converged on the scene.

The tile floor of the six-by-nineteen-foot vestibule was awash with blood. Ordinarily this gruesome circumstance might have benefited police, because the killer surely left a trail of bloody footprints. Unfortunately, so did almost everyone else, and his tracks were quickly obliterated. The sharp crack of the .45 had touched off a surge of humanity from both the upstairs hall and the Jockey Club to the lobby to see what had happened.

"There were blood trackings leading everywhere," recalled Van Bokkelen afterward, in criticizing the initial phase of the police investigation. "People were stepping over the body and tracking blood away in many directions. The crime scene was absolutely bobbled . . . the worst I can think of."

In all probability the killer retreated briefly, then quickly melted into the crowd gathered to gape at the corpse. Later, perhaps after ordering a drink to divert suspicion from himself, he might have calmly departed with the rapidly thinning crowd.

Of the seventy-five men and women later called before a Lake County grand jury investigating the politician's execution, only one, a firefighter named Mark Warholic, could say that he had seen Given in the vestibule talking to another man before the shooting. But Warholic, who was on the way to the restroom, paid them scant attention and was unable to give authorities even a sketchy description of the suspect.

Neither Van Bokkelen nor Jack F. Crawford, prosecuting attorney for Lake County who assembled a team of experienced police investigators to assist Van Bokkelen in the case, regarded the killing as the work of a professional assassin. Nor did they feel it was carefully planned. Both agreed that, more likely than not, the killing was an act of spontaneous rage.

One of the things that piqued police curiosity was what Given had been doing at a predominantly black shindig in the first place. "By being there he was courting the blacks," Crawford suggested.

The population of the gritty industrial city hugging the bottom of Lake Michigan was fairly equally divided among blacks, whites, and Hispanics, with each clawing at the ladder of political power. Given's highly visible appearance at the Spann affair was seen as an effort to help solidify the shaky political alliance between the Democratic white power bloc and the emerging black political forces against the growing strength of local Mexican-Americans and Puerto Ricans.

The investigation into Given's murder was unprecedented in Lake County for its scope, intensity, and duration. Virtually every law enforcement agency in the county had a piece of it, from the initial work done by East Chicago detectives and the Lake County police Metro Squad, to follow-up investigations by Indiana State Police and the FBI.

As part of the grand jury probe of the shooting, two dozen people known to have been nearest the door when Given was shot were brought back to the club to reenact the slaying. Each wore the same clothing as before and occupied the same position in the hall. To simulate the murder, a detective fired a blank pistol. At the sound of the shot the twenty-four witnesses retraced their movements, following the precise routes they took from tables, chairs, the bar, and other locations. This drill was to help the grand jurors determine whether the killer could have slipped out of the building unnoticed. Their conclusion: he could not.

Meanwhile the investigation took a dramatic and unexpected turn.

In going over the crime scene, police had found an empty brass shell casing in a corner of the vestibule about nine feet from the body. This important clue, which indicated the weapon had been a .45-caliber pistol, could be scientifically traced to the murder gun.

A short time later police and coroner's deputies came up with a second highly significant find—the fatal slug itself. It, too, could be linked to the murder weapon through ballistics tests. The bullet was recovered from the street about sixty feet north of the double-glass doorway through which it had crashed after passing through Given's head.

Inspector Paul DiCharia of the East Chicago crime laboratory took possession of both the shell casing and the slug, and etched his initials into each for future identification. He then placed them in separate evidence containers and locked them in a desk drawer in the crime lab. DiCharia would later explain that he did not seal the boxes, according to procedure, or drop them down the chute of the evidence room, also customary, because he figured detectives on the next shift might want quick access to them as the only physical evidence in the case.

He was also unaware that a set of keys to the locked drawer were kept elsewhere in the same desk in an unlocked drawer. At least eight people had ready access to the crime lab in the East Chicago station, and any one of them could have gotten into the desk.

On Wednesday morning, May 20, DiCharia removed the two evidence boxes from the desk drawer, sealed them, and turned them over to FBI agents in Gary to be sent to the FBI lab in Washington for analysis. Two weeks later an alarmed FBI agent contacted DiCharia and demanded, "Who's kidding who?"

"What do you mean?" the inspector asked.

"The evidence you sent us has been tampered with!"

"You're kidding!"

"The rim of the shell casing has been twisted, like someone took a hammer to it, and the primer mark on the bottom of the casing has been punched and scratched to obliterate the distinct markings left by the pistol's firing pin."

Furthermore, the FBI lab man continued, the blood-stained slug bore fresh file marks across the lands and grooves that had been etched into it as it spun through the pistol barrel. The file marks clearly had been made after DiCharia had initialed the object.

Question: Why was the evidence altered? Could it be that the murder weapon belonged to a person who could not dispose of it, possibly because it was checked out to him in connection with his job? If so, why merely mutilate the evidence and put it back? Why not dispose of it forever? Or did the killer—or an accomplice—think the act would go unnoticed?

"It certainly appears that someone in the police department did the tampering, or aided the tamperer," an angry Crawford declared on learning of the incident.

The mutilation of key evidence touched off a storm of criticism of the East Chicago police department, which resulted in Van Bokkelen being brought into the case to try to salvage what was left of it.

"The tampering was the dumbest thing to happen in the case," he said. "It presumably was done in the belief that the casing and slug might be traced to the killer. That possibility still exists."

Despite the mutilation of the evidence, ballistics experts were able to narrow down the murder weapon to one of five versions of the .45-caliber pistol, including the standard U.S. military issue and a small palm model manufactured in Europe.

Slowly, as the murder probe progressed, Van Bokkelen and his "core group" of investigators, including East Chicago Detective Sergeant Augusto "Gus" Flores, state police detectives James Brehmer and Raymond Vukas, and Agent Philip Hultgen of the FBI, ruled out every possible suspect except one.

The suspect, a high ranking Hispanic official of the East Chicago police department, was in attendance at the Spann function the night Given was murdered. He admitted under questioning that he was at the Elks Club specifically to keep tabs on Given at the behest of another city official, who was not publicly identified.

At the time of the shooting he was a member of East Chicago's "20–20" club, a political organization started by twenty Latinos who each paid twenty dollars in dues. Police investigators determined that Given and members of the 20–20 club were not on friendly terms.

The suspect admitted that he once owned several palm guns—of the type that might have fired the fatal .45-caliber slug—but when asked to produce the weapons for ballistics tests he said they were stolen from him or sold to a man who was later killed in Mexico.

The Metro Squad was advised that, of some 100 East Chicago police officers and civilian personnel who took lie detector tests at their request, the Latino police official alone failed to score a passing grade. He later contended that he flunked the polygraph because he was nervous, and steadfastly denied any wrong doing. When asked by Crawford and Van Bokkelen to take a follow-up lie test to clear his name he refused, and resigned from the force.

Investigators subsequently turned up a witness who said he had seen Given exchanging angry words with the same police official only minutes before the fatal shot was fired. The witness said he overheard Given threaten the lawman, "I'll see you walking a (expletive) beat again!"

DiCharia also quit the East Chicago department and moved to the Georgia seacoast town of St. Marys, where he became a sergeant on the small town police force. Five years after the slaying he contacted East Chicago authorities and told them he had lied about having no knowledge of the evidence tampering.

"I was a widower with five kids to raise. I lied to protect my job. I had no political connections," he said. "A son-of-a-bitch in our own department got the evidence. I was set up. That [tampering] was directed at me because the evidence was in my custody. Nobody wants this case solved more than me."

UPDATE

Detectives and special prosecutor Van Bokkelen are convinced that the killing was not planned, but that Given was killed on the spur of the moment by the East Chicago police official in the heat of an argument. The city was in the midst of a political power struggle, and Given was playing king-maker, making enemies on one side as he was garnering friends on the other. Both he and the suspect were known for their quick tempers. After resigning from the police force the suspect, realizing the investigation was now focused on him and nobody else, packed up his belongings and moved from the state.

The account given by the witness, placing the police official at Given's side moments before the slaying, jibed with other circumstances investigators had pieced together. The witness was a convicted auto thief, however, and prosecutors felt his credibility on the witness stand would leave a lot to be desired.

No one was ever charged in the homicide, although Van Bokkelen said he felt there was enough evidence to take into court and let a jury decide. "There are days when I feel we are this close to naming the killer," he said, holding his thumb and forefinger inches apart. "But the case isn't a sure winner on a platter. It was always regarded as a high-risk case."

The decision not to prosecute was made by Crawford, a rising star on the political scene, who later became Indiana's first lottery director. Following a 1989 sex scandal involving his relationship with a woman employee of his office, Crawford resigned and went into political exile.

BOOK XI

MURDER AT RANDOM

TAKE TWO CAPSULES AND CALL THE CORONER

On Wednesday morning, Sept. 29, 1982, twelve-year-old Mary Kellerman, a seventh grader at Schaumburg's Jane Addams Junior High School, gulped down two Tylenol capsules with a glass of water to try to kick a budding head cold before skipping off to class. A short time later she became violently ill in her home in Elk Grove Village, and before members of her family could do anything for her she was dead.

That same morning a twenty-seven-year-old postal worker, Adam Janus, complained of chest pains shortly after driving his neighbor's daughter home from nursery school in Arlington Heights. He went to the kitchen cabinet, got out the bottle of Extra-Strength Tylenol, and took two capsules. By noon he, too, was dead.

Meanwhile, over in Winfield, twenty-seven-year-old Mary Reiner was feeling a bit woozy. She had just come home from Central Du Page Hospital, where she had given birth to her fourth child two days earlier. By 3:45 that afternoon she was so violently ill she had to be rushed back to the hospital, where she died before doctors could determine the nature of her illness.

At four o'clock that afternoon, thirty-one-year-old Mary McFarland, the mother of two sons, complained of a "tremendous headache" while at work in the Illinois Bell Phone Center in the Yorktown shopping mall in Lombard. She became so ill, in fact, that someone called an ambulance which rushed her to Good Samaritan Hospital in Downers Grove, where she died of undetermined causes. Investigators found a bottle of Extra-Strength Tylenol in her purse.

Back in Arlington Heights, at the home of Adam Janus, the deceased postal worker, his brother, Stanley, twenty-five, and Stanley's nineteen-year-old wife, Theresa, had driven over from Lisle to make funeral arrangements. Neighbors had brought over some coffee, and commiserated with the young couple as they sat around Adam's kitchen table. At 5:44 P.M. Stanley was stricken so ill that his college student wife called an ambulance. By the time the emergency vehicle arrived at 5:51 she, too, had become violently ill. A short time later they, too, were among the unexplained dead.

That evening a United Airlines flight from Las Vegas touched down at O'Hare International Airport at 8:15 P.M. Paula Jean Prince, a thirty-five-year-old flight attendant from Chicago, left the plane as soon as the last passenger had disembarked. She hadn't been home in several days, and she had a turnaround that would require her to be on a flight the next morning, so she wouldn't get much sleep.

On the way to her North LaSalle Street apartment she was dropped off at the Walgreen drugstore at North Avenue and Wells Street, where she picked up a bottle of Extra-Strength Tylenol. She then walked to her apartment around the corner, put down her suitcase, took two capsules, and got ready for bed.

"We knew Paula was supposed to fly out again on Thursday, so we didn't miss her," her sister, Carol, said later. "But on Friday, when we couldn't locate her, we got concerned."

She and a friend, Jean Regula, went to Paula's apartment at 5:15 P.M. and found her dead on the bathroom floor.

Police were now conducting five separate investigations into mysterious deaths in the northwest suburbs of Elk Grove Village and Arlington Heights; in the western suburbs of

Winfield and Lombard; and in Chicago itself. It would be a full eighteen hours before investigators discovered a common denominator that linked the tragedies. A reporter for the City News Bureau in Chicago, poring over coroner's reports, first made the Tylenol connection. He called it to the attention of a deputy coroner, who passed the information on to police—just in case there might be something to it.

It was a bit farfetched, but authorities were grasping at straws. Arlington Heights authorities questioned neighbors of Adam Janus. They learned that while they were sitting around the kitchen, Stanley and Theresa Janus, under the stress of making burial arrangements for Stanley's brother, had taken Tylenol from a bottle on the kitchen counter to settle their nerves. It was the same bottle Adam had used before he collapsed.

The contents of the bottle were analyzed, and four of the remaining forty-five capsules were found to contain cyanide.

Investigators went to Mary Reiner's home in Winfield, where they determined that four pills out of forty-seven remaining in a Tylenol bottle there were also laced with cyanide. Elk Grove Village detectives found six poisoned pills in a bottle of fifty-one in the medicine cabinet at Mary Kellerman's home. In Mary McFarland's home in Elmhurst authorities found a Tylenol bottle with forty-four pills remaining—six of which were loaded with cyanide. In Paula Prince's apartment on LaSalle Street police found the Tylenol she had bought on the night she died. Of the twenty-three capsules still in the container, four contained deadly cyanide.

A near panic set in among regular pill users after Dr. Edmund R. Donoghue, Cook County's deputy chief medical examiner, warned the public against taking Tylenol until the investigation could be concluded. "It would appear that most or all of the Tylenol compound had been emptied out of certain capsules, and cyanide was substituted," he said. The remaining capsules found in the victims' homes contained sixty-five milligrams of the poison, well above the fifty milligrams considered lethal.

The race was now on to determine where the victims, or their families, had purchased the Tylenol. Adam Janus had obtained his medication at the Jewel Food Store in Arlington Heights. After his death other grief-stricken members of his family, who had assembled in his home, proceeded to pass around the bottle of Tylenol—but only his brother, Stanley, and Stanley's wife were unfortunate enough to pour out tainted capsules. It was the luck of the draw—headache roulette.

Other bottles of Tylenol laced with cyanide were found still on the shelves in stores in Schaumburg, Wheaton, and Chicago.

All of the suspect containers were from lot No. MC 2880. Johnson & Johnson's McNeil Laboratories, manufacturer of the product, quickly pulled it from the market and offered refunds to customers who had purchased containers from that lot. Walgreen's, Jewel, Osco, F.W. Woolworth, and other stores removed Tylenol from their shelves.

Meanwhile at McNeil's plant in Fort Washington, Pennsylvania, samples from lot MC 2880 were tested and found to be pure. Clearly, the Tylenol had been tampered with after it left the factory.

The terror quickly spread across the country in the form of copycat poisonings and false alarms.

The FBI entered the case as the Tylenol manufacturer posted a $100,000 reward for information leading to the arrest and conviction of whoever tampered with the medication.

A number of other Chicago area residents became ill and were hospitalized for cyanide poisoning after taking Tylenol, but none had ingested toxic levels of the substance.

As the investigation progressed there was yet another murder. John Stanisha, a forty-six-year-old Chicago father of three daughters, was considered the eighth victim of the tragedy, even though he had not taken any of the poison pills. Stanisha, a computer consultant, was shot to death by forty-nine-year-old Roger Arnold, a Jewel Food Stores warehouse employee, who mistakenly thought Stanisha had implicated him in the investigation. Arnold was sentenced to thirty years in prison for the slaying.

By week's end a Tylenol Task Force of more than 100 local, state, and federal investigators was involved in the case, working under the direction of Illinois Attorney General Tyrone Fahner.

In all probability the killer purchased a bottle of Extra-Strength Tylenol, took it home, poured out the medication and refilled the capsules with potassium cyanide. He then made the rounds of area drug and food stores, slipping several capsules out of Tylenol bottles on the shelves and replacing them with the poisoned ones.

Investigators surmised that the killer put the contaminated capsules on all the shelves on the same day, September 28. All of the poisoned packages were up front on the shelves, where a customer would reach for them first.

"He wanted a lot of people to die in a short period of time," said Illinois State Police Master Sergeant Richard Tetyk.

"Whoever laced the capsules with cyanide did an amateurish job. Some capsules were not even rejoined properly," Fahner said. "There is no meaningful way you can deal with a madman hell-bent on doing something like this."

"Because the deaths all occurred in connection with the same instance, the person responsible is considered a mass killer," State Police Captain Edward Cisowski pointed out. "Mass killers like a Richard Speck [the slayer of eight student nurses in Chicago in 1966] commit such a crime at one time, whereas serial killers like Ted Bundy [executed for murders in Florida] repeat their actions over and over again."

Psychiatrists portrayed the killer as a Dr. Jekyll-and-Mr. Hyde type. On the surface, they suggested, he was probably a man in his mid-twenties or early thirties who led a sane ordinary life. But back in the innermost corners of his mind he was plagued with doubts and illusions that the random killings could boost his sense of self-worth and achieve the notoriety that life had denied him.

Dr. Robert Stein, the Cook County medical examiner, speculated that the killer had probably committed suicide, and thus would never be discovered.

It was not long, however, before authorities had in custody a suspect who exactly fit the portrait painted by the psychiatrists. He was thirty-five-year-old James Lewis, a tax consultant, whose wife had worked for a travel agency. Lewis was sitting in the main branch of the New York City public library on December 12 when a well-dressed man walked up and tapped him on the shoulder.

When Lewis looked up inquisitively the man showed him a badge and said, "Come with me, please." His arrest culminated an intense investigation.

The week after the seven random victims died after taking Tylenol, Lewis had sent an extortion letter to the manufacturer demanding $1 million "to stop the killing."

The letter, which bore a New York postmark, touched off a manhunt by hundreds of New York detectives and FBI agents. It was eventually traced through handwriting analysis to Lewis, who was living there.

Although he was one of more than 2,000 leads or suspects being checked out at the time, suspicion was fueled when investigators quietly dug into the letter writer's background. They learned that he was wanted by postal inspectors for credit card fraud in Kansas City, Missouri, where he had also been indicted in 1978 for the grisly murder of an elderly resident. He was freed in the homicide case on legal technicalities.

Lewis and his wife, LeAnn, fled Kansas City in December of 1981 as U.S. Postal Service inspectors converged on their bungalow with a search warrant to obtain evidence in the credit card scheme. The couple came to Chicago, where they changed their names to Robert and Nancy Richardson.

Lewis got a job as a tax preparer, but was fired after a violent outburst in the office where he worked. His wife worked as a travel consultant, but lost her job when the agency went out of business. The couple left Chicago and moved to New York in September 1982—the same month the Tylenol deaths occurred.

Under questioning by federal authorities, Lewis admitted sending the million-dollar extortion letter to Johnson & Johnson, but denied going around to Chicago and suburban stores and slipping cyanide into random Tylenol containers.

"Look, if you didn't do it, we'd like you to take a lie detector test," authorities told him. "It will be an easy way to exonerate yourself in these murders." But Lewis refused, and to this day has balked at going on the lie box. "Those things are unreliable scientifically," he said. "I do not believe that polygraphs are accurate."

Lewis was returned to Kansas City, where he was convicted of credit card fraud and sentenced to ten years in prison. He was then transferred to Chicago, where he was tried in U.S. District Court for extortion in the Tylenol case, convicted, and sentenced to another ten years. Judge Frank J. McGarr ordered that the ten-year Tylenol sentence would not begin until after Lewis had completed the other ten-year sentence—effectively rendering him a twenty-year stretch. He is now confined to the federal prison in El Reno, Oklahoma.

Is Lewis also the Tylenol killer?

The investigation to determine whether he, or someone else, was the killer continues. Findings of the State Police Criminal Investigations Division have produced more than 20,000 pages of reports, a plethora of computerized data, and cost the taxpayers as much as $4 million. Some 6,500 leads have been checked out, and 400 possible suspects were scrutinized extensively.

Pointing to the unusual character of the investigation, Jeremy Margolis, Illinois Inspector General, said, "We lacked a crime scene and we lacked a motive, the two inroads to move into the solution. All that was left was the cyanide."

In all, the amount of cyanide that had taken seven lives, poisoned many others, caused a nationwide panic, and hit the taxpayers' pocketbooks for $4 million, had cost the killer about fifteen cents.

UPDATE

For Johnson & Johnson, the nightmare was the beginning of a years-long struggle to restore consumer confidence in their products. The drug industry, itself, spent millions to develop tamper-resistant packages and bottles.

Lawmakers enacted tough legislation to deter tampering, and framework agencies of the Tylenol Task Force, principally the State Police, FBI, and Federal Drug Administration, remain in place today, poised to respond without delay to any episode of drug tampering.

The $100,000 reward offered for the killer has never been claimed.

"More than eight years after the murders James Lewis remains our most viable suspect, because of the extortion letter he wrote to Tylenol's manufacturer," said Captain Cisowski.

Lewis' mandatory release date is in March of 1996. Some investigators would like to be able to ask him point blank, "Did you or did you not do it?"

"We've just got to know; to talk to him without any hidden microphones or criminal charges against him," one investigator said. "After all the deaths and man hours and money expended, we'd like to know one way or the other."

BOOK XII

MISSING AND
PRESUMED . . .

MYSTERY IN CANDYLAND

On Saturday, Oct. 27, 1990, a DeKalb County farm owned by Helen Vorhees Brach went on the auction block. It was the last bit of business to be taken care of in disposing of the estate of the mysteriously missing candy heiress. Other Brach properties in Glenview, Schaumberg, and Danville, plus homes in Ohio and Florida and another farm in Indiana, had been sold off earlier, one by one.

Although no one in authority knows what really happened to her, Mrs. Brach was declared legally dead in 1984. The money from each sale could thus go into a charitable foundation, as stipulated in her will.

"If you take the proceeds from the estate, as well as $7 million in taxes that have been recovered, the value of the Brach Foundation is now in excess of $50 million," said Edward Donovan, Jr., a lawyer who is handling the missing woman's affairs.

As a result, Helen Brach, heir to the vast Brach candy company fortune, will go down in history as the wealthiest person ever to disappear without a trace.

Helen Marie was born in 1911 in Unionport, Ohio, to Daisy Rowland and Walter Vorhees, who celebrated a hurry-up marriage just four months and three days earlier. She could trace her pedigree all the way back to her great-great-great-grandfather, Jacob Voorhees (the family later shortened the name), a German immigrant who settled in America around 1670.

A strikingly beautiful woman with reddish-gold hair, Helen was married and divorced by the time she was old enough to vote.

She was working as a hatcheck girl at a Miami Beach country club in 1950 when she met sixty-one-year-old Frank V. Brach, president of the E.J. Brach & Sons Candy Company of Chicago. She became his third wife the following year, at the age of thirty-nine. After Frank's death in 1970 she continued to live with her three dogs and her houseman, an ex-convict named Jack Matlick, on Brach's seven-acre estate in north suburban Glenview.

She became known as a woman who doted on animals, kept a diary, delved into psychic writing, and enjoyed big cars. Her fleet included a dark lavender Rolls Royce convertible, a pink Cadillac convertible, a salmon-colored Cadillac sedan, a fire-engine red Cadillac, and a pearl pink Lincoln Continental.

The last thing that is definitely known about Helen Brach is that she checked out of the Mayo Clinic in Rochester, Minnesota, on Feb. 17, 1977, with a clean bill of health. She had a ticket on a 2:00 P.M. Northwest Orient Airlines flight to Chicago. Airline records show the ticket was used, although nobody remembers the woman who used it.

Jack Matlick, the houseman, claims Mrs. Brach arrived home on schedule, and he drove her back to O'Hare International Airport to board a flight to Fort Lauderdale on the morning of February 21—four days after she was last seen alive by anyone else.

Police investigating Mrs. Brach's disappearance could find no record of any ticket purchased in her name to go to Fort Lauderdale or any other destination, however. Nor could authorities find Mrs. Brach's diaries—which Matlick conveniently claimed to have burned at her request. What they did learn was that Helen Brach had been the victim of a clever embezzlement scheme in which someone had forged her name to more than $13,000 worth of checks benefiting none other than Jack Matlick. They also learned that the weekend before Mrs. Brach disappeared, Matlick had purchased a large meat grinder.

A nationwide search for Mrs. Brach failed to turn up any trace of her, and no one was ever arrested in connection with her disappearance.

In 1988 a Mississippi convict named Maurice Ferguson led police to the Minneapolis area, where he claimed he buried "the candy lady" at the behest of Silas Jayne, a prominent Chicago horseman. Mrs. Brach was known to have had dealings with Jayne, which did not turn out to her liking. Authorities learned that Jayne, who died in 1978, had once been a cellmate of Ferguson while serving a prison term in connection with the murder of his own brother.

It sounded like a hot lead, but the celebrated body hunt turned out to be nothing more than a stunt Ferguson dreamed up to get out of his cell for awhile. No body was found, then or ever.

Although rewards of up to $250,000 were offered for information concerning Helen Brach's whereabouts—alive or dead—nothing was ever heard from her again.

The investigation into her disappearance continues to be actively pursued by Glenview police and detectives of the Illinois State Police Criminal Investigation Division. "I am optimistic," said State Police Lieutenant David Hamm.

Relatives of the missing woman also hired a private detective, Ernie Rizzo, to investigate the disappearance. In her book, *Thin Air*, author Pat Colander said, "Ernie Rizzo's final conclusion was that Mrs. Brach had become a missing person at the hands of Jack Matlick."

More specifically, Rizzo theorized, the ground was too frozen to dig a grave at the time the candy heiress disappeared, so her body was run through the large meat grinder Matlick had brought home and fed to her three dogs.

UPDATE

The specter of Helen Brach rose once again in the waning days of 1990, when her name came up during a federal investigation into Chicago area horse traders suspected of defrauding wealthy matrons. One name mentioned during the investigation was that of Richard J. Bailey, a stable owner accused in lawsuits filed by three wealthy widows of taking advantage of them on horse deals. Bailey, federal agents recalled, had once been a frequent escort of Mrs. Brach. At the time of her disappearance he invoked his rights against self-incrimination when authorities sought to question him.

As investigators dug deeper into the horse trading mess, agents of the U.S. Bureau of Alcohol, Tobacco and Firearms received a tip that an unidentified skeleton found in a forest preserve near the Indiana state line twelve years earlier was that of Helen Brach.

Hoping to clear up the Brach mystery for once and for all, Assistant U.S. Attorney Steven Miller obtained an order to exhume the bones, which had been buried in a pauper's grave in a south suburban Willow Springs cemetery.

Cook County Medical Examiner Dr. Robert Stein was almost beside himself. "It's a waste of time, money, and energy," he declared. "That body is not Mrs. Brach. It was obvious when we first discovered the body in 1978 that it wasn't her."

The skeletal remains of a white woman, believed to have been in her sixties, were found by a young couple strolling in the Wentworth Woods near 159th Street in Calumet City on October 1 of that year. The apparent homicide victim had been stuffed into a steamer trunk or foot locker, which had subsequently burned away, leaving only leather straps and the charred skeleton with its hands missing.

With the disappearance of Mrs. Brach still fresh in their minds, Glenview detectives and Illinois State Police investigators prevailed upon Dr. Stein to compare the bones to X-rays of the missing candy heiress. Stein determined that the skeleton was more than two inches shorter than Mrs. Brach, and had worn dentures. He estimated that the woman, whoever she was, had been without her own teeth for a good ten years, whereas Mrs. Brach had been to a dentist shortly before her disappearance.

Calumet City police theorized that the remains might have been dumped in the forest preserve by criminals from nearby Indiana, since other Indiana homicide victims turned up in the area from time to time. Efforts to identify the victim were unsuccessful, and the bones were given a pauper's burial.

Dr. Stein was indignant that authorities were now going to dig up the skeleton and perform another examination. "My medical reports were very accurate the first time," he asserted.

Never-the-less, the bones were disinterred shortly before Christmas and brought back to the medical examiner's office. Incredibly, the skeleton now had no head.

Charles Reilly, retired Calumet City fire chief who was present when the remains were originally discovered, consulted photographs he had taken at the time. "It had a skull in 1978, you can be sure of that," he said.

John Cadwalader Menk, the court appointed attorney for Mrs. Brach, determined that the skull disappeared shortly thereafter when someone in the Cook County medical examiner's office packed it up and sent it somewhere, since forgotten, in an effort to identify it. It probably rests today on the dusty shelf of some pathologist, who wonders where it came from and what to do with it.

Some investigators, pointing to the abundance of intrigue surrounding the Brach case, have hinted that the skull was deliberately lost, or destroyed, perhaps by whoever was responsible for Mrs. Brach's disappearance and presumed murder. More likely, however, it was packed off by a political employee who quit, retired, or moved on to another job and forgot about it.

Meanwhile the re-exhumed skeleton, minus the head, was reexamined by Dr. Stein, who brought in another forensic pathologist and an anthropologist to confirm his original conclusions. On December 27, two days after Christmas, all agreed that Dr. Stein was right the first time around.

But that wasn't good enough for Jerry Singer, a spokesman for the Bureau of Alcohol, Tobacco and Firearms. He ordered DNA (genetic) tests comparing the exhumed skeleton with samples of genetic material recovered from Mrs. Brach's home after she disappeared. Singer had no idea how long the tests would take, but asserted, "There's no timetable. It's not finished yet."

In late February 1991, the results of the DNA tests came back marked "inconclusive."

"This is silly," Stein declared. "It's definitely not Helen Brach. As far as we're concerned, the case is closed."

Either way, the big mystery remains: Who did what to Helen Brach, and why?

SNATCHED RIGHT OUT OF HER SHOES

One thing is known for sure about Molly Zelko. She is legally dead. That is a matter of court record. How she got that way remains a mystery that might never be resolved.

Amelia "Molly" Zelko, still a rather attractive woman at the age of forty-seven, was the epitome of the "crusading newspaper editor" in her day—an executive of a small-town weekly who wasn't afraid to take on anyone, including the mob.

That is not to say she wasn't afraid. She declared more than once that she feared that her life was in danger. But that did not stop her from going ahead and doing what she thought was right.

Molly ran the *Joliet Spectator*. Her official title was secretary-treasurer and business manager, but in truth she ran the whole shebang ever since her business partner, Bill McCabe, was beaten to within an inch of eternity by local thugs.

The *Spectator* was published every Thursday, which meant the paper "went to bed" on Wednesday evenings, which meant everybody worked late Wednesdays. Normally Molly would be in the office until 1:00 or 1:30 A.M. taking care of last minute details before the press runs. On the night of

Sept. 25, 1957, she cleared her deadlines earlier than usual and was on her way out the door at 11:27 P.M.

"So long, everybody. I'll see you tomorrow," she said cheerfully, as the printers locked the plates on the presses.

Molly climbed into her black 1955 Chrysler and headed for the apartment she maintained in one of Joliet's fine old homes at 413 Buell Street, several blocks away. Police know that she got there, because they found her car parked at the curb in front of the house Thursday morning. The doors were unlocked, and the keys were under the front seat where Molly had a habit of stashing them.

But it was what *else* the lawmen noticed that caused them grave concern. One of Molly's shoes was on the trunk of her car. The other was on the parkway between the curb and the sidewalk, where a passing bus driver had tossed it after he found it lying in the road.

A pair of empty shoes. That was the last trace anyone ever found of feisty Molly Zelko.

Because of Molly's importance in the community, Police Chief Joseph Trinza assumed personal command of the investigation into her disappearance. Police broke down the locked door to her second floor apartment, but there was no sign of her. Nor was there any indication that she had spent the night there. Her bed was unmussed, and the towels in the bathroom were dry.

If Molly had driven straight home after leaving the paper at 11:27, she would have arrived in two or three minutes. "I want a complete canvass of the neighborhood," Chief Trinza told his detectives. "Maybe somebody saw or heard something."

Somebody had, and the news was not encouraging. "I heard screaming around 11:30 last night, but I thought it was some teen-agers horsing around," one neighbor told detectives. A second neighbor also heard the screams. "I went to the window but I couldn't see anything so I went back to bed," she said.

Both neighbors said they heard a car door slam, and heard a car drive away, right after the screams.

Someone, it would appear, had snatched Molly Zelko right out of her shoes. The position of the shoes—one on the trunk of her car and the other in the road—indicated she was kicking and struggling as she was being forced into another automobile.

Chief Trinza ordered a missing person bulletin sent out over the police network. The subject was described as five feet four inches tall, 120 pounds, dark hair, and dark brown eyes. When last seen she was wearing a dark suit, white blouse, and a small hat. And, from all indications, she was in her stocking feet.

The investigation disclosed that area residents had seen a strange man lurking in the neighborhood. "I noticed this man walking past Molly's house last Sunday, and he didn't look like he belonged around here," one resident of the area reported. "I called my husband, but by the time he got to the front door, the person was gone."

Although police suspected otherwise, robbery was not ruled out as a motive. Molly was known to possess a platinum diamond bracelet worth $2,300; a ring with a one carat diamond surrounded by four smaller ones, valued at $1,700; and a $300 dinner ring. She presumably was wearing her jewelry when she vanished, since no trace of the bracelet or rings was found during a thorough search of her apartment.

Molly, who never married, also owned a very elegant seventeen carat diamond valued at well over $20,000. That rock, alone, would have been motive enough for robbery. Her friends knew, though, that she did not have that with her. C.H. Peterson, chairman of the Will County Republican Central Committee, told police a curious story:

"Molly gave me the diamond a month ago to keep for her. I put in in my safe deposit box with her name on it. It's still in my box at the bank." Why Zelko had taken this precaution remains to this day one of the mysteries in her disappearance. You just don't take an extremely valuable piece of jewelry and turn it over to someone else to hold unless you are concerned that something is liable to happen to it.

Indeed, robbery could not immediately be ruled out as a motive. But it was what had happened to Molly's partner, McCabe, that caused authorities far greater concern.

An outspoken law-and-order man, William R. McCabe, seventy-three, the father of five daughters, lived on a 160-acre farm near Lockport. An attorney, he served in the Illinois House of Representatives from 1912 to 1922, and as mayor of Lockport from 1923 to 1925. He had law offices in Chicago, where he specialized in criminal law, from 1922 to 1930, and from 1932 to 1936 he served as state's attorney of Will County, of which Joliet is the county seat.

Molly served as McCabe's secretary during his term as the county's chief prosecutor. When he acquired control of the *Joliet Spectator* in 1936, he took the twenty-six-year-old secretary along to help run the paper.

The *Spectator* enjoyed a turbulent history under the McCabe-Zelko regime, with crusades against gambling and bitter editorials against politicians suspected—or known—of having their hands in the cookie jar. In 1938 a deputy sheriff, angered over an editorial, accosted McCabe on the street and beat him.

But the crusades continued, and the paper continued to make enemies as it gained readers. By 1941 Molly owned a 33 percent interest in the paper. By 1953 she and McCabe were equal partners, each holding 48 of the 100 shares in the *Spectator*.

Of the four remaining shares, one was owned by a private citizen, and the other three were placed in trust with Frank Masters, Jr., the Will County state's attorney, under an agreement that they would go to the survivor on the death of either Molly or McCabe.

The "survivor" pact was worked out after McCabe suffered his second frightening beating, from which he barely survived.

He was driving home from the paper to his Lockport farm on an April day in 1948 when two men abducted him and drove him to a lonely country road. There, in the quiet of the countryside, the two thugs beat the sixty-four-year-old newspaper crusader with spiked clubs, breaking both his legs and one of his arms. Then, as he lay battered and bleeding on the ground, they relieved him of forty dollars—a bonus for their work.

The beating left McCabe in broken health, and had a profound effect upon Molly and her career. He spent an entire year in the hospital, recovering from his injuries, while Molly took care of the paper.

From his hospital bed McCabe charged that the beating was carried out on orders of Francis Curry, the millionaire slot machine boss of Will County and reputed representative of the crime syndicate in the Joliet area. McCabe had warned Curry editorially not to run for Republican committeeman from Joliet's Sixteenth Precinct.

Whether Curry was responsible for the beating was never established as a certainty, but Molly developed an undying hatred for him and his associates, and under her direction the *Spectator* launched an all-out blitz against gamblers and gambling in Will County.

So great was her obsession that in her "Around the Town" column of June 20, 1957, she even went so far as to ridicule an account of a social function in Curry's home that appeared in a rival Joliet publication.

McCabe blamed Curry for her subsequent disappearance. On October 9, two weeks after Molly's shoes were found by her abandoned car, McCabe wrote to FBI Chief J. Edgar Hoover, asking his help in the search.

"Due to the underlying gangster and criminal background in this county, I am fearful she has been kidnapped," he told Hoover. "I am certain this is not a voluntary disappearance. I have known Miss Zelko for years and she has been closely associated in my newspaper fights against crime and corruption."

Though the feds said they could not enter the case unless it could be proved that Molly had indeed been kidnapped, they did make their facilities available to local authorities in connection with the hunt.

Police questioned Curry, along with a number of other gamblers, night club owners, politicians, and others who had drawn the wrath of Molly Zelko's typewriter. They learned zilch.

There was no question but that Molly lived in fear of her own life, despite her bold crusader front.

In a letter to a friend in which she referred to McCabe's near fatal beating she wrote, "Everything since that night seems terrifying and not one day since, can I say has been a happy one. Everything in life seems to center around that night and each day brings more sorrow and grief because of that night."

Several months before her disappearance, in the midst of her paper's crusade against pinball machines in Joliet, she confided to a close friend, "I fear something might happen to me."

Friends told police that Molly feared somebody might try to plant a bomb under her car. On one occasion she offered to trade automobiles with another woman, but the woman would have no part of it.

Yet another friend told investigators that about two months before she disappeared Molly telephoned her late at night and asked her to come to the *Spectator* office. "I'm in trouble and I'm afraid I'm going to get my head blown off," Molly told her.

The woman said she went to the newspaper office as Molly had requested, but could not get in. "The lights were turned off, and Molly wouldn't let me in. I finally drove away, and as I did so I noticed that two men in another car were following me," she said, still shaken over the experience.

Police learned that Molly once told another friend she had no fear of being abducted because, "I'd leave something behind." There was much talk of her keeping secret files, but a police search of her apartment and office turned up nothing of evidentiary value.

There was also a rumor that Molly maintained a file, with orders to destroy it in the event of her death. Her secretary told police that after Molly disappeared, a man who identified himself as her brother came to the *Spectator* office and specifically asked for a package of letters and documents wrapped in a "pink ribbon." "My sister wanted those papers destroyed," he explained. "I told him I didn't know of any such package," the secretary told investigators.

A safe deposit box rented jointly with McCabe after they signed the trust agreement in 1953 was opened in the presence of police officials for the first time since it had been leased. It was found to contain only personal and business papers, along with the trust agreement dealing with the three *Spectator* shares that would give the survivor complete control of the paper.

Molly's own forty-eight shares were not there. They were subsequently found in the safe deposit box of a sister.

Investigators were mystified as to why Molly, with two safe deposit boxes at her disposal—her own and her sister's—had gone to Peterson a month before she vanished and asked him to keep her most valuable diamond in his bank box.

If Molly had been around, incidentally, she would have inherited the three shares in trust and become the *Spectator*'s major stockholder. McCabe died less than a year after her disappearance, on Aug. 13, 1958, at the age of seventy-four.

In October of that same year a Joliet man out looking for a job stumbled upon the badly decomposed body of a woman in a ditch at 138th Street and Thornton Road in the suburb of Blue Island, northeast of Joliet. The body, about five feet two inches tall, was clad in a slip and brassiere and a pale green dress. A coroner's pathologist estimated she had been thirty to forty-five years old, and had been dead for at least six months.

A Joliet detective, armed with Molly's dental charts, hustled to Chicago to confer with Coroner Walter E. McCarron. The coroner, a flagrant publicity hound, would have loved to have gone on television to announce that Molly Zelko had been found, but it was not to be. The dental charts didn't match.

A month later James V. Rini, a convict and former Chicago crime syndicate terrorist, confessed to the Senate Rackets Committee in Washington that he and two other hoodlums kidnapped and murdered Molly Zelko. The late Robert F. Kennedy, chief counsel for the committee, passed the following story on to Illinois investigators:

Rini and two companions forced Miss Zelko into their car at gunpoint as she got out of her Chrysler in front of her home. With Rini behind the wheel, the gunmen drove to a farm several miles north of Joliet. Once there one of the two men who had held Miss Zelko captive in the back shot her in the head. After she was killed Rini and the others buried her in a grave that had been prepared in advance and covered her body with quicklime.

Rini told the Senate committee he embarked on the mission of murder at the behest of Chicago crime syndicate chieftains who paid him $3,000. These included Curry, Frank LaPorte, overall gambling boss in Will County and southern Cook County, and mob boss Willie "Potatoes" Daddano, he claimed. He identified the triggerman in the Zelko slaying as hoodlum Frank Mustari.

Kennedy flew to Chicago to accompany Senate investigators and Rini to the farm Rini described, where they were joined by Illinois State Police.

For two days the lawmen dug up the farmyard, at a point designated by Rini, but found nothing. They also put out feelers for Mustari, the alleged gunman, and learned that he had been slain during the attempted murder of a tavern keeper three months before Molly disappeared.

Confronted with this gross contradiction in his story Rini, who had been serving a ten-to-fourteen-year prison sentence for damaging coin machines, burglary, and robbery, admitted his "confession" was a hoax. He said he had hoped to gain preferential treatment from the Senate committee, which was investigating juke box and coin machine gangsters in the Chicago area.

Kennedy, infuriated at being taken in by the hoax, whacked Rini across the seat of his pants with the flat part of a shovel and sent him back to prison.

Police continued to search high and low for Molly, or her body. They even used helicopters and enlisted the aid of lawmen in adjoining counties to look into out of the way places. The hunt continued uninterrupted for one solid year, without results. After that the investigation just plain petered out, because there was nothing left to investigate.

"We've had rumors of all kinds. We've checked them all out, with the aid of other departments, to no avail. We're not getting anywhere with this case," Chief Trinza said. "We're still hoping we'll get some break. As it stands, Miss Zelko is another missing person."

No trace was ever found of Molly Zelko. In addition to her shoes and her Chrysler, she left that seventeen-carat diamond that had been intrusted to Peterson, a mink coat, and some miscellaneous fur pieces—but no cash that anyone could find.

Oh, yes. She left behind one other thing: The most puzzling mystery Joliet has ever known.

UPDATE

On Jan. 5, 1965, slightly more than seven years after she disappeared, Molly Zelko was declared legally dead. Her will, disposing of an estate estimated at $36,200, was admitted to probate and her brother, Frank, of Joliet, was named executor of the estate.

A SUMMER OUTING TO ETERNITY

From the moment the red sun climbed over the horizon on Saturday morning, July 2, 1966, Ann Miller knew it was going to be a real sizzler. The twenty-one-year-old Lombard horse-woman gave her dark brown hair a lick and a promise as she stood in front of the mirror. Then she got her two-piece blue bathing suit with a red belt out of the dresser drawer and wriggled into it. She pulled her blue denim shorts on over the swimsuit, slipped on a light polo shirt and stepped into her sneakers. She casually tossed her white bathing cap, towel, comb, and thermos into a beachbag and ducked out of the house to get an early start on the long Fourth of July weekend.

After backing her eleven-year-old Buick out of the drive on Rochdale Circle she headed for Westchester, where she picked up Patty Blough, nineteen, at her home on Drury Lane. As Blough was leaving the house she called over her shoulder, "We'll be home early, Mom, 'cause Renee has to make dinner for her husband."

The two young women drove to Chicago's West Side where nineteen-year-old Renee Bruhl, the only married one of the group, was waiting for them at her home in the 5800 block of West Fulton Street.

By 8:00 A.M. they were well on their way to Indiana Dunes State Park, hugging the Lake Michigan shore some sixty miles southeast of the city on the Indiana side of the line. Along the way they stopped at a drugstore to pick up a $1.53 bottle of suntan lotion.

The air temperature had already climbed to 88 degrees by the time they arrived at the park two hours later, with light winds coming in off the lake. By eleven o'clock the thermometer would register a sweltering 90 degrees, and at noon the mercury would hit 92.

Patty Blough, Ann Miller, and Renee Bruhl were among 8,600 sun worshippers in 2,178 automobiles to pass through the park gate that Saturday. After Ann found a parking spot in the sprawling lot they hiked down to the beach, nearly three-quarters of a mile east of the pavilion. Patty and Renee left their shoes in the car and walked barefoot.

The trio picked out a spot and spread their blanket on the side of a dune under three poplar trees that might give them some shade from the blistering sun. Then they peeled down to the swimsuits they had worn beneath their street clothes.

The deeply suntanned Patty, who stood five feet four inches tall and had soft brown hair and brown eyes, wore a bright yellow two-piece bikini with ruffles. Renee, the tallest of the three at five feet nine inches, with brown hair and hazel eyes, had on a brown swimsuit with a pattern of green flowers and solid leaves. Ann, the little one at five-foot-two, carefully folded her blouse and denim shorts and placed them at the edge of the blanket.

The spot they had selected was about 100 yards from shore, and as the beach became more crowded the three sunbathers on the blanket were hardly noticed.

Toward nightfall a young Chicago couple, Mike Yankalasa and Frances Cicero, flagged down Park Ranger Bud Connor and called his attention to the abandoned blanket on the sand.

"There were three girls. They left all their belongings on the blanket around noon and never came back," they told him.

"They were out in the water, talking to some guy in a boat. Then they got aboard and took off, heading west."

"Yeah? What kind of a boat?" asked Connor.

"It was a white outboard with a blue inside, maybe fourteen or sixteen feet long."

"O.K. Thanks, kids. I'll take it from here."

The ranger was only mildly curious. Small boats with suntanned, shiny-teethed young men aboard were always pulling in close to shore, trying to pick up girls. No doubt the young ladies had gone off on a lark that was turning into a moonlight cruise.

Patty Blough had trustingly left behind her yellow robe, a pair of sunglasses, a transistor radio, a white print towel, and her wallet containing five dollars. Renee Bruhl left a large towel, her shorts, blouse, cigarettes, the bottle of suntan lotion, twenty-five cents in coins, and her pocketbook containing about fifty-five dollars in checks. Ann Miller left her thermos bottle on the blanket, along with her shorts, shoes, polo shirt, bathing cap, and comb.

Connor carefully picked up the blanket by its corners, so none of the items would tumble out, and took it to the office of Park Superintendent William Svetic for safekeeping.

"Thanks, Bud. Some gals'll come looking for this stuff and be glad nobody ran off with it," Svetic told the ranger.

But they never did. The blanket and belongings were set aside and all but forgotten as the harried park staff coped with the holiday weekend crowd.

Early Monday morning—July 4—Svetic got a telephone call from a man who identified himself as Harold Blough.

"My daughter and two of her girlfriends went to the park Saturday and they haven't come home. They left Chicago around eight o'clock and should have gotten to the park around ten," he said apprehensively. "I've checked with the other girl's families, and they haven't heard anything either."

"All right Mr. Blough. Thanks for calling. I appreciate your concern, and I'll get back to you," Svetic told the worried father. Suspecting there might be a connection, the park superintendent surveyed the items left behind on the blanket. They included a key ring with a miniature Illinois license plate, number 265–487. He asked the rangers to check the parking lot. Sure enough, there was a 1955 Buick four-door with license plates matching the key ring. Inside the car were several items of clothing, and shoes belonging to Renee Bruhl and Patty Blough.

At 8:50 A.M. Svetic put in a call to Indiana State Police, who were quartered just south of the park on Indiana Highway 49. A squad was on the scene within minutes.

At 10:00 A.M. Trooper Harry Young inventoried the items left behind on the blanket, including the key ring. Then he contacted Illinois authorities and asked them to run a check on the license plates on the Buick.

At 10:20 A.M. Chicago police advised the trooper that the car was registered to Ann Miller of suburban Westchester. A check with Westchester police disclosed that a missing person report had been filed on her by family members the night before.

The empty beach blanket and abandoned car suddenly became the focal points of an urgent police matter.

The state police, who had jurisdiction over the park, called in First Sergeant Edward Burke, a sixteen-year veteran of the force, who was regarded as one of the best detectives in the department. The thirty-nine-year-old investigator joined troopers at the scene, went over the evidence with them and interviewed park employees, trying to piece together what might have happened to the trio.

At 3:50 P.M., after satisfying himself that the women were nowhere in the immediate vicinity, Burke alerted the U.S. Coast Guard and requested a sweep of the southern end of Lake Michigan. The Coast Guard estimated that between 5,000 and 6,000 small boats had been on the lake between Chicago and the Indiana Dunes State Park on Saturday, when the women disappeared. Identifying the craft on which they might have gone joyriding would have been impossible.

With two days already elapsed before police got into the case, Burke knew that each passing day would make the mystery tougher to solve. Witnesses would become more vague in details. The wind and weather would obliterate possible clues in the ever-shifting sand.

The first thing Tuesday morning the detective ordered an all-out search of the 2,180-acre park and the adjoining shoreline, extending all the way to Michigan City near the Indiana-Michigan line.

Search parties, coordinated by Svetic and State Police First Sergeant Albert Hartman, spread out over the sprawling parkland, over sand dunes, through thick woods, and across quiet meadows containing some of the finest flora anywhere in the Middle West. Among them were forty-two soldier volunteers from a nearby Nike missile base, and ten members of the Porter County Sheriff's Posse on horseback.

In sifting through the contents of nineteen-year-old Renee Bruhl's purse, meanwhile, detectives found something rather disturbing. The abandoned purse contained an unmailed letter to her husband of fifteen months, Jeffrey. The missive, written two weeks earlier, suggested Renee wanted to leave her husband because he spent too much time with friends, working on hot-rod cars. For reasons known only to herself, she never delivered the message, but carried it in her purse.

"This note could suggest a planned disappearance, but I don't buy it," Burke told other detectives. "Leaving the letter behind like this would have given the plot away."

Police questioned the husband, a twenty-one-year-old accounting student. He assured them there had been no marital problems that he knew of. Members of the missing woman's family discounted the importance of the note, suggesting Renee might have written it during a fit of depression and then forgot about it.

As darkness enshrouded the park at the end of the fourth day, Burke ordered a beach buggy patrol of the shoreline. "If the three girls did indeed drown on Saturday, their bodies are due to surface and float to shore," he explained grimly.

On Wednesday, July 6, the search shifted to a six-mile stretch of beach west of the park extending to Ogden Dunes, an area of woods and expensive homes. Burke ordered the action after state police received two telephone tips—one from an Indianapolis couple, and the other from two men who lived in the Chicago suburb of South Holland.

Both parties reported seeing three young women get into a boat containing a well-tanned male in his early twenties, with dark, wavy hair and wearing a beach jacket. After the women climbed aboard, the boat took off in a westerly direction.

The witnesses recalled that one of the women was wearing a yellow swimsuit. That could have been Patricia Blough.

Later that same day debris from a wrecked boat washed ashore three miles west of the park where the women were last seen. Searchers found pieces of styrofoam and metal, believed to have been parts of three boat seats, along with oil and gasoline cans and a piece of oil-soaked wood.

The discovery was made near the Northern Indiana Public Service Company's Bailly Generating Station, which maintained a water intake crib about a quarter-mile out in the lake. Police theorized that a boat might have smashed into the crib in the dark and broken up.

Curiously, neither the police nor the Coast Guard had any record of any boat having been reported missing. The Civil Air Patrol flew over the area in search of additional debris but spotted nothing.

"As of this time we have no evidence of a connection between the debris and the missing women," Burke told news reporters congregating at the scene.

The air and sea hunt resumed Thursday as Civil Air Patrol planes from two states crisscrossed the lower end of the lake south of a line extending from downtown Chicago to New Buffalo. The Coast Guard dispatched ten cutters, one airplane, and one helicopter to aid in the search. Two army choppers also joined in the operation.

As the aircraft soared overhead, dozens of scuba divers working from an army amphibian "duck" explored the lake bottom from a point opposite where the women's blanket was found to an area as far west as the steel mills at Burns Ditch.

At the same time Coast Guard cruisers were checking every boat along the Lake Michigan shore in Illinois, Indiana, and Southern Michigan. The search would continue uninterrupted for a solid week.

Back at Dunes Park, Svetic urged anyone with bloodhounds to come and join in the search, and asked the owners of private cabins along the shore to check their properties for signs of the missing sunbathers. The sheriff's posse checked out some 250 cabins, talking to anyone they could find at home, and peering through the windows of those that appeared unoccupied.

The park superintendent also appealed to the public for anyone who might have seen the three women enter a boat to contact him. In all he received more than 100 calls from citizens hoping to help. Typical of the calls was one from a druggist who insisted he had seen Blough in his shop several days before the disappearance.

"She was in here and bought a couple of those love story magazines, three birthday cards, a pair of earrings, and three pairs of stockings," he told detectives.

Other sightings, by callers who had seen pictures of the women in the newspapers, were reported in Michigan, Illinois, and Wisconsin. Various other callers, who had been in the park over the weekend, thought they saw the women enter a boat with three men, two men, or one man.

A lifeguard told investigators he had seen the women get into a boat with three men on board. This seemed the best lead yet, until the witness changed his mind and said he did not think they were the same girls.

In the end, the best lead appeared to be the original one, from the teen-aged couple who told the ranger they had seen the women get into a small boat containing one man. This account was subsequently backed up by the South Holland and Indianapolis witnesses.

Later Thursday, Coast Guardsmen located three Michigan City men who said they had attempted, without success, to pick up three women at the beach with their boat on

Saturday. "They were standing in the water up to their chins," one of the boaters related. "This one girl said, 'I can't go. I'm married,' and the other two girls said they wouldn't go with us either."

The men's report refueled speculation that the women might have drowned after all. Six scuba divers were sent into the chilly lake to probe the sandy bottom. They worked throughout the night as floodlights reflected eerily off the water to the monotonous drone of an electric generator. The diving continued all day Friday, without result.

"The presence of shoes left behind on the blanket is a pretty good indication that they had gone into the water, either for a swim or a boat ride," Burke said, in reviewing details of the disappearance with the park superintendent. "But the fact that they left behind their purses and other personal stuff is a pretty good indication that they intended to come back in a short time."

"Well, Ed, I'm 90 percent sure they were victims of an accidental drowning," Svetic suggested.

"I don't buy that, Bill," the detective argued. "We've checked with the families, and all three were good swimmers. Patty Blough was capable of swimming twenty to thirty miles. True, one girl could have gone down—maybe cramps or something—but not all three of them. I can't see that at all."

"What about the boat angle?"

"As far as the families know, none of the girls had friends with boats. As a matter of fact, all three of them were heavily into horseback riding."

Patty Blough owned a thoroughbred named Hank, which was presently stabled at a track near Winnipeg, Manitoba, where it had won a race two weeks earlier. Before acquiring Hank she owned a saddle horse, which she boarded in the same stable that Ann Miller kept her animal. That was where the two first met.

"So far we have nothing to indicate foul play," Burke emphasized. "But nothing has been found to indicate what else might have happened to them, either."

By the end of the week Burke and Svetic, who had been all but working around the clock, were satisfied that the three women were nowhere in the park, dead or alive, and the search was called off.

The volunteers returned to their jobs, the soldiers hiked back to the Nike base, and Sheriff William Seidel led his mounted posse back to their station.

Patty's fifty-nine-year-old father, Harold Blough, who had caught only intermittent snatches of sleep during the week long ordeal, sat on the ground exhausted and ran his hand over his unshaven face.

"We can't be sure of anything right now," he said. "They could have been drowned or taken away in a car. I can't seem to keep my thoughts straight."

Pulling the plug on the search left nothing but routine nuts-and-bolts police work, interviewing friends, relatives, and coworkers, in an effort to come up with one common denominator that might bring the jigsaw pieces together.

Patty Blough worked as a secretary for Commonwealth Edison Company. She had previously worked for six months as a secretary for Sears, Roebuck & Company after graduating from Proviso West High School in Maywood. She had become an expert swimmer while spending her summers at a lake cottage owned by her parents in Wisconsin.

"She learned to swim up in the North Woods when she was two years old. She could swim for hours," her father told police.

Ann Miller had no problems that anyone was aware of at the swank Oak Brook Polo Club, where she worked exercising horses; and Renee Bruhl, who had been a high school classmate of Blough's, seemed happy working at her job as a credit clerk in a Loop department store while her husband finished school.

The weekend after the disappearance every visitor to the park was made aware of the incident. Under Burke's direction, 5,000 circulars containing photos and descriptions of the women were distributed throughout the area.

Meanwhile Harold Blough, a lieutenant in the Illinois Civil Air Patrol, carried on a personal search for his daughter and her two friends. Along with A.W. Hardt of west suburban Hillside, a Civil Air Patrol major, and Detective Fred Miller of the Westchester Police Department, Blough flew over the Lake Michigan shoreline from Calumet Harbor to Michigan City in a four-passenger Cessna 210.

The three made several passes along the beach and over wooded areas and summer homes, taking aerial photographs which Blough would pore over endlessly, looking for any indication of his daughter's fate.

"If I can just find one small fact that will be of use to the police . . ." he said hopefully.

Renee Bruhl's father, Joseph Slunecko, expressed confidence that the three were still alive. He said he felt they had voluntarily left the area but were "too frightened" to return after seeing the stir the disappearance had caused.

Blough did not see it that way at all. "In my heart I feel this is an abduction. My daughter is a regular reader of the newspapers. If she were free to move, she would have read newspaper accounts of the search for her and her friends, and she would have come home. If she were running away she would have taken more clothing, and her contact lenses, her cosmetic case, and the keys for her car. Besides, she was completely wrapped up with her horse. She would not have run out on Hank," he insisted.

That weekend, while police in Indiana searched in vain for his owner, Hank won $900 in a horse race at Winnipeg.

The next lead in the baffling case came from a Ligonier, Indiana, man, who had been panning the dunes beach with his movie camera on the Saturday of the disappearance. He turned the film over to investigators. From the home movie, and from the hundreds of interviews of possible witnesses, authorities were able to narrow their search to two boats—a cabin cruiser, twenty-six to twenty-eight feet long; and a sixteen-foot or eighteen-foot trimaran runabout, possibly a sailboat being powered by its auxiliary motor.

"The smaller boat is fairly distinctive because of its three-hulled design," Burke told his detectives.

"We know it was made of fiberglass, and was operated by a man in his early twenties, well tanned, with dark wavy hair and wearing a beach jacket. Three girls wearing the same colored bathing suits as Renee Bruhl, Patricia Blough, and Ann Miller, were seen getting into this boat. Miss Blough—or the person we believe to have been Miss Blough—sat up front beside the man. The other girls sat behind."

The cabin cruiser in question was spotted by Gary attorney Robert Blatz and his wife, about three hours after the women were seen getting into the smaller boat.

Witnesses told Burke the trio had wandered around the beach, getting something to eat, and going off into the dunes. "This raises the possibility that they came back to the beach in the runabout and waited for the young man to get his friends, who owned the cabin cruiser," the detective suggested.

According to Blatz, the cruiser came up close to the beach in the same area where the smaller craft had been. "One man left the cruiser and went directly to the beach and talked to the three girls," the witness asserted. "The girls accompanied the man to the cruiser, boarded it, and it put out into the lake."

Blatz, who observed the incident from a distance, said he was too far away to determine the facial features of the young women, so he could not be sure that they were Blough, Bruhl, and Miller. Burke said there appeared to be no question, however, that the women seen earlier aboard the smaller boat were Patty, Ann, and Renee.

Harold Blough issued another plea for information about his daughter, or about the whereabouts of the white trimaran with a turquoise colored inside.

"We've just got to break this thing. Each day that goes by gets worse," he said. "My wife is heartbroken. Every time the telephone rings, a knife goes through her heart. She is afraid of what she will hear. We want Patricia back very badly. There must be someone who can help us."

Divers even went down at the generating station's water intake crib three miles west of the park, to satisfy themselves that the women had not been sucked into the pipes while swimming.

Meanwhile a thorough background investigation turned up skeletons in the closets of all three women that their families did not necessarily know about.

"Each of the girls had personal problems that could have motivated them to stage what would appear to be a possible drowning accident," Burke wrote in a log he kept on the case.

Through their mutual interest in horses, Patty Blough and Ann Miller had come in contact with men who had criminal arrest records, the files showed. On the night before they disappeared, neither of them had come home.

And in March, about four months before the disappearance, friends of Blough noted an injury to her face that "could have been caused by a fist." When they asked about it, she confided that she was in some sort of trouble involving "some syndicate people" she knew. A friend of hers from Oak Park told investigators, "Patty told me, 'I'm going to leave and nobody will find me.'"

Burke learned that Blough had a boyfriend named John Paul Jones, whom he described in his log as an ex-convict and rodeo cowboy. At his request, FBI agents twice interviewed Jones in California in connection with the disappearance. He confirmed a romantic involvement with the missing horsewoman, but denied any knowledge of her whereabouts.

In delving into Ann Miller's personal life, investigators learned that she had confided in friends that she was three months pregnant, and was planning to move into a home for unwed mothers.

As for Renee Bruhl, her marriage was anything by idyllic. Shortly after she disappeared her husband joined the Army.

All three of the missing women, police learned in talking to those who knew them best, possessed what Burke's log described as "a certain youthful immaturity in judgment." They might well indeed have innocently gone off with someone who did not have their best interests in mind.

July moved into August, which faded into September, and still no word of the missing trio or the distinctive tri-hulled boat on which they were last seen.

In early autumn a Pontiac, Michigan, man told authorities that a girl with whom he shared a seat on a bus to Detroit resembled one of the missing woman. "When the bus arrived in Detroit the girl was met by two others, who looked very much like the other two missing ones," he said.

The possible sighting gave rise to new hopes that they really had run away and were alive and well, but Harold Blough knew his daughter better than that.

"All three are either dead, or being held some place against their will," he insisted. "Patricia was an adult girl who was given every freedom. If she wanted to go somewhere her mother and I would not object. She did not have to run away.

"And she loved that horse. No one could take care of the horse but her. If she wanted to run off, she would have made arrangements for someone to take care of Hank, but she didn't make any arrangements. There's something sinister about this. I hope I'm wrong, but I'm afraid I'll never see my daughter alive again."

The distraught father continued his one-man air search, flying countless missions over the southern end of Lake Michigan in chartered planes, looking for any sign of his missing daughter or her yellow bathing suit. He even flew down to Nassau to check out a false report that Patty had been seen there.

On the outside chance that the three women were still alive and working somewhere outside the area, their families printed 5,000 new circulars containing previously unpublished pictures of their daughters, and sent them to friends and relatives in other states. The flyers were also distributed among police departments in Florida, Arizona, California, and in cities with major horse tracks.

On July 2, 1968, the second anniversary of the disappearance, police received an unconfirmed report that Blough was seen riding in a pickup truck pulling a horse trailer in Moneta, a small town in Wyoming.

Burke dutifully contacted Wyoming authorities and asked them to check it out. "Due to the fact all of the girls liked horses, it can be assumed that they would frequent rodeos, dude ranches, riding stables, and racetracks," he advised.

He also traded information with police in San Francisco, after finding a cryptic mention in Blough's diary of "Fresno, Golden Gate Fields."

Sergeant Burke retired in 1971 after five solid years of trying to unravel the baffling case. He spent the next four years working for the U.S. government as a police advisor in South Vietnam, and was among the last Americans evacuated by helicopter from Saigon in 1975.

From there he went to Saudi Arabia as security chief for the King Faisal Medical Center in Riyadh.

Harold Blough, the determined father who refused to give up, retired and moved to Florida, but kept communication lines open to Burke in Arabia, exchanging theories about the mysterious disappearance of his daughter and her two friends.

After Burke retired the case was taken over by State Police Sergeant Michael Carmin. One day in the fall of 1975, when he and Trooper Lou Weber were sifting through the mountain of paperwork accumulated during the unending investigation, they came across a letter written to Indiana authorities from a spiritualist in Montana.

"I visualize a cabin on Lake Michigan, not too far from where the girls' beach blanket was found. There is a dark colored sand. There are rickety wooden stairs leading up from the beach to the cabin on a bluff, with a lawn chair outside with its bottom out," the spiritualist wrote. The medium's letter went on to say that the women's bodies were buried there.

"This piques my curiosity," Carmin said, passing the note to Weber. "There's no indication in the file that anyone ever looked into this aspect. The cabin described in the letter probably fits the location of several places. I think we owe it to the families of these girls to check it out."

Weber agreed. "At this point, hey, even a letter from a psychic is worth taking a look at."

Weber went out and checked the general area, driving his police cruiser as far as the narrow roads would take him near Beverly Shores, and then proceeding on foot. Nestled in a small cove flanked by wooded dunes, less than two miles east of the spot where the young women had spread their beach blanket nine years earlier, he came upon an old cabin. He returned to State Police headquarters with his eyes bulging.

"There's a place out there exactly like the one described in the letter, sergeant," he told Carmin.

Flushed with excitement that they might have stumbled onto something, Carmin, Weber, and two rookie patrolmen tossed some shovels into their cars and returned to the scene. A brisk wind off the lake whipped sand around their ankles as the four uniformed men huffed up the rickety wooden stairs leading from the beach at Indiana Dunes State Park.

"There's the cabin," Weber pointed out when they reached the top of a bluff overlooking the southern end of Lake Michigan. "See, in the yard—the dark colored sand and the lawn chair with the bottom busted out—just like she said."

The only comment Carmin could muster at the moment was, "What an eerie coincidence."

"If a crime was committed, this would be the place for it," Weber remarked. "No one could see into the cove from the beach, only from a boat on the lake. It's that secluded."

"Okay, guys. This is where we dig," Carmin said, regaining his composure. "This is crazy. Let's get at it."

Throughout that day and the next, and the next, the four lawmen sweated, puffed, groaned, and cursed as they kicked their shovels into the sandy soil, half expecting with each turn of the spade to uncover a human skull, a rib cage, or a thigh bone.

They turned over every inch of yard around the isolated cabin, but the only reward they got for their labor was sore backs. At the end of the third day Carmin called the dig to a halt. "Well, that's it," he said dejectedly. "Nothing!"

Exhausted, the unsuccessful hunters trooped back to their squad cars, tossed the shovels into the trunks, and drove off into the autumn sunset to report yet another disappointment in the will-o'-the-wisp search for Ann Miller, Renee Bruhl, and Patty Blough.

Over the years, various investigators who have worked on the case have narrowed their theories as to what might have happened to the young women to four possibilities:

1. They were involved in a horrible boating accident that left no physical trace of anyone aboard. This is doubtful, however, since no boat was reported missing at that time.

2. They were victims of an abduction that turned to murder aboard a boat.

3. Death, possibly murder, occurred after they left the boat in a bizarre climax to what had been planned as a "voluntary" disappearance.

4. Ann Miller's pregnancy might have led to an abortion death, with her two friends slain to keep them from talking.

"If violence occurred, it involved all three together. I strongly believe all three are dead," said Burke. "Otherwise, I am certain at least one of them would have made contact with her family. One of them would have felt the need to get back in touch."

Detective Burke, now retired in sunny Florida, is still working on the case in his own mind, because something inside will not let him forget the empty blanket on the sandy beach. "I seldom pass a day without thinking about the case," he said. "It nags at me. I feel sure some day the answer will surface. Perhaps a criminal caught by police in another crime will admit this one."

UPDATE

There is one more frightening theory which a number of investigators subscribe to, but may never be able to prove.

On June 14, 1965, Cheryl Lynn Rude, a twenty-two-year-old horsewoman, was blown to smithereens when a Cadillac owned by horseman George Jayne exploded at Jayne's Tri-Color stable in northwest suburban Palatine. Police deduced the bomb had been intended for Jayne, who was engaged in a bitter feud with his brother, Silas Jayne, owner of a rival stable. George Jayne was latter assassinated, and Silas went to prison for his role in his brother's murder.

During the George Jayne homicide investigation in 1970, Illinois Bureau of Investigation agents learned that Silas had once boasted to a sheriff in El Reno, Oklahoma, while on a horse-trading expedition, "I got three bodies buried under my house." Before IBI agents could interrogate the Oklahoma lawman he was killed in an accident.

But this much is known. Miller, Blough, and Bruhl were all avid horsewomen, and all frequented George Jayne's Tri-Color stables, now the site of Harper College. In going through the women's effects investigators found George Jayne's phone number, and the number of Silas Jayne's wife, in one of their purses.

A south suburban man who worked for Silas Jayne had owned a blue-and-white power boat, which he often took to the Indiana Dunes. When IBI agents went to check out the boat several years later they were told it had been destroyed by fire.

Authorities suspect that one or all of the missing women might have seen who planted the bomb that killed Cheryl Rude in George Jayne's car, and had to be silenced.

"There was always a strong suspicion on my part that their disappearance had something to do with the car bombing," said former Westchester Police Sergeant Fred Miller, who subsequently retired to northern Wisconsin. "They all did their share of riding horses at George's stables. They may have overheard something about that crime that led to their deaths."

Silas Jayne, a suspect in several other homicides as well, died in 1987 after serving seven years in prison for engineering his brother's murder.

EPILOGUE

Somebody out there knows something. What happened to the girls at the dunes? It had to take more than one person to abduct three athletic young women the likes of Ann Miller, Patty Blough, and Renee Bruhl. Who plugged Broadway Bill and Wendy McDade? It would have required at least one gunman to hold them captive while another drove the car to the Chiwaukee Prairie dumping ground. Who snatched Evelyn Hartley from her baby-sitting job? Where is Sal Pullia?

Despite the $100,000 reward in the Clem Graver case, nobody ever tried to claim it.

Dedicated police officers throughout the country, and Chicago in particular, have an enviable record of bringing killers to justice. Unsolved murders are the exception—not the rule—but they keep popping back into the headlines because, until they are solved, they will never go away.

Most homicides are cleared within hours, and it is not unusual for dogged investigators to work around the clock until they can make an arrest.

Sometimes all it takes is just one tip. A name. A description. The brutal murder of a twenty-two-year-year old woman in downstate Illinois was recently solved when a frightened witness finally came forward after more than two years of wrestling with her conscience. In Chicago, detectives solved a homicide that had been on the books for twenty-five years.

Who killed the Grimes sisters, the Schuessler brothers and Bobby Peterson? Who chopped off Judith Mae Andersen's head and cast it adrift in a bucket in Montrose Harbor?

What happened to Timothy Hack and Kelly Drew? Where are Molly Zelko and Helen Brach? Who invaded Valerie Percy's bedroom? Why would anyone want to shoot Charles Merriam? Who laced the Tylenol with cyanide?

Somebody knows. But perhaps he or she is reluctant to come forward and get involved for any number of reasons. Homicides are scary crimes. We understand fear of reprisal, fear for one's family, fear of self-incrimination.

But do the right thing. We'll make it easy for you. If you know anything at all about any of the unsolved murders recounted in these pages—or any other unsolved homicide—write to the authors in care of Bonus Books, 160 East Illinois Street, Chicago, IL 60611. We'll see that the information gets to the proper authorities, and that they do something about it.

REWARD INFORMATION

For Information on the Murder or Abduction of:

Judith Mae Andersen	$50,000
Helen Brach	$250,000
Beth Buege	$5,000
Maria Caleel	$50,000
Salvatore Canzoneri	$75,000
Julie Cross	$100,000
Richard Esparza	$10,000
Patricia Wisz Field	$10,000
Clem Graver	$100,000
Barbara and Patricia Grimes	$11,000

Sherry Gordon and Theresa Hall	$7,000
Timothy Hack and Kelly Drew	$10,000
Donna Hartwell and Frank Matous	$50,000
Elvia Johnson	$1,000
Lisa Kopanakis	$9,000
Ben Lewis	$10,000
Charles Merriam	$100,000
Valerie Percy	$50,000
Concepcion Reyes	$6,000
John and Anton Schuessler and Robert Peterson	$130,000

Adam Janus

Stanley Janus

Theresa Janus

Mary Kellerman ———————————————— $100,000

Mary McFarland

Paula Prince

Mary Reiner

Not surprisingly, no reward was ever offered in any of the mob hits. The "Outfit" has its own way of taking care of unfinished business.

ABOUT THE AUTHORS

Between them, Edward Baumann and John O'Brien have covered every major crime in Chicago and the Middle West in the past four decades. For the past fifteen years they have worked together as a team.

Baumann, a native of Kenosha, Wisconsin, served with the Army Air Corps in the South Pacific during World War II. He worked as a reporter or editor on the *Waukegan News-Sun*, *Chicago Daily News*, Chicago's *American*, *Chicago Today*, and the *Chicago Tribune* before turning to free-lancing full time in 1988. He is a past president of the Chicago Press Club, former chairman of the Chicago Press Veterans Association, a director of the Chicago Newspaper Reporters Association, and winner of two Chicago Newspaper Guild Page One Awards for investigative reporting. In 1988 his peers honored him as Chicago Press Veteran of the Year.

O'Brien, who was born in Chicago, served with the U.S. Marine Corps before becoming a crime reporter for the *Chicago Tribune*. His assignments have taken him to police stations and county morgues from coast to coast. He has done in-depth stories on criminal justice in Michigan and California, exposes on child abuse in Texas and political dirty tricks in North Dakota, covered mob chief Tony Accardo in Florida, and joined investigators in tracking three suspects in a fortune in stolen cash all the way to the British West Indies. In 1989 he shared the *Tribune*'s Edward Scott Beck Award for investigative reporting.

Baumann and O'Brien are also the authors of *Chicago Heist*, the true story of America's biggest and most bizarre cash theft, and more than 300 internationally published detective magazine articles. Baumann is also the co-author, with Kenan Heise, of *Chicago Originals: A Cast of the City's Colorful Characters*.

INDEX

Abbatacola, Elena, 3–5
Abt, Ronald, 182
Accardo, Tony, 247
Adler, Artie, murder of, 234
Aiuppa, Joseph "Doves," 241, 243, 252, 253
Alden, Amy, murder of, 42, 46
Alderisio, Felix "Milwaukee Phil," 253
Aleman, Harry, 226
Allen, Detective Lee, 114
Allotta, Officer James, 43–44
Allsop, Detective Don, 34
Alterie, Leland Varain, murder of, 278, 279
Amatuna, Salvatore "Samoots," murder of, 275–77
Andersen, Bobby, 5
Andersen, Jimmy, xiii, 3–4
Andersen, Judith Mae, murder of, xiii, 3–5, 7, 9, 11–12, 13, 18, 30
Andersen, Ralph, 4, 5
Anderson, Frances, 286, 293

Anderson, Thomas "Shaky Tom," 286, 293
Andrews, Marcy Jo, disappearance of, 94–95
Anonymous phone calls
    in the Callahan case, 164
    in Grimes sisters murder case, 21, 22, 23
    in Hawkins case, 307
Arnold, Roger, 324–25
Austin, Richard, 29, 30

Babcox, Coroner Robert H. "Mickey," 196, 197, 201, 203, 219
Bailey, Richard J., 334
Banks, Detective Commander Robert, 305
Barker, Marie Ann, 168, 174–75
Barry, Lieutenant Edward, 144
Baum, Joan, 218
Beatings
    Betteley, Judith, 41
    Davis, Jody Lynn, 94–95

Flanagan, Barbara, 41, 45
Goodman, Philip "Philly,"
  263–65
Hulse, Darlene, 124–27
Kandel, Sally, 41, 45
Morecraft, Kathleen, 41
Raftopoulos, Gus, 110–11
Beck, Ben, 86
Beck, Berit, murder of, 85–88
Beck, Dave, 85, 87
Beck, Diane, 86
Bedner, Joanne, 94
Bedwell, Edward L. "Bennie,"
  28, 29
Begner, Captain Maurice, 30,
  290
Bergstrom, Police Chief Keith,
  113, 114
Bermuda Triangle, of murder,
  39–40
Betteley, Judith, murder of, 41
Big Cat. See Lewis, Benjamin F.
Big Nine, 298
Bjork, Dr. Robert, 194
Black politicians, 283–95, 297,
  306–9, 311
Blasi, Dominick "Butch," 242
Blatz, Robert, 356
Blough, Harold, 348, 354, 355,
  356, 358, 359
Blough, Patty, disappearance
  of, xiv, 346–63
Bobowski, Dr. Stanley, 71
Bodner, Officer William, 42
Boeck, Renata, 172
Bolton, John H., murder of,
  297
Bonet, Nai, 172
Borak, Catherine, 22
Borowski, Deputy Bob, 211,
  214, 215
Bostetter, Lieutenant Michael,
  194

Brach, Frank V., 332
Brach, Helen Vorhees, disap-
  pearance of, ix, 331–36
Brach Foundation, 331
Braun, Lieutenant Frank, 141,
  142
Brickhouse, Jack, 98
Broadway Bill. See Callahan,
  William H.
Brown, Al, 260
Brown, Detective Bernie, 236
Brown, Joseph, 285, 290
Brown, Sheriff Thomas, 196,
  197, 202, 203
Bruhl, Jeffrey, 350
Bruhl, Renee, disappearance
  of, xiv, 346–63
Bruno, Captain Michael, 36,
  38
Brzeczek, Police Superinten-
  dent Richard, 250
Buccieri, Fiore "Fifi," 231–32,
  259
Buege, Beth, murder of, 89–90
Buege, Bonnie, 90
Buege, Robert, 90
Buerger, Chief Deputy Harry,
  154, 155
Bulman, Lloyd, attack on, 207–8
Burke, First Sergeant Edward,
  xiv, 349–51, 353, 356, 357–
  58, 359, 361
Butcher of Plainfield, 65
Butler, Michael, 70
Byrne, Ranger John J., 15

Caifano, Marshall, 225
Cain, Richard, 238, 241
  murder of, 221–26
Caleel, Annette, 69, 73, 74
Caleel, Dr. Richard, 69, 73, 74
Caleel, Maria Louise, murder
  of, 69–74, 75

Callahan, Charles, 171
Callahan, Commander
    William, 267–68
Callahan, Eleanor, 171, 176
Callahan, Jr., William, 171
Callahan, William H., murder
    of, 158–77
Calvise, Frank, 213, 215
Cannon, Senator Howard, 248
Canzoneri, Cori, 188
Canzoneri, Jamie, 188
Canzoneri, Karen, 188–89,
    191–92
Canzoneri, Linda, 192
Canzoneri, Robert, 192
Canzoneri, Salvatore "Sam,"
    murder of, 188–92
Canzoneri, Thomas, 192
Capri, Anna, 100, 101
Carmin, Sergeant Michael,
    359–61
Carney, Assistant Chief Robert,
    194
Carpino, John, 304–5
Cerone, John, "Jackie the
    Lackey," 231, 304
Cesaro, Sam "Sambo," 253
Champaign News-Gazette re-
    ward, 74
Chicago Crime Commission, x
Chicago Sun-Times, 96, 102
Chicago Tribune, 164, 165
    reward, 12
Chiwaukee Prairie, 158–59
Christofalos, George, 218
    murder of, 219–20
Church, Richard "Rick,"
    181–86
Cicero, Frances, 347–48
Cisowski, Captain Edward,
    325, 328
Cline, Lieutenant Philip, 150,
    151–52

Colander, Pat, 333
Colby, Marlene, 192
Concia, Aulette, 172
Congreve, William, 257
Conlisk, James B., 217
Connor, Park Ranger Bud,
    347–48
Cook, Barry Zander, 6–12, 18
Cook, Charles, 8, 11, 12
Corpse in the hearse. See Kal-
    denberg, Mary Ellen.
Corruption, 308–9
Costas, John, 229–30
Counterfeiters, 207, 210
Cozzo, Sam "Jelly Belly," 224
Crane, Walter. See Callahan,
    William H.
Crawford, Jack F., 312, 315,
    316, 317
Crichton, Detective Dale, 160,
    163
Crimaldi, Charles "Chuck,"
    232–33, 235–36, 238
Crisanto, Alex, 71–72
Cross, Julie, murder of, 207–10
Cults, 155
Cummings, Shelley, 192
Curin, Commander Kenneth,
    167
Curry, Francis, 341, 342, 344

Dacey, James, 296
Daddano, William "Willie Pota-
    toes," 230, 344
Daley, Mayor Richard J., 284,
    285
Daley, Police Chief Robert H.,
    76–79
Daley, Richard M., 303, 304
D'Arco, John, 303
Dato, Edward, 158–59
Davis, Jody Lynn, murder of,
    93–95

Dean, Irene, 29
Death threats
  in Hawkins case, 307
  in Isaacs case, 138
  in Kupcinet case, 100–1, 102
  in Merriam case, 133, 134
DeCarolis, Rose, 166–67, 173–74
Deeley, Detective Chief Patrick,
  6, 8, 9, 18, 28, 301
De Laurentis, Salvatore "Sollie
  D," 191
Delph, Catherine, 144
Delph, Dennis, murder of,
  143–45
De Mora, James, 277
Dennis, Dr. David, 254–55
DePalma, Jerome, 242
DeStafano, Mario, 231, 233,
  235
DeStefano, Anita, 233
DeStefano, Michael, murder
  of, 236
DeStefano, Sam, ix, 214, 230,
  231, 232–33, 234–37
  murder of, 237–38
Deutsch, Sidney, 284
Deviant sexual behavior, 5–6,
  17–18, 19, 32, 41, 64–65,
  230, 232, 235
DiCharia, Inspector Paul, 314,
  316
DiLeonardi, Commander
  Joseph, 218, 219, 220
Dioguardi, Detective David,
  270, 271
Disappearance
  of Andrews, Marcy Jo, 94–95
  of Blough, Patty, 346–63
  of Brach, Helen Vorhees,
    331–36
  of Bruhl, Renee, 346–63
  of Graver, Celinus "Clem,"
    299–302

of Hartley, Evelyn Grace,
  47–65
of Miller, Ann, 346–63
of Pullia, Sal, 303–5
of Zelko, Amelia "Molly,"
  337–45
Dismemberment, of victims, 5,
  65, 114
Donaldson, Undersheriff
  James, 202
Donnelly, Deputy Chief
  William, 189
Donoghue, Dr. Edmund R.,
  323
Donovan Jr., Edward, 331
Dorff, Coroner Thomas J., 161,
  164–65, 168, 175, 176
Dorff, Vi, 164–65
Dorfman, Allen, murder of,
  246–51, 255
Dorfman, Lynn, 247
Dorfman, Paul "Red," 246–47
Double agent, 223
Douglas, Roger, 213–14
Drake, Bertha, 276
Drew, Kelly, murder of, 153–55
Drug overdose, of Hartwell,
  Donna, 156–57
The Dry and Lawless Years,
  276
Dunham, Lieutenant James,
  63–64

Eavesdropping devices, 11
Edward Gein, America's Most
  Bizarre Murderer, 64
Elrod, Sheriff Richard, 309
Embezzlement, 172–73, 177,
  333
English, Charles "Chuckie,"
  242, 243
  murder of, 244–45
The Enterprise, 288

Epplen, Sergeant Lee, 261
Esparza, Rebecca, shooting of, 149–52
Esparza, Richard, murder of, 149–52
Esparza, Stephanie, 149
Eto, Ken, 260
Etzel, Captain A.W., 102
Evans, Coroner John, 109, 113, 114
Evans, Harold James "Jimmy," 82–83
Evidence tampering, 314–15, 316
Ewing, Russ, 113, 114
Extortion, 217, 253
    letter, 326, 327

Faegenburg, Gary, 119
Fahner, Tyrone, 325
Falcon, Leon, 157
Farrell, Sharon, 100
Fazio, Lou, 232
Fecarotta, John, murder of, 259–62, 268
Feigel, Harry, death of, 222–23
Ferguson, Dr. Lawrence, 150–51
Ferguson, Maurice, 333
Ferriola, Joseph "Joe Nagaul," 245, 253, 256, 262
Feuerriegel, Robin, murder of, 46
Field, Patricia Wisz, murder of, 91–92
Fisher, Dorothy, 21
Fisher, Police Chief Ernest, 123
Fitzgerald, Kimberly, 45
Fitzgerald, Sergeant Charles, xiii, 6–8, 10–12
Fitzpatrick, Sergeant Timothy, 71, 73, 74

Flanagan, Barbara, murder of, 41, 45
Flanagan, Captain Frank, 286, 290, 292
Flanagan, Renee, murder of, 41, 45
Fletcher, Bob, 184–85
Ford, Reverend Robert, 289
Foreman, Jonathan, 70
Foreman, Leo, murder of, 235–36, 238
Fosco, Detective Chris, 214

Gagliano, Joseph "Joe Gags," 304
Gagliano, Salvatore, 304
Gallagher, John, 213
Gallagher, Margaret, murder of, 7–8, 9, 10
Galuski, Patricia, 192
Gambling, 191, 244, 266, 341
Garland Building, 14
Gauger, Detective James, 89, 90
Gaynor, Michael, murder of, 296
Gebardi, Vincent, 277
Gehrke, Chris, 182
Gein, Ed, 64–65
Genna, Angelo, murder of, 275
Ghost employee, 260
Giancana, Salvatore (Sam) "Momo," 235, 238, 239, 265
    aliases of, 240
    murder of, 242–43
Gilbert, Sergeant James, 289
Given, Jay N., murder of, 310–17
Gladden, Jerry, ix–xi
Goddard, Marcia, 97, 98–99
Goddard, Mark, 97, 98–99
Gollmar, Judge Robert H., 64–65

Gonzales, Santiago Rosa, 260
Goodman, Philip "Philly," 266
  murder of, 263–65, 267, 268
Gordon, Blanche, 32
Gordon, Sherry, murder of,
  31–34
Granady, Octavius, murder of,
  297
Granata, William J., murder of,
  297
Graver, Amelia, 299
Graver, Celinus "Clem," ix
  disappearance of, 299–302
Graver Detail, 300, 301
Griffin, Richard J., 209
Grimes, Barbara, murder of,
  xiv, 3, 18, 20–30
Grimes, Joseph, 21
Grimes, Loretta, 20–22, 25, 29
Grimes, Patricia, murder of,
  xiv, 3, 18, 20–30
Grimes, Sr., Joseph, 22, 24
Grimes, Theresa, 21
Gross, Charles, murder of,
  297–98
Guzzino, Nicholas, 258

Hack, Pat, 154
Hack, Timothy, murder of,
  153–55
Hall, Patricia, 31–33
Hall, Theresa, murder of, 31–34
Hamm, Lieutenant David, 333
Handlon, Steven, 111
Hanson, Julie, murder of, 41
Hardt, A. W., 355
Harmon, James, 259–60
Harmon, Jerry, 212–13, 214–15
Hartley, Carolyn, 47
Hartley, Dr. Richard, 47, 49–
  51, 53
Hartley, Evelyn Grace, disap-
  pearance of, 47–65

Hartley, Tom, 47
Hartwell, Donna, death of,
  156–57
Harvey, Michelle, 307
Hathaway, Robert T., 99, 100
Hauser, Detective Kenneth,
  241–42
Hawkins, Gerald, 307
Hawkins, Mayor William, mur-
  der of, 306–9
Hawkins, Nancy, 307, 309
Healy, Patrick, 250, 262
Heckscher, Patrolman
  Rudolph, 7
Hegarty, FBI Chief Edward D.,
  249, 255
Heidinger, Detective Peter, 10
Henderson, Coroner Thomas,
  71
Henderson, Lieutenant Ed,
  209
Hessberger, Dr. Robert, 137
Hijackings, 231, 232, 260, 300–1
His Way: The Unauthorized
  Biography of Frank Sina-
  tra, 240
Hoffa, Jimmy, 246–48
Hohf, Dr. Robert, 76
Hohf, Nydia, 76
Hohimer, Francis Leroy, 83
Hohimer, Harold, 83
Hoodlum squad, x
Hoover, Dr. Rick, 113, 114
Houlihan, Sergeant James, 309
Howell, Police Commissioner
  Robert, 307
Hubbard, Detective Robert,
  160, 163
Hubbs, Preston, 264
Hudson, Dick, 253–54
Hulse, Darlene, murder of,
  124–27
Hulse, Ronald, 124, 126, 127

Incledon, Deputy Chief George, 263
Income tax evasion, 266
Insurance fraud, 292
Isaacs, Dr. Burton, murder of, 136–38
Isaacs, Ilene, death of, 136
Isaacs, Marlene, attack on, 136–37

Jackson, Norman, 83
Jackson, Sergeant Arthur, 308
Jackson, William "Action," murder of, 229–33
Jacobs, Bob, 133–34
Jakucyn, Patrolman Joseph, 144
Janecek, Officer John, 249
Janus, Adam, murder of, 321, 322, 323, 324
Janus, Stanley, murder of, 322, 323, 324
Janus, Theresa, murder of, 322, 323, 324
Jayne, George, 362
murder of, 19
Jayne, Marion, 19
Jayne, Silas, 18–19, 333, 362, 363
Jennings, Lee Clark, 45
Jewish faction, 267
John Reid & Associates, 8
Johnson, Commander Earl, 262
Johnson, Elvia, murder of, 122–23
Johnson, Jason, 122, 123
Johnson, Officer Allen, 71
Johnson, Patrolman Bruce, 293, 294
Johnson & Johnson, 324, 328
Joliet Penitentiary, 9–10, 11
Joliet Spectator, 337, 340, 341

Jones, John Paul, 357
Jones, Prosecutor Fred R., 127
Josephson, Alma M. "Joe," 56–63
Joyce, Leah, 190
Juice man, 229–30, 231
Jury tampering, 248

Kade, Dr. Harold, 98
Kahoe, FBI Agent E. Michael, 254
Kaldenberg, Cecil, 36
Kaldenberg, Daniela, 36
Kaldenberg, Eddie, 36
Kaldenberg, Mary Ellen, murder of, 35–40
Kandel, Sally, murder of, 41, 45
Keane, Detective Robert, 169
Kearney, William, 229
Kearns, Dr. Jerry, 15, 25–26, 144
Keating, Sergeant James, 214
Keating, Sergeant William, 291
Kellerman, Mary, murder of, 321, 323
Kelley, Kitty, 240
Kelly, Detective Patrick, 113, 114
Kennedy, Detective Frank, 113
Kennedy, Robert F., 344, 345
Kid Riviera. See Williams, Jimmy.
Kiely, John M., 266
Kihm, Detective Captain Leo, 52, 53
Killackey, Chief of Detectives John, 238
Killackey, Lieutenant John, 286
King, Carol, 29
Kinz, Michael, 253
Kiser, Detective Roger, 108, 109, 110, 111, 114

Kittel, Police Chief Ronald, 86
Klatzco, Police Chief Richard,
    137, 138
Knyuch, Paul, 152
Kolarik, Gera-Lind, 114
Kolbasuk, Police Chief Nick,
    212
Kopanakis, George, 107, 108
Kopanakis, Lisa, murder of,
    107–11
Kopanakis, Niki, 107, 108
Kopanakis, Sophia, 108, 110
Koppel, Harold, 149
Korshak, Sid, 98
Koziol, Detective John, 74
Kozlarek, Edward, 45
Kozlorek, Deborah, murder of,
    45
Kranz, Walter, 23, 25
Krenn, Edwin, 158–59
Kuczynski, Stanley, 293–94
Kulbiski, Deputy Coroner Mat-
    thew, 176, 177
Kup—A Man, An Era, A City,
    102–3
Kupcinet, Esther Solomon, 96
Kupcinet, Joseph, 98
Kupcinet, Irv, 96, 98, 101,
    102–3
Kupcinet, Karyn, murder of,
    96–103
Kurczewski, Norbert, 155
Kusper, Stanley, 304

LaBarber, Patricia, 149
LaBarber, Sergeant Russell,
    149
Lackard, Sergeant John, 74
Lamb, Police Agent Robert, 82,
    83–84
Lane, Clem, 11
Lange, David, 103
Lange, Hope, 103

LaPorte, Frank, 344
LaRose, Joseph, murder of,
    139–42
Lawford, Peter, 239
Lazarus, Victor, murder of,
    266–68
LeFebvre, Dr. Kenneth, 151
Lewis, Benjamin F., murder of,
    283–95
Lewis, Ella, 287, 289
Lewis, James, 326–28
Lewis, LeAnn, 326
Liberman, M. David, 138
Liebach, Linda, 192
Lincoln Park, 7
Livingston, Victor, 15
Lohman, Sheriff Joseph, 24,
    26–29
Loizzo, Thomas F., 187
Lombardo, Joseph "Joey the
    Clown," 245, 248
Long, FBI Agent Robert, 187
Long, Police Chief George C.,
    52, 59
Loudan, Bonnie, 132
Luckman, Sid, 98
Lulinski, Chester, 145
Lundgren, Waldorf, 14
Lyle, Judge John H., 276–77
Lynch, Lieutenant John, 16

McBride, Detective Howard,
    241–42, 243
McCabe, William R., attack
    on, 337, 340–41
McCarron, Coroner Walter E.,
    15, 26–27, 343
McCormick, Edith Rockefeller,
    158–59
McDade, Edwin E., 170
McDade, Scott, 170
McDade, Wendy, murder of,
    158–77

McDade, William. *See* Callahan, William H.
McFarland, Mary, murder of, 321–22, 323
McGarr, Judge Frank J., 327
McGuire, Phyllis, 239
McGurn, Machinegun Jack, 276–77
  murder of, 277
McMahon, Captain George, 294
McNeil Laboratories, 324
Malchow, Frederick J. "Freddie," 81–82, 83, 84
Maloney, James, 173, 176
Mamches, William, 99, 100
Manson, John Edward. *See* Rubin, Edward Stephen.
Marak, Lieutenant Leonard, 120, 121
Marchbanks, Donald, murder of, 139–42
Margolis, Jeremy, 327
Marinaro, Gary, 305
Marks, Albert, 29
Marovich, Judge George M., 118
Masters Jr., Frank, 340
Matlick, Jack, 322, 323
Matous, Frank A., murder of, 156–57
Menk, John Cadwalader, 335
Merlo, Mike, 276
Merriam, Carol, 133
Merriam, Charles E., grandfather, 132
Merriam, Charles E., murder of, 131–35
Merriam, Charles J., 132
Merriam, Robert E., 132
Meyers, Sergeant Cheryl, 207
Mickels, Sara, 288
Micus, James, 29

Miller, Ann, disappearance of, *xiv*, 346–63
Miller, Charles, 134
Miller, Detective Fred, 355
Miller, Robert, 304
Miller, Sergeant Fred, 362–63
Miller, Steven, 334
Milone, Richard, 45
Missing babysitter mystery. *See* Hartley, Evelyn Grace.
Mr. Smile. *See* Isaacs, Dr. Burton.
Mokry, Detective Patrick, 269–70, 271–72
Monte Cristo bowling alley, 14
Montrose Harbor, 5
Morecraft, Kathleen, murder of, 41
Moriarty III, Michael J., murder of, 95
Morris, Lieutenant Joseph, 14, 28
Morse, Arthur, 98
Morton, Samuel "Nails," 278
Moss, District Attorney Milton O., 83
The Mourning Bride, 257
Mueller, George, 186
Mueller, Sheriff Keith, 155
Mullen, Mary, 288
Mullen, Sheriff Charles "Pat," 254, 256
Muranaka, Detective Anthony, 9–10, 11
Murderer's Row, 8–9
Murder Mansion, 203
Murphy, Sergeant George, 14–15, 18
Mustari, Frank, 344

Nelligan, Thomas, 165–67
Neurauter, John R., 291
Nevergall, John, 82

New York Daily News, 169–70
Newey, Paul D., 222–23
Newman, Major Thomas, 135
Nick the Barber. *See* Raftopoulos, Gus.
Nicosia, Captain George, 120, 131, 132
Niewiandomski, Ernest, 14
Nitti, Frank, 297
No. 265, murder of, 269–72
Nowicki, Casey, 94–95

O'Banion, Dion, 278
O'Connor, Police Commissioner Timothy J., 300
Ogilvie, Richard, 221, 223, 224
Olkwitz, Dianne, murder of, 39
Olson, Lieutenant Ray, 135
Organized crime, 221–26, 229–72
  murders, x
Organized Crime Task Force, x
Organized Crime Unit, 241
Ormson, Lieutenant Lee, 160

Palermo, Dominick, 258
Panczko, Joseph "Pops," 251
Patrick, Lenny, 264, 265
Pecoraro, Rose, 276
Percy, Gail, 76
Percy, Loraine, 75, 76, 77
Percy, Mark, 76
Percy, Roger, 76
Percy, Senator Charles, 39, 75, 76
Percy, Sharon, 76, 77, 78
Percy, Valerie Jean, murder of, 39, 75–84
Peterson, C. H., 339, 343
Peterson, Dorothy, 14
Peterson, Malcolm, 14, 17, 18

Peterson, Robert, murder of, xiv, 13–19. *See also* Schuessler-Peterson boys murders.
Petrocelli, William "Butch," 220
Petyo, Patrolman George, 229–30
Philbin, Investigator John, 226
Phillipe, Kathryn, 172
Pikelis, Walter, 299, 300
Pilewicz, Richard, 42–43
Pilewicz, Rosemarie, 42–44
Pilewicz, Violet, 42–43
Pitzman, Police Chief Herbert J., 183, 184, 185, 187
Pless, Dr. John, 254–55
Pluim, Michael L., 88
Plummer, Robert, 203
Poisoning
  of Janus, Adam, 321
  of Janus, Stanley, 322
  of Janus, Theresa, 322
  of Kellerman, Mary, 321
  of McFarland, Mary, 321–22
  of Prince, Paula Jean, 322
  of Reiner, Mary, 321
Police
  scandal, 217
  strike, 308
Political violence, 283–317
Pollard, George, 163–64
Polygraph testing, 56–57
Pomeroy Jr., Donald, 143–44
Pornography war, 220
Powis, Robert E., 209
Prescott, Leonard, 23–24
Prescott, Marie, 23–24
Prignano, Albert J., murder of, 297
Prince, Carol, 322
Prince, Paula Jean, murder of, ix, 322, 323
Prine, Andrew, 98, 99, 100–1

Probst, Marlene, 211
Probst, Officer Ralph, murder of, 211–15
Proschwitz, Investigator Kurt, 197, 201
Psychics, 194
Pullia, Frank, 305
Pullia, Karen, 304, 305
Pullia, Sal, disappearance of, 303–5

Quinlan, Amy, 181

Racketeering, 252, 259
Raftopoulus, Demetra, 110–11
Raftopoulos, Gus, murder of, 110
Ragen, Warden Joseph, 10
Ransom notes, 22
Rao, Charles, 171
Rao, Eleanor, 169, 171, 172
Rao, Jr., Paul, 175
Rash, Police Chief Robert, 189
Rasmusen, Dr. Viggo, 48
Rasmusen, Janis, 48, 50
Raucci, Sergeant Dennis, 157
Regula, Jean, 322
Reichert, Coroner Ewald, 154
Reilly, Charles, 335
Reiner, Mary, murder of, 321, 323
"The Relentless Pursuer of Evildoers," 6, 12
Rewards, 12, 18, 30, 34, 59, 74, 83, 92, 111, 123, 135, 152, 155, 157, 192 194–95, 209, 290, 300, 324, 328, 333, 365, 367–68
Reyes, Concepcion "Connie," murder of, 193–95
Richardson, Coroner Barbara, 122, 189
Richardson, Nancy, 326

Richardson, Robert, 326
Richie, Sergeant Beverly, 307
Rinaldi, Dana, murder of, 119–21
Rinaldi, Joseph, 120
Rini, James V., 344
Ritter, Colleen, attack on, 181–83, 185
Ritter, Henry, 186, 187
Ritter, Matthew, attack on, 181–82
Ritter, Raymond, murder of, 181–87
Ritter, Ruth Ann, murder of, 181–87
Ritter, Steven, 186
Rizzo, Ernie, 333
Roberts, Patrolman John, 43
Robinson's Woods, 15
Roemer Jr., FBI Agent William F., 234, 245
Rosenberg, Floyd W., 100–1, 102
Rosenberg, Seth, 169, 177
Rothschild, Christine, murder of, 39
Rottman, Lieutenant Daniel, 189
Rouse, Billy, 197, 199, 200–1, 202, 203
Rouse, Bruce, murder of, 196–203
Rouse, Darlene, murder of, 196–203
Rouse, Kurt, 197, 199–200, 203
Rouse, Robin, 197, 199, 201, 202
Roviaro, Albert John, 258
Rowland, Daisy, 331
Rubin, Edward Stephen, 99, 100
Rude, Cheryl Lynn, death of, 362

Rum wars, 275
Russell, Malcolm, murder of, 139–42
Ryan, Dennis, 202

Sander, Phil, 158, 159–60
Sanson, Dr. John, 161
Scalzetti, Richard. See Cain, Richard.
Scarpelli, Gerald, 220
Schenk, Sergeant Charles, 120
Scherping, Captain John H., 222
Schmeer, Gordon, 168
Schmeer, Willa, 168
Schuessler, Anton, murder of, xiv, 13–19. See also Schuessler-Peterson boys murders.
Schuessler, Eleanor, 14, 17
Schuessler, John, murder of, xiv, 13–19. See also Schuessler-Peterson boys murders.
Schuessler, Sr., Anton, 14, 17, 18
Schuessler-Peterson boy murders, xiii, 3, 13–19, 27, 28, 30. See also Peterson, Robert; Schuessler, Anton; Schuessler, John.
Schwartz, Detective Warren, 135
Scott, Sam, 304
Scully, Ole, murder of, 221
Seifert, Daniel, 248
Serpico, John, 260
Serpico, Ralph "Babe," 303
Sexual assaults, 5–6, 12, 32, 41, 122
Sheafe, Larry, 209
Sheppard, Lieutenant Ed, 88
Shimon, Joseph, 240

Shine, Detective Thomas, 151
Shooting
of Alterie, Leland Varian, 279
of Andersen, Judith Mae, 3–12
of Bolton, John H., 297
of Cain, Richard, 221–26
of Callahan, William H., 158–77
of Canzoneri, Salvatore "Sam," 188–92
of Christofalos, George, 219–20
of Cross, Julie, 207–10
of Delph, Dennis, 143–45
of DeStefano, Michael, 236
of DeStefano, Sam, 237–38
of Dorfman, Allen, 246–51
of English, Charles "Chuckie," 244–45
of Esparza, Richard, 149–52
of Fecarotta, John, 259–62
of Giancana, Salvatore (Sam) "Momo," 242–43
of Granady, Octavius, 297
of Gross, Charles, 297–98
of Hawkins, Mayor William, 306–9
of Isaacs, Dr. Burton, 136–38
of Jayne, George, 19
of Kozlorek, Debbie, 45
of LaRose, Joseph, 139–42
of Lazarus, Victor, 266–68
of Lewis, Benjamin F., 283–95
of McDade, Wendy, 158–77
of Marchbanks, Donald, 139–42
of Matous, Frank A., 156–57
of Merriam, Charles E., 131–35
of Moriarity III, Michael J., 95

of No. 265, 269–72
of Prignano, Albert J., 297
of Probst, Officer Ralph,
211–15
of Rinaldi, Dana, 119–21
of Rouse, Bruce, 196–203
of Rouse, Darlene, 196–203
of Russell, Malcolm, 139–42
of Scully, Ole, 221
of Stanisha, John, 324–25
of Thanasouras, Mark,
216–20
Sicilian Beau Brummel. *See*
Amatuna, Salvatore
"Samoots."
Sicilian societies, 275–77
Sinatra, Frank, 239, 240
Singer, Jerry, 336
Sinnott, Assistant U.S. Attor-
ney Stephen, 118
Skinner, Samuel, 219
Slunecko, Joseph, 355
Smerciak, Ed, 143–44
Smith, Derrick, 288
Smith, James H., 290
Snow, Dr. Clyde, 271
Sonquist, Sheriff Gerald, 160,
161, 162–64, 165, 166, 176
Sosynski, Sy, 149
South Bend Medical Founda-
tion, 113
Spann Jr., N. Atterson, 311
Spanos, Detective Thomas, 237
Spear, Dr. Ivan M., 167
Spencer, Raymond, death of,
250–51
Spilotro, Ann, 257
Spilotro, Anthony "Tony," 235,
248, 259, 263, 264, 267, 268
murder of, 252–58, 265
Spilotro, Dr. Patrick, 255
Spilotro, Michael, murder of,
253–58

Spiotto, Michael, 225
Spyglass Murder Case. *See*
Gallagher, Margaret.
Stabbing
of Caleel, Maria Louise,
69–74
of Granata, William J., 297
of Hanson, Julie, 41
of Kaldenberg, Mary Ellen,
35–40
of Kopanakis, Lisa, 107–11
of Olkwitz, Dianne, 39
of Percy, Valerie Jean, 39,
75–84
of Ritter, Raymond, 181–87
of Ritter, Ruth Ann, 181–87
of Rothschild, Christine, 39
Stanisha, John, murder of,
324–25
Stein, Dr. Robert, 134, 269,
326, 334–35, 336
Stein, Dr. Robert J., 187
Stephens, Lieutenant Gary,
186
Stibich, John, 294
Strangulations
of Buege, Beth, 89–90
of Gordon, Sherry, 31–34
of Hall, Theresa, 31–34
of Johnson, Elvia, 122–23
of Kupcinet, Karyn, 96–103
of Peterson, Robert, 13–19
of Reyes, Concepcion "Connie," 193–95
of Schuessler, Anton, 13–19
of Schuessler, John, 13–19
Sultan, Jerome, 191
Sunday Matinee Murders. *See*
Peterson, Robert;
Schuessler, Anton;
Schuessler, John.
Survivor pact, 340
Sutton, Pearl, 290

Svetic, Park Supt. William,
348–49, 350, 352–53
Szczepanski, Deland, 254

Tapper, Albert, 116, 117
Tapper, Alan, 112, 115
Tapper, Dr. Edward, 112, 115–
17, 118
Tapper, Dorothy Goods, mur-
der of, 112–18
Task Force on Organized
Crime, 190
Tattooed waitress case. See
Davis, Jody Lynn.
Taylor, Matthew, 72
Teamsters Union insurance
business, 246–47
Teller, Sergeant Sheldon, 190
Teller, Sheldon, 29, 30
Terrell, Sergeant Charles, 156,
157
Tetyk, Master Sergeant Rich-
ard, 325
Thanasauras, Mark, ix
murder of, 216–20
Thin Air, 333
Thomas, Dorothy, 290
Thomas, Ora Goods, 113, 114
Thomas, Walter, 113
Thompson, Roosevelt, 288
Three Gun Louie. See Alterie,
Leland Varain.
Tocco, Albert "Caesar," 256,
257–58
Tocco, Betty, 257–58
Toman, Coroner Andrew J., 77,
80, 230
Torture
of Foreman, Leo, 235–36
of Jackson, William
"Action," 229–33
of Spilotro, Anthony, 252–58
of Spilotro, Michael, 253–58

of victims, 113–14, 230, 232,
234–36, 270
Trick-or-treat murders. See
Gordon, Sherry; Hall,
Theresa.
Trinza, Police Chief Joseph,
338–39, 345
Turney, Detective James, 237
20–20 Club, 315
Tylenol tampering case,
321–28
Tylenol Task Force, 325, 328
Tyson, Sheriff Richard E., 125,
126

U.S. Universal, Inc., 139–42
Unknown cause of death
of Beck, Berit, 85–88
of Drew, Kelly, 153–55
of Feuerriegel, Robin, 46
of Field, Patricia Wisz,
91–92
of Grimes, Barbara, 20–30
of Grimes, Patricia, 20–30
of Hack, Timothy, 153–55

Vaci, Emil "Mal," murder of,
256
Vallas, Coroner Chris, 32
Vallee, Detective Walter, 7
Van Bokkelen, Joseph S., 310,
312, 315, 316–17
VanderMolen, Carolyn, mur-
der of, 44–45
VanderMolen, Sally, 44
Vanick, Lieutenant Howard,
307, 308
Vaughan, Police Chief Patrick,
32, 33–34
Violent Criminal Apprehen-
sion Program (VICAP), x
Vische, John F., murder of,
139–42

Vito, Frank, 300
Voorhees, Jacob, 332
Vorhees, Walter, 331

Wacks, FBI Agent Peter, 248
Waller, Judge Jane, 192
Walsh, Lieutenant George, 97,
    98–100, 102
Warholic, Mark, 312
Wavro, Coroner Edward, 38
Weber, Trooper Lou, 359–61
Weil, Joseph "Yellow Kid," 267
Weiner, Irwin, 248, 249
Welborn, Officer Jeff, 71
Wellin, Ruby, 289–90
Wellner, Rick, 155
Whalen, Frank G., 8, 10
White, David, 286
Williams, Jimmy, 286–87, 293
Williams, Morris, 288

Williams, Roy, 248
Williams, Raymond, 300–1
Wilson, Charles, 54–55
Wilson, Orlando W., 216, 217,
    285
Wilson, Sergeant Rutherford,
    150
Winchell, Walter, 102
Wisz, Patricia, 91, 92

Yankalasa, Mike, 347–48
Yehle, Patrolman Gregory, 59
Yoquelet, Detective Sergeant
    David, 127
Young, Captain Robert, 194

Zahn caper, 224
Zelko, Amelia "Molly," disap-
    pearance of, 337–45
Zelko, Frank, 345